AF651309

Concept Publishing Co.
Rs 750/--

Committees and Commissions in India
1976

Concepts in Communication
Informatics & Librarianship-50

General Editor : **S.P. Agrawal**

Committees and Commissions in India 1976

Volume 14

A Concept's Project

Compiled by a team of professionals
guided by
VIRENDRA KUMAR

CONCEPT PUBLISHING COMPANY, NEW DELHI 110059

All rights reserved. No part of this work may be reproduced, stored in a retrieval system, or transmitted, in any form or by any means, electronic, mechanical, photocopying, microfilming, recording or otherwise, without the prior written permission of the copyright owner and the publisher.

ISBN 81-7022-483-7 (Vol. 14)

First Published 1993

© Publisher

Published and Printed by
Ashok Kumar Mittal
Concept Publishing Company
A/15-16, Commercial Block, Mohan Garden
NEW DELHI 110059 (India)

Lasertypeset by
Printing Express
H-13, Bali Nagar
NEW DELHI 110015

GENERAL EDITOR'S INTRODUCTION

In the context of the changing world, the role of the government – be it at central, state or local level – is becoming more prevasive in the modern society. Everyday, it has to encounter new problems and face new issues which demand quite a new thinking and novel strategies to overcome them. Thus, the increasing role of the government in every sphere of people's life has broadened its functions and responsibilities tremendously and enlarged its activities to such an extent that the government machinery of its own can hardly manage its affairs. Moreover, its functions are becoming more complicated and complex requiring the assistance of outside specialists, technocrats and specialized agencies.

In view of this, the modern government has to set-up committees and commissions and working or study groups on various problems and issue from time to time. In the light of the recommendations of these committees and commissions, the government takes decisions on key issues and problems. Often the government is obliged to seek the assistance of a committee to evaluate some of its schemes in operation so that on the basis of the evaluation reports of the committee, it may either continue, modify or scrap the on-going schemes. In other words, the committees or commissions, etc., exercise a great deal of pivotal force in shaping the policies and programmes of the government and for this purpose submit a large number of reports.

In these volumes of *Committees and Commissions in India*, now being published under the *Concepts in Communication Informatics and Librarianship (CICIL)* series, an attempt has been made to cover the period from 1974 onwards. The volumes include the vital data about only those reports of the committees and commissions which have been constituted by the Central Government. We have made every endeavour to include the digest of all the important reports on various vital issues of great importance and on major areas of national development.

We have also an ambitious plan to publish the digests of the important reports of the committees and commissions appointed by different state governments, the semi-government organisations and the learned bodies as also the reports published during the period of the British Government.

The publication has been brought out under the guidance of Shri Virendra Kumar, specialist in his own right with vast experience of working in Government Documents Section in the Central Secretariat Library and having the privilege of the blessings of Dr. S.R. Ranganathan – the father of Indian Library Science. I also put on record the collaborative help provided by Shri M.W.K. Sherwani.

We are sure that this compilation will prove a very useful reference tool for researchers, serious students and scholars of the public administration and political science, administrators, policy-makers, educationists and historians.

S.P. AGRAWAL

PREFACE

This volume of *Committees and Commissions in India* attempts to understand the activities of the various Committees and Commissions during the period 1974.

A 'Commission' is a governmental agency created to perform a particular function such as special investigations or on governmental regulations of business. It is appointed mainly when it is thought that a matter involves some financial questions. There are other reasons for which a Commission is appointed, e.g., in matters pertaining to welfare of the State and its citizens and or improving the efficiency in an administration. The status of a 'Committee' is also the same as that of a 'Commission', but it does not possess as wide powers as are enjoyed by a Commission and has to limit itself to specific work assigned to it under its terms of reference. While arriving at decisions in the form of recommendations, a Commission or Committee ensures that such decisions are representative of interests of various types of people and also a safeguard against abuse of power.

A Committee or a Commission comprises a Chairman, the Members and Member Secretary (sometimes there is also an Assistant Secretary). In some cases, there are even One-man Commissions and the enquiry in such Commissions is entrusted to an Officer-on-Special Duty.

The Chairman of a Commission is a person well-versed mostly in legal matters and is often a retired judge of a High Court or the Supreme Court of India. Occasionally, a Member of Parliament is also appointed as the Chairman of a Commission. On the other hand, the Chairman of the Committee is mostly a specialist in the subject of the Committee. He can be a Leader or a Convenor also, if he heads a Panel, a Study Group or a Delegation, etc.

The Members of a Commission, Committee, Panel, Study Group etc., are specialists in their respective fields and provide valuable guidance to the Commission or the Committee in making recommendations.

The Member-Secretary or Secretary is generally nominated from among the experienced officials who have the requisite competent knowledge of the subject on which the Commission or the Committee is appointed.

Committees and Commissions in India provides in chronological order vital information about Committees and Commissions appointed by the Government from time to time. Information for each Committee or Commission is presented in a compact form in four parts, namely; Constitution; Appointment; Terms of Reference and Recommendations.

CONTENTS

COMMISSION OF INQUIRY TO ENQUIRE INTO THE ALLEGATIONS AGAINST THE ERSTWHILE CHIEF MINISTER AND OTHER MINISTERS OF TAMIL NADU, 1976 – FIRST REPORT[1] (SARKARIA COMMISSION OF INQUIRY)

One Man Commission Shri R.S. Sarkaria
Secretary Shri K.A. Ramasubramaniam

Appointment

S.O. 74(E). Whereas the Central Government is of opinion that it is necessary to appoint a Commission of Inquiry for the purpose of making an inquiry into a definite matter of public importance hereinafter specified;

Now, therefore, in exercise of the powers conferred by section 3 of the Commissions of Inquiry Act, 1952 (60 of 1952), the Central Government hereby appoints a Commission of Inquiry consisting of a single member, namely, Shri Justice R.S. Sarkaria, Judge, Supreme Court of India.

And whereas the Central Government is of opinion, having regard to the nature of the inquiry to be made by the Commission and other circumstances of the case, that all the provisions of sub-section (2), sub-section (3), sub-section (4) and sub-section (5) of the Commission of Inquiry Act 1952 (60 of 1952) should be made applicable to the Commission, the Central Government hereby directs, in exercise the powers conferred by sub-section (1) of the said Section 5, that all the provisions of the said sub-sections (2), (3), (4) and (5) of that action shall apply to the Commission.

On November 4, 1972, Shri M.G. Ramachandran, M.L.A. of Tamil Nadu State Assembly sent a Memorandum to President of In-

---

1. Madras, Director of Stationery and Printing, 1976, 4 Vols.

dia Praying for the appointment of a Commission of Inquiry:

"(a) Against the entire Cabinet of the Tamil Nadu Government,
(b) Against all the District Secretaries of the ruling Karunanidhi D.M.K.,
(c) Against the officials against whom specific charges have been made in the accompanying annexure, (see original report), and
(d) Against such other officials and such other persons who are involved in abetting with corrupt Ministers and Officials."

In the Annexure to this Memorandum, he made several allegations containing charges primarily against Shri M. Karunanidhi, the then Chief Minister of Tamil Nadu and his Cabinet Colleagues.

Shri M. Kalyanasundaram, M.P., and five others, viz., S/Shri K. Baladhandayudham, M.P., K.T.K. Thangamani, M.L.A., K.T. Raju, P. Manickam, M.V. Sundaram and S. Narayanan, all of the Communist Party of India, submitted a Memorandum, dated November 6, 1972, to the President of India making similar allegations chiefly against Shri M. Karunanidhi and his companion Ministers of the D.M.K. Government.

On receiving those memoranda, the Prime Minister on November 15, 1972, wrote to Shri Karunanidhi for his comments on the allegations made by the Memorialists. Thereupon, Shri M. Karunanidhi sent two letters, dated December 14, 1972, one of which was a covering letter and the other contained his comments and "detailed answers to the specific charge made by the memorialists." Thereafter, S/Shri M.G. Ramachandran and M. Kalyanasundaram submitted their rejoinders, dated January 10, 1973 and February 5, 1973 respectively to the Prime Minister. The Prime Minister sent copies of these rejoinders to Shri M. Karunanidhi for further comments. In reply thereto, Shri M. Karunanidhi sent his further comments on these rejoinders and a note to the Prime Minister under cover to his letter dated May 28, 1973.

The aforesaid Memoranda, rejoinders and the comments and answers given by Shri M. Karunanidhi to the Prime Minister, were published by the then Government of Tamil Nadu and the Central Government in regard to these matters, which obviously remained under consideration till the issue of the Central Government Notification, dated February 3, 1976 constituting this commission.

It was against the background set out above that the Government of India in the Cabinet Secretariat, Department of Personnel and Administrative Reforms appointed a Commission of Inquiry for the purpose of making an inquiry into a definite matter of public importance in exercise of the powers conferred by Section 3 of the Commission of Inquiry Act, 1952 (60 of 1952), vide their Notification No. 381/3/76-AVD.III dated February 3, 1976.

Terms of Reference

(a) to inquire into the following allegations namely:

(i) the allegation contained in the Memorandum dated December 1, 1975 received from Sarvashri K. Manoharan and G. Vishwanathan, addressed to the President,

(ii) such of the allegations contained in the Memorandum dated November 4, 1972 received from Shri M.G. Ramachandran and Memorandum dated November 6th and December 20th, 1972 received from Shri M. Kalyanasundaram, M.P., as are specified in the Annexure (see original report) to this notification;

(b) to inquire into any irregularity, impropriety or contravention of law on the part of any person in relation to any matter referred to in the allegations aforesaid;

(c) to inquire into any other matter which arises from or is connected with or incidental to, any act, omission or transaction referred to in the allegations aforesaid.

And whereas the Central Government is of opinion having regard to the nature of the Inquiry to be made by the Commission and other circumstances of the case that all the provisions of sub-section(2), sub-section (3), sub-section (4) and sub-section (5) of the Commission of Inquiry Act 1952 (60 of 1952) should be made applicable to the Commission, the Central Government hereby directs, in exercise the powers conferred by Sub-section (1) of the said Section 5, that all the provisions of the said Sub-section (2), (3), (4) and (5) of that action shall apply to the Commission.

Contents

Part I – Narrative of the Proceedings of the Commission From 3rd

February 1976 to 3rd December 1976; Introductory; Preliminaries; The First Sitting; Preparing the material for the inquiry; Preliminary Objections to Affidavits; Further Proceedings under Rule 5(5); Circumstances leading to withdrawal of Respondents (Except Shri Aditanar) from the Proceedings; Evidence and Arguments; Appendix I-VII. Part II – Discussion .of Evidence and findings on Allegations; Chapters I to 9; Summary of Conclusions; Part I.

Summary of Conclusions

Allegation No. 3 (Tractor)

The allegation that Messrs Wallace Cartwright & Co., London, paid for the purchase of the Tractor from Messrs Massey Ferguson, London, and that the tractor was misused in Shri Karunanidhi's farm in Tiruvarur in Thanjavur district, has not been substantiated. The inordinate delay in registering the tractor in question as well as the fact that some tractors were actually engaged in ploughing Shri Karunanidhi's lands, might have created reasonable suspicion in the mind of the Memorialist, Shri M.G. Ramachandran and led him to believe: "It all smells a rat."

Allegation No. 11(a) — Nathan Publications

(a) It has been cogently proved that Shri Anbil Dharmalingam had intimate relations with Shri Kasthuri Chettiar and his brother, Shri Pandurangam Chettiar, Partners of Nathan Publications, and they had joint business interests.
(b) From the evidence which mainly consists of authentic Income-tax records, registered documents, the statements of Income-tax officials, officials of the Registration Department, Village Headman, etc., it is abundantly clear that Shri Anbil Dharmalingam and his family members, and Shri Kasthuri Chettiar and Shri Pandurangam Chettiar, were not affluent prior to 1967 and there was a spurt in their affluence and prosperity after the D.M.K. came into power in 1967.
(c) The appointment of Nathan Publications as distributors of text books for two Development Districts during 1970-71, was in contravention of the rules and norms of property. Shri V.R. Nedunchezhiyan, the then Education Minister, was respon-

sible for preferring Nathan Publications over Palaniappa Brothers, who had quoted 5.5 per cent as against Nathan Publications' 6 per cent and had also done satisfactory work during the previous two years, as distributors for Trichy North District. He was also responsible for violating the principle laid down in G.Os. 432 and 600, of appointing one Distributor for one Development District, without any adequate reasons. He was also responsible for taking a decision on a proposal directly put up to him as Chairman of the Executive Committee of the Text Book Corporation, in violation of the normal procedure, and thus confronting the other two members of the Executive Committee with a fait accompli. Since Shri Kasthuri Chettiar and Shri Pandurangam Chettiar, Partners of Nathan Publications, were staunch members of the D.M.K. Party and Shri Anbil Dharmalingam's sister Dhanamanickam, was also a partner in this concern, the conclusion is inescapable that the appointment of Nathan Publications in violation of the rules and the norms of propriety, was clearly with the motive of favouring either members of supporters of the ruling party.

Allegation No. 11(b) — Aerial Spraying

The following charges have been established by cogent, convincing and reliable evidence, oral, documentary and circumstantial:

Regarding Aerial Spraying Contracts of 1970-71

I. *Against Shri Anbil Dharmalingam* —

(i) That Shri Anbil Dharmalingam acting in concert with and through V. Rajagopal, entered into an agreement with the Operators whereby he agreed to receive gratification in the shape of commission as a motive or reward for securing for the operators who were Members of the Indian Agricultural Aviation Association, Bombay, by inducing with the exercise of his personal influence, the Chief Minister, Shri M. Karunanidhi of the Government of Tamil Nadu, and the Director of Agriculture, Tamil Nadu, Shri Hari Bhaskar, contacts for the aerial spraying of crops from helicopter during 1970-71, in Tamil Nadu, at the rate of Rs. 9 per acre;

(ii) That in pursuance of the aforesaid arrangement, a firm, in the name of Ponnee Agencies, was floated in which Mrs. N.D. Mahalakshmi, a 'dummy' partner was inducted, only to cover and conceal the share which Shri Anbil Dharmalingam was to receive equally with Rajagopal of 66 per cent of the commission collected from the Operators;

(iii) That in pursuance of the aforesaid arrangement, Shri Anbil Dharmalingam, actually received Rs. 20,000 in cash on 14 July, 1970, towards his share of the "Commission", through V. Rajagopal collected from the Operators.

II. *Against Shri Karunanidhi, the then Chief Minister*—

(i) That on November 17, 1970, Shri Karunanidhi abusing his official position, as the Chief Minister of the State of Tamil Nadu, accepted, through his Private Secretary, Vaithialingam, a sum of Rs. 25,000 as illegal gratification, from H.P. Rao, Managing Director of Pushpaka Aviation (P) Ltd., Bombay, as a motive or reward for awarding to the said Company aerial spraying contract during the year 1970-71 in respect of an acreage of 1.5 lakhs at the rate of Rs. 9 per acre, a rate which was in excess of what that Company itself had originally quoted;

(ii) That in awarding the aerial spraying contracts of 1970-71 at the rate of Rs. 9 per acre to the Operators who were members of the Indian Agricultural Aviaticn Association, Bombay, Shri Karunanidhi, being influenced by extraneous considerations, abusing his official positions as Chief Minister, and acting in utter disregard of the norms of propriety, fair practice and good administration, designedly stalled and foiled the rightful move of Shrimati Sathyavani Muthu the then Agriculture Minister, to fix the rate at Rs. 8.25 per acre, through negotiations with the Operators;

(iii) That in awarding the aforesaid contract in 1970-71, to Pushpaka Aviation, at the rate of Rs. 9 per acre, as against their original quotation of Rs. 8 per acre, Shri M. Karunanidhi the then Chief Minister, actuated by the said corrupt motive of pecuniary gain to himself, improperly and designedly brushed aside the proposal of the Secretary for Agriculture, for making an, attempt to persuade Pushpaka Aviation (P) Ltd., in the first instance, to agree to do the spraying work at their original quotation of Rs. 8 per acre.

Regarding the Contracts of 1971-72

I. *Against Shri M. Karunanidhi, the then Chief Minister* —

(i) That on 13th August 1971, Shri M. Karunanidhi, abusing his position as Chief Minister of Tamil Nadu, received through his Private Secretary, Vaithialingam, and illegal cash gratification of Rs. 25,000 in the shape of advance commission, from H.P. Rao, Managing Director of Pushpaka Aviation (P) Ltd. Bombay, as a motive or reward for doing acts in connection with his official functions, such as prompt clearance of the bills of that Company for payment, the delivery of signed contract-deed to them and the allocation of more acreage to that company for spraying etc.;

(ii) That on 18th September 1971, Shri Karunanidhi, abusing his official position as Chief Minister, preemptorily demanded, through his Private Secretary, Vaithialingam, from the Operators, payment of illegal gratification, in the shape of commission at 90 paise per acre immediately in advance, without any vouchers, off-the record, as a condition or motive for allowing payment of their pending bills, and for allocating them further work, and eventually forced the Operators to agree to pay commission of 90 paise per acre in advance, in two instalments at 45 paise per acre in respect of the acreages covered up to 19th September 1971;

(iii) That on 22nd September 1971, in pursuance of the aforesaid demand, and imposed arrangement, Shri Karunanidhi, abusing his official position as Chief Minister, received through his Private Secretary, Vaithialingam, a total sum of Rs. 1,17,273 from the seven Operators including Cambata, Captain, Krishnap and others, as a motive or reward for doing acts connected with his official functions, such as releasing payment of their pending bills in respect of the work done up to 19th September 1971 and for allocating further work at the contractual rate of Rs. 11 per acre, etc.;

II. *Against Shri Anbil Dharmalingam* —

(i) That Shri Anbil Dharmalingam, abusing his official position as the Minister for Agriculture, acting in concert with V. Rajagopal, and initially negotiating through V. Rajagopal and later after direct talks with the Operators, on July 2, 1971, finalised an arrangement whereby he agreed to award to the Operators aerial contracts in 1971-72 at the rate of Rs. 11 per acre in consideration of their paying 'commission' at the rate of 80 paise per acre to and through the firm Ponnee Enterprises, managed by V. Rajagopal.

III. *Against Shri Karunanidhi and Shri Anbil Dharmalingam* —

(i) That in 1971, Shri Karunanidhi and Shri Anbil Dharmalingam abusing their official positions as the Chief Minister and the Minister for Agriculture, Tamil Nadu, respectively, conceived in concert a plan to bring down the Aviation Operators to their heels and make them submit to their extortionate demands for gratification in the shape of commission, and in implementation of that plan issued verbal instructions to the Government officials, particularly, Vaithialingam, Vedanarayanana and Hari Bhaskar, and through them took the following steps:

(a) The contract deeds, in duplicate, signed by the Operators were obtained from them by the Director of Agriculture with the representation that one copy of the same would be returned to them in due course after being signed and completed on behalf of the Government; but with the solitary exception of Pushpaka Aviation, whose Managing Director had with less resistance and little delay complied with the peremptory demand of the Chief Minister to pay him the gratification, such copies of the signed contract deeds were never returned to the Operators, despite repeated requested made by them;

(b) By giving the Operators to understand that for 1971-72 they had been awarded the contracts at Rs. 11 per acre, they (Operators) were induced to undertake large-scale aerial spraying operations and incur heavy expenditure in compliance with the work allocation orders in which the rate at which they were to be paid for the spraying, was deliberately not specified;

(c) the secretary and the Director of Agriculture were directed with a view to ensure regular payment of the commission by the Operators, that payments in respect of the arrears of the preceding year (1970-71) as well as for the work done during 1971-72 in anticipation of signing of the formal contract, could be settled and the signed contracts handed over only to those Operators who had paid the commission as demanded by the

Ministers;

(d) In order to ensure better control over the settlement of the bills of the Operators settling of their bills which had been delegated to the District Agriculture Officers, was designedly centralised and they were asked to send all the bills to the Office of the Director of Agriculture for "scrutiny" — the only scrutiny exercised at the Directorate being whether the "commission" had been paid or not, as stipulated by the Ministers;

(e) Such orders releasing payment or for clearance of the bills were issued by the Director of Agriculture, only when the concerned Operator/Operators had paid the commission in respect of a particular area covered during a period by the spraying operations, in advance, without vouchers, and the fact of such payment was communicated to the Director by the Chief Minister/the Minister directly or through Vaithialingam or Vedanarayanana;

(f) The non-return of the signed contract, deeds, was designed to serve a double purpose (i) to emasculate the Operators from the enforcing payment of their bills or seeking redress through Courts; (ii) to keep the Operators under constant threat and fear that the Government might by signing these Contracts, at any time, impose a penalty at the rate of Rs. 5 per acre on the allocated acreage, on the slightest excuse of a default on the part of the Operators in the performance of the contract.

(ii) That in causing the issue of work allocation orders and the commencement of spraying work by the Operators, before the execution and completion of the formal contract-deeds, Shri Karunanidhi, the then Chief Minister and Shri Anbil Dharmalingam acted with grave irregularity and impropriety in wilful contravention of Article 166 of the Madras Financial Code and Article 299 of the Constitution;

(iii) That in July, 1971, Shri Karunanidhi and Shri Anbil Dharmalinga, abusing their official positions as Chief Minister and the Minister for Agriculture, respectively, acting in accordance with a pre-arranged plan conceived in concert by them, and in disregard of the norms of propriety, fairness and the rules, and actuated by corrupt motives, induced under pressure Vedanarayanana, Secretary for Agriculture, against the latter's better judgement, to put up a proposal (which was eventually approved by them) for rejecting on some excuse the tender of H.S. Shoba Singh (P) Ltd. for the year 1971-72, even though it was the lowest, i.e., Rs. 9.50 per acre, and for accepting the quotation of Rs. 11 per acre from the other Operator-members of the Association, even though the same was in excess of the ceiling rate of Rs. 10 per acre fixed by the Government of India;

(iv) That Shri Dharmalingam, the then Minister for Agriculture, Tamil Nadu, acting in pursuance of a pre-arranged plan conceived in concert with Shri Karunanidhi, Chief Minister, abusing his official position as Minister, and actuated by corrupt motives, first, on 19th July 1971 and again on 21 July 1971, demanded from the Operators, who met him on these dates, illegal gratification in the shape of commission at the rate of Re. 1, or at least, 90 paise per acre, to be paid through an agent other than V. Rajagopal, or the Ponnee Enterprises.

(v) That Shri Anbil Dharmalingam, acting in pursuance of a pre-arranged plan conceived by him in concert with Shri Karunanidhi, the then Chief Minister, and by abusing his official position as Minister for Agriculture, directly received from the Operators illegal gratifications in amounts and on dates noted below, as a motive or reward for doing acts connected with his official functions.

(a) Rs. 1,41,650 in cash on 11th October 1971.
(b) Rs. 41,714 in cash on 25th October 1971.
(c) Rs. 52,676 in cash on 6th November 1971.
(d) Rs. 53,359 in cash on 25th November 1971.
(e) Rs. 64,502 in cash on 23rd December 1971.
(f) Rs. 17,603 from H.P. Rao after 25th November 1971.
(g) Rs. 16,242 from P.G. Dastoor after 25th November 1971.

Total Rs. 3,87,746

(vi) That Shri Karunanidhi, being the Chief Minister and Shri Anbil Dharmalingam, the Agriculture Minister of Tamil Nadu, during the period from April 1973 to 3rd February, 1976, abusing their official positions in the State Government, and actuated by ulterior motives, attempted to stall, thwart and frustrate the investigation under the Code of Criminal Procedure, 1898, of the criminal case, R.C. No. 2/73, registered on 5th April 1973 under Ss. 120B, 161, 162, 163, 165 and 165A I.P.C. and S.5(2) read with S.5(i)(d) of the

Prevention of Corruption Act, 1947, by refusing to allow the Investigating Officers of the Central Bureau of Investigation to scrutinise fully and freely official records in the custody of the Government and its Departments, relating to the award of the aerial spraying contracts of 1970-71, 1971-72, nor allowed the said investigating officers to take over any documents, whatever, from such records, despite the assurance given on their behalf by the then Governor of Tamil Nadu in his letter dated July 16, 1974, addressed to the Minister of State, Ministry of Home Affairs, Government of India, New Delhi.

IV. *Against Shri Anbil Dharmalingam* —

It has been *prima facie* established, that during 1971-72, while as Minister for Agriculture, Tamil Nadu, Shri Anbil Dharmalingam received pecuniary benefits from V. Rajagopal in the shape of payment by the latter towards the petrol consumed in the cars used by Shri Anbil Dharmalingam or his son, Poyyamozhi, and also towards other household expenses of Shri Anbil Dharmalingam, exceeding Rs. 11,080, in the aggregate, and Shri Dharmalingam never reimbursed V. Rajagopal with regard to those expenses. These acts of Shri Anbil Dharmalingam were connected with his misconduct in receiving or agreeing to receive gratification in the shape of 'commission' from the Operators in respect of the aerial spraying contracts in question through V. Rajagopal and the firms floated by him. This misconduct of Shri Anbil Dharmalingam was also against the Code of Conduct for Minister laid down by the D.M.K. Government, themselves.

Allegation No. 12 (S. Kandappan, M.L.A.)

(Favour to father-in-law of Shri Kandappan)

(a) From the evidence placed before the Commission, it has been established that there was some discrepancy between the declaration of wealth field by Shri S. Kandappan for the year ending 31st March 1972, and his Income-tax return for the same year, but it is not possible to conclude that he had intentionally field a false declaration of wealth.

(b) The loan of Rs. 1,77,000 granted by the Tamil Nadu Industrial Investment Corporation to Shri S.P. Rangaswami Gounder, proprietor of Messrs Mani Rice and Oil Mills, Tiruchengode, and father-in-law of Shri S. Aandappan, was sanctioned without proper verification and in violation of the guidelines laid down in the rules of the Corporation. The disbursement of Rs. 74,550 to Shri Rangaswami Gounder in one lump-sum was made in a hurry and without any kind of scrutiny. The officials of the Corporation were also induced by a false statement made by Shri Gounder that he had already purchased and installed an Expeller. The loan was definitely misused and was not spent for the purpose for which it was sanctioned; although it has not been established that it was spent by Shri Gounder for opening Arrack shops. The officials of the Corporation failed to take effective follow-up action in the Board's resolution foreclosing the loan. Recovery action has been initiated only after imposition of the President's rule.

Shri Madhavan, the then Minister for Industries, had exercised pressure on the officials of the Corporation at the time of the sanction and disbursement of the loan as well as for delaying follow-up action on the Board's resolution of foreclosure.

Allegation No. 15 (New Globe Theatre)

It has been fully proved that in moving, piloting and getting passed the Amendment Bills 4 of 1972 and 24 of 1973 introducing certain amendments to the Madras City Tenants Protection Act, 1922, S/Shri Karunanidhi, the then Chief Minister, P.U. Shanmugham, the then Revenue Minister and S. Madhavan, the then Law Ministers, were actuated with the oblique motive to benefit Shri Varadaraja Pillai. It has not been established beyond all manner of doubt that the respondents had received any illegal gratification from Shri Varadaraja Pillai for causing these amendments. The evidence on record, however, establishes a strong possibility, verging on probability, falling short of positive certainty, in favour of the allegation that the aforesaid amendments were got enacted in consideration of the receipt of some gratification by S/Shri Karunanidhi and P.U. Shanmugham.

Allegation No. 16 — Mud for Officers and Money for Ministers

(Favour to Editor *Broadway Times*).

The order of Shri Karunanidhi withdrawing the prosecution against Shri Mathew Cherian of *Broadway Times* summarily, and capriciously, when the prosecution had been sanctioned after due consideration and in consultation with the Law Department, was definitely an act of favouritism and also amounted to interference with the course of justice.

The order of Shri Karunanidhi rescinding the order blacklisting the firm, Thompson & Co., against the advice of all the senior officers as well as of the then Minister for Industries, Shri Madhavan, and without even waiting for his two other Cabinet colleagues, views in the matter, was definitely an act of favouritism.

Shri Karunanidhi's judgement in both the case seems to have been influenced by the fact that Shri Mathew Cherian was very close to his nephew, Shri Maran.

The allegation that Shri Karunanidhi kept corrupt officers like Shri P.K. Nambiar and Shri Pasupathy in key posts so as to fill up his coffers, has not been substantiated. The appointments of Shri P.K. Nambiar as Revenue Commissioner in the Board of Revenue and Shri Pasupathy as Secretary, Revenue, were made in accordance with their seniority in the I.A.S. Cadre and considering other relevant aspects. It cannot be said that either of these appointments was improper. As far as Shri Vaithialingam is concerned, this will be dealt with separately while dealing with Allegation No. 9, which specifically relates to him.

Allegation No. 19 (A.L. Srinivasan)

(a) It has been established that Shri Karunanidhi's decision, that Shri A.L. Srinivasan should be given a Brewery licence was in violation of the prescribed procedure and the established norms. Shri Srinivasan was not of sound financial standing and did not, therefore, satisfy the first criterion for selection laid down by Shri Karunanidhi, himself. He had not even applied in the prescribed form, and he did not have a piece of land for locating the project when Shri Karunanidhi took this decision, which was an act of favouritism to a close associate.

(b) The allegation that Shri A.L. Srinivasan tried to forcibly acquired ownership of about 100 acres of land in the vicinity of Madras City through the influence of the Chief Minister and the Revenue Board, has not been substantiated.

Allegation No. 22(C) — Shri Anbil Dharmalingam

(Eviction of tenants from Thathachari Estate)

The allegation that Shri Anbil Dharmalingam helped Shri Thathachari, a landlord, to evict his tenants forcibly from the lands in their possession, has not been substantiated.

Allegation No. 22(D) — Shri Anbil Dharmalingam

(Jangamarajapuram Murder Case).

It has been established beyond doubt that the investigation of the Jangamarajapuram murder case was conducted in a most improper, partial and perfunctory manner. In connection with the investigation and prosecution of this case, several acts of impropriety, partiality and irregularity were designedly committed by the Investigating Officer, Superintendent of Police and Public Prosecutor, to save the three accused who were closely related to the Minister, Shri Anbil Dharmalingam, from prosecution with consequent failure of justice. There is, however, no direct evidence to show that Shri Anbil Dharmalingam or any other Minister had spoken to them or influenced them in the conduct of the investigation or the prosecution of the case.

The erstwhile D.M.K. Government did not direct the filing of an appeal against the order of acquittal passed by the trial court, nor did they direct any action to be taken to get the strictures expunged. Nor did they proceed against the Police Officers whose faulty and biased investigation had led to the failure of justice. Shri Anbil Dharmalingam in his counter affidavit also made a wrong statement that the D.M.K. government has called for explanations from the concerned Police Officers, which were found to be acceptable. No such explanation was ever called before the imposition of the President's rule in Tamil Nadu. Although these circumstances do raise a strong suspicion that the Investigating Officer, Superintendent of Police and the Public Prosecutor misconducted themselves, possibly under influence or interference from Shri Anbil Dharmalingam or any of his Cabinet colleagues, the evidence adduced before the Commission is not sufficient to establish this fact beyond doubt.

2

COMMISSION OF INQUIRY TO ENQUIRE INTO THE ALLEGATIONS AGAINST THE ERSTWHILE CHIEF MINISTER AND OTHER MINISTERS OF TAMIL NADU, 1976 – FINAL REPORT[1] (SARKARIA COMMISSION OF INQUIRY)

One Man Commission Shri R.S. Sarkaria
Secretary Shri K.A. Ramasubramaniam

Appointment

S.O. 74(E). Whereas the Central Government is of opinion that it is necessary to appoint a Commission of Inquiry for the purpose of making an inquiry into a definite matter of public importance hereinafter specified;

Now, therefore, in exercise of the powers conferred by section 3 of the Commissions of Inquiry Act, 1952 (60 of 1952), the Central Government hereby appoints a Commission of Inquiry consisting of a single member, namely, Shri Justice R.S. Sarkaria, Judge, Supreme Court of India.

And whereas the Central Government is of opinion, having regard to the nature of the inquiry to be made by the Commission and other circumstances of the case, that all the provisions of sub-section (2), sub-section (3), sub-section (4) and sub-section (5) of the Commission of Inquiry Act 1952 (60 of 1952) should be made applicable to the Commission, the Central Government hereby directs, in exercise the powers conferred by sub-section (1) of the said Section 5, that all the provisions of the said sub-sections (2), (3), (4) and (5) of that action shall apply to the Commission.

On November 4, 1972, Shri M.G. Ramachandran, M.L.A. of Tamil Nadu State Assembly sent a Memorandum to President of In-

---

1. Madras, Director of Stationery and Printing, 1976, 4 Vols.

dia Praying for the appointment of a Commission of Inquiry:

"(a) Against the entire Cabinet of the Tamil Nadu Government,
(b) Against all the District Secretaries of the ruling Karunanidhi D.M.K.,
(c) Against the officials against whom specific charges have been made in the accompanying annexure, (see original report), and
(d) Against such other officials and such other persons who are involved in abetting with corrupt Ministers and Officials."

In the Annexure to this Memorandum, he made several allegations containing charges primarily against Shri M. Karunanidhi, the then Chief Minister of Tamil Nadu and his Cabinet Colleagues.

Shri M. Kalyanasundaram, M.P., and five others, viz., S/Shri K. Baladhandayudham, M.P., K.T.K. Thangamani, M.L.A., K.T. Raju, P. Manickam, M.V. Sundaram and S. Narayanan, all of the Communist Party of India, submitted a Memorandum, dated November 6, 1972, to the President of India making similar allegations chiefly against Shri M. Karunanidhi and his companion Ministers of the D.M.K. Government.

On receiving those memoranda, the Prime Minister on November 15, 1972, wrote to Shri Karunanidhi for his comments on the allegations made by the Memorialists. Thereupon, Shri M. Karunanidhi sent two letters, dated December 14, 1972, one of which was a covering letter and the other contained his comments and "detailed answers to the specific charge made by the memorialists." Thereafter, S/Shri M.G. Ramachandran and M. Kalyanasundaram submitted their rejoinders, dated January 10, 1973 and February 5, 1973 respectively to the Prime Minister. The Prime Minister sent copies of these rejoinders to Shri M. Karunanidhi for further comments. In reply thereto, Shri M. Karunanidhi sent his further comments on these rejoinders and a note to the Prime Minister under cover to his letter dated May 28, 1973.

The aforesaid Memoranda, rejoinders and the comments and answers given by Shri M. Karunanidhi to the Prime Minister, were published by the then Government of Tamil Nadu and the Central Government in regard to these matters, which obviously remained under consideration till the issue of the Central Government Notification, dated February 3, 1976 constituting this commission.

It was against the background set out above that the Government of India in the Cabinet Secretariat, Department of Personnel and Administrative Reforms appointed a Commission of Inquiry for the purpose of making an inquiry into a definite matter of public importance in exercise of the powers conferred by Section 3 of the Commission of Inquiry Act, 1952 (60 of 1952), vide their Notification No. 381/3/76-AVD.III dated February 3, 1976.

Terms of Reference

(a) to inquire into the following allegations namely:

(i) the allegations contained in the Memorandum dated December 1, 1975 received from Sarvashri K. Manoharan and G. Vishwanathan, addressed to the President;

(ii) such of the allegations contained in the Memorandum dated November 4, 1972 received from Shri M.G. Ramachandran and Memorandum dated November 6th and December 20th, 1972 received from Shri M. Kalyanasundaram, M.P., as are specified in the Annexure to this notification;

(b) to inquire into any irregularity, impropriety or contravention of law on the part of any person in relation to any matter referred to in the allegations aforesaid;

(c) to inquire into any other matter which arises from or is connected with or incidental to, any act, omission or transaction referred to in the allegations aforesaid.

Contents

Volume I – Mekala Pictures; Anjukam Pictures; Immovable Properties of Chief Minister Thiru M. Karunanidhi at Gopalapuram, Madras; Anjukam Pathippagam; Son's house at Tiruvarur, Thirumati Dharma; Thiru Amritham, Nephew; Thiru Vaidyalingam, P.A. to Chief Minister; Veeranam Project; Family Concerns of K.K. Angappa Chettiar and Brothers; *Volume II* – Disposal of Samayanallur Power Station; Sugar Scandal; *Volume III* – Tanjore Co-operative Marketing Federation; Kodaikanal-Palani Road; D.M.K. Party and Private Trusts — (A) The Madras D.M.K. Charitable Trust; (B) The Madurai District DMK Charitable Trust; (C) Navalar Nenduchezhian Educational Trust; (D) Perarignar Anna Arakkattalai; (E) Mandran Trust; (F) Rama Arangannal Arakkattalai; (G) Kalaignar Karunanidhi Charitable Trust; (H) Anna Trust; (I) Dr. Vetrichelvi Anbazhagan Trust; Conclusion on (A) to (J); Vallanadu Land Development Bank; Tanjore Urban Bank Affairs; Tanjore Central Co-operative Bank Affair; Dharmapuri District Central Co-operative Bank Affairs; *Volume IV* – Using State Machinery and Armed Gangs to Organise D.M.K. Trade Unions — (i) Simpson Company Affairs, (ii) Sarada Studio Affairs, (iii) State Electricity Board Affair; Intimidation and attack on the Press; Misuse of State Apparatus for Party purposes; Misuse of police to marshall opposition — (a) incident on 27th August 1972 at Singampuneri in Ramanathapuram District; (b) incident in October 1971 at St. Xavier's College, Palayamkottai in Tirunelveli District; (c) incident in the month of September 1971 at Kadayampatti near Bhavani Coimbatore District; (d) incident in November 1971, at Karivalamuandanallur in Tirunelveli District; (e) incident in January 1972 — attack on Trade Union Leaders; (f) incident on 26th February 1972, at Namakkal in Salem District; (g) incident on 27th February 1972, at Tirupatur Town in Ramanathapuram District; (h) & (i) incidents at Peddanaickenpalayam, Sattur, Manmadurai, etc.; Saklhi Pipes Ltd.; Summary of Conclusions; General Observations; Annexure 'A' Statistical Information regarding Affidavits, etc., received. . . .

Conclusions

Allegation No. 1

It has been established that even after become in a Minister/Chief Minister of the Tamil Nadu Government, Shri Karunanidhi continued to be a beneficial partner on the firm, Mekala Pictures, and his wife, Srimathi Dayalu, was only an ostensible partner or a benamidar for him. This fact, however, does not fall within the mischief of the Code of Conduct for Ministers; it has not been indubitably established that the continued to participate in the conduct and management of this firm after taking office as Minister.

In view of what has been found by the Income-tax Department during their special investigation, it is assumed that in the books of Mekala Pictures, fictitious cash credits have been introduced through one Rama Vellaiyan and certain records and documents relating there to have been fabricated. The evidence on record only shows that these cash credits and fabricated documents relating thereto, were introduced at the instance of Shri Maran. In the absence of cogent proof, it cannot be said that Shri Karunanidhi was aware that these cash credits were fictitious and the entries and documents related thereto, false and fabricated.

Allegation No. 2

Even on the assumption that fictitious loans and cash credits have been introduced and entries related thereto fabricated in the books and records of Anjukam Pictures, it has not been indubitably established by cogent and convincing evidence that these cash credits were introduced at the instance of, or in concert with, Shri Karunanidhi.

The evidence on record indicates that the distributors at the time of acquiring the distribution rights for the picture "Pillai-O-Pillai", did not anticipate losses, but, on the contrary, hoped to make handsome profits since the family members of the chief minister and his son were associated with the picture. There is no evidence to show that he had purchaed the distribution rights under the influence or pressure of Shri Karunanidhi.

This allegation has thus, not been substantiated against Shri Karunanidhi.

Allegation No. 4

The Commission would refrain from giving any finding with regard to the post-memoranda additions and improvements to the building at 7-A, IV street, Gopalapuram or with regard to the improvements, additions, etc., made prior to the date of Shri Karunanidhi's assumption of office as Minister. Similarly, the question whether the house was under-valued at the time of its purchase, is not related to alleged misuse or abuse of his official position as Minister/Chief Minister by Shri Karunanidhi. These matters concern the Income-tax authorities. The evidence adduced before the commission shows that the value of additions made to the building in 1973, would be roughly Rs. 20,000, which is substantially in accord with Shri Karunanidhi's case.

The Commission would not like to record any finding as to whether certain cash-credits introduced in the accounts of Mekala Pictures are factitious or not. Assuming that they are fictitious, it can only lead to the inference that Mekala Pictures, at the relevant time, had unaccounted income to conceal which it introduced in fictitious cash credits. It cannot be indubitably said that Shri Karunanidhi had unaccounted money, which he, with the connivance of his nephew, Shri Maran, under the guise of these fictitious cash credits, converted into white money.

This allegation has thus not been proved beyond reasonable doubt.

Allegation No. 5

Although the circulation as well as the advertisement revenue of "Murasoli" had a high spurt after the advent of the D.M.K. to power, there is no evidence, whatever, to show that Shri Karunanidhi exercised any influence, pressure or inducement in any manner to cause or contribute to this spurt.

The accounts furnished before the commission for the sums expended on the construction of the new "Murasoli" building are not self-explanatory and will have to pass scrutiny before they are accepted. But Maran's failure to give satisfactory sources from which he raised the money for construction of this building, would not necessarily load to the inference that Shri Karunanidhi had financed this unaccounted money.

The allegation has thus, not been established beyond all manner of doubt.

Allegation No. 6

The allegation that Shri Karunanidhi's son's house at Tiruvarur has been substantially improved at high cost, has not been substantiated.

Allegation No. 7

There is *prima facie* evidence that the two sales — one made by Smt. Dharma in favour of Kapali and other, made by Kapali in favour of Dharma's mother, Sivabhagyathammal, in respect of house No. 9, First Cross Street, Raja Annamalaipuram, were sham transactions. Out of Rs. 63,000 alleged to have been spent by Smt. Dharma over the purchase of this house from Srimathi E.L. Viswasam, it is possible that Rs. 23,000 could have been met by her out of her own savings. It must, however, be inferred that the balance of Rs 40,000 came from Shri Karunanidhi. There is, however, no evidence to show that this amount as acquired by him by corrupt means or through abuse of has office or power as chief Minister.

There has been an infringement of Rule 1 (a) of the Code of Conduct for Ministers on the part of Shri Karunanidhi, as he failed to show this house owned by his second wife, Smt. Dharma, and the relevant particulars related thereto, in his Property Statement.

There is no evidence to show that the properties acquired by Kapali were acquired with funds supplied by Shri Karunanidhi.

Allegation No. 8

This allegation has not been established since there is no evidence to show that House No. 7, IV Street, Gopalapuram, Madras, was the benami property of Shri Karunanidhi. The Commission does not consider it necessary to express any final opinion as to whether the valuation of the property, belonging to Shri Amritham, nephew of Shri Karunanidhi, made by the Income-tax Department is correct or not.

Allegation No. 9

The allegation that Shri Karunanidhi shielded and favoured Shri M. Vaithialingam, knowing him to be corrupt and having assets disproportionate to his known sources of income, has not been substantiated.

The imputation under Allegation No.16, that Shri Karunanidhi showed favouritism in promoting Shri Vaithialingam to the I.A.S. and in his posting as Deputy Secretary has not been established.

Allegation No. 10

It has been established that Shri Karunanidhi, abusing his official position as Chief Minister, actuated with the motive to unduly favour Sathyanarayna Bros. with the award of the contract for Veeranam Project, directed the Chief Engineer, Shri Hussain, to tailor his recommendations on the tenders in such a manner as would enable the Government to accept the tender of Sathyanarayana Bros.

In both the original and first revised assessments, the Executive

Engineer, Sivaraman, had rightly evaluated the tenders of M/s. Tarapore and Co. and M/s. Sathyanarayna Bros. According to these assessments, the tender of M/s. Sathyanarayna Bros. was not the lowest. It became the lowest only when an opportunity was given to them to withdraw some conditions through negotiations and when Hussain arbitrarily deducted about Rs. 85 lakhs from the assessed tender value of M/s. Sathyanarayna Bros. to make their tender substantially lower than that of M/s. Tarapore and Co. In so misconducting himself, Hussain was obviously complying with the imperative directions of Shri Karunanidhi conveyed through Vaithialingam at the cost of fairness, propriety and public interest. Thereupon, the Government, i.e., the Minister Shri Sadiq Pasha, acting in concurrence with the Chief Minister, Shri Karunanidhi accepted it post-haste and provisionally awarded the contract to Sathyanarayna Bros., without satisfying themselves as to the technical feasibility of the vacuum-concrete process and the capacity of Sathyanarayna Bros. to manufacture pipes of the requisite specifications and equality by that process. And all this was done in contemptuous disregard of the notes of caution sounded by the technocrats of the Central Public Engineering Organisation, and the Executive Engineer, Shri Sivaraman.

There is, no doubt, that Karunanidhi was interested in the contract being given to Sathyanarayna Bros. for some extraneous consideration. In this connection circumstances have been firmly established.

Purushotham's friendship with Maran and his exploiting this friendship to influence Karunanidhi and through him, Hussain;

The supply of materials worth about Rs. 59,202 by Purushotham for construction of 'Murasoli Building' without accepting payment from Maran—a fact admitted by Maran himself.

With regard to the alleged payment of illegal Iratifiction of Rs. 29 lakhs in seven instalments by Purushotham to Karunanidhi, the story of Purushotham is not such that it can be rejected brevimanu. But as he is admittedly an accomplice, his evidence cannot, as a matter of caution, be acted upon without corroboration in material particulars by independent evidence. The corroboration available is not adequate in extent and specificity and this evidence on record goes no further than establishing a preponderance of possibility, coming peridouly close to probability, in favour of this charge. The charge of accepting illegal gratification has thus, not been indubitably established against Shri Karunanidhi.

The decision to entrust the Veeranam Project to M/s. Sathyanarayna Bros. was, undoubtedly, a major administrative blunder. Huge advances were given to this firm not covered by the Contract Agreement, against simple indemnity bonds. The Accountant-General had adversely commented on this.

Public money to the extent of nearly Rs. 6 crores was squandered over this project as rightly pointed out in the report of the Technical Committee set up by the State Government, the project cannot now be brought to its successful conclusion unless the foreign collaborators, M/s Vacrete, accept full responsibility for the manufacture, testing, laying and jointing of the pipes. To the public exchequer, it would mean an additional burden of several crores and to the public looking long for adequate water supply, a tortuous wait for at least two years more. The responsibility for this huge waste of public money must rest squarely on Shri Karunanidhi and Shri Sadiq Pasha.

Allegation No. 13

The evidence on record has substantively established the following circumstances:

Close association of J.K.K. Angappa Chettiar and his brothers with the Chief Minister, Shri M. Karunanidhi, Revenue and Sales Tax Minister, Shri P.U. Shanmugham, and Law and Industries Minister, Shri Madhavan.

One Venkatakrishnan had field a petition alleging evasion of sales tax by the J.K.K. group and their benamidars. The Intelligence Wing of the Commercial Taxes Department made perfunctory investigation into this complaint.

Some material portions of the official records relating to this cases are missing and appear to have been deliberately suppressed.

These circumstances are not of a determinative tendency and do not conclusively point towards the guilt of the respondents. The Sales Tax Officers concerned, knowing that the J.K.K. group were closely associated with the Ministers might have shown diffidence in taking vigorous action against them. There is, however, no evidence to show that they were influenced by Ministers. There is also no evidence to show that sales tax to the tune of Rs. 7 lakhs and a penalty of Rs. 7 lakhs, was leviable on the firms belonging to the J.K.K. group, as has been alleged by the Memorialists.

This Allegation has thus, not been substantiated.

Allegation No. 14

It has been proved with a preponderance of probability from the evidence on record, that Shri O.P. Raman, then Minister of Electricity, abusing his official position, obtained the illegal gratifications, as noted below, from the purchasers of the plant and machinery of the Samayanallur Thermal Power Station, for securing to them repeated extensions of time for dismantling and removing the plant and equipment, and also for directing the officers of the State Electricity Board to deliver to the purchasers spares and accessories not covered specifically by the list of spare attached to the specifications:

(a) Rs. 50,000 from Nachimuthu Chettiar a few days after 25th September, 1972 at his residence in Madras.
(b) Rs. 25,000 on or about 10th January, 1973 from Nachimuthu Chettiar and Malayalam, at his residence in Madras.
(c) Rs. 30,000 on 13th May, 1973 from Malayalam in the Inspection Bungalow at Samayanallur.
(d) Rs. 25,000 from Nachimuthu Chettiar and Malayalam in the 2nd week of August 1973.

There is not a scintilla of evidence to show that in receiving there gratifications, Shri O.P. Raman was acting in concert with Shri M. Karunanidhi, the then Chief Minister.

The sources of finance for investment of about Rs. 90,000 made by Shri O.P. Raman towards construction of a house and improvements on agricultural lands, while functioning as Minister, are suspicious, but there is no definite link between these investments made between February 1974 and March 1976 and the illegal gratifications in questions received by him from Nachimuthu Chettiar and Malayalam between September 1972 and August 1973.

Allegation No. 17

It has been established with a preponderance of probability.

That in January 1970, Shri P.U. Shanmugham and Shri M. Karunanidhi, while being the Food Minister and the Chief Minister, respectively, of the State of Tamil Nadu, abusing their offices and official powers, taking undue advantage of the critical situation resulting from the unprecedented accumulation of stocks with the Sugar Mills in the state, and both acting in concert, demanded from the Sugar Mills in the Private Sector through Shri Maruthai Pillai, President of their Association (S.I.S.M.A.), Madras Branch gratifications at particular rates on sales of levy sugar particular periods in respect of Particular Releases, as a motive or reward for appointing the Sugar Mills as wholesalers-cum-retailers of levy sugar on behalf on the state; and (b) in pursuance of the aforesaid arrangement, Shri Karunanidhi, then Chief Minister, received from the nine Sugar Mills, namely: E.I.D. Parry, Deccan Sugars, Cauvery Sugars, Sakthi Sugars, South India Steel and Sugars, Madura Sugars, Thiru Arooran Sugars, Kothari Sugars and Aruna Sugars, collectively, through Maruthia Pillai, illegal gratifications in cash aggregating Rs. 13,21,296 in the following manners:

(1) Rs. 3,77,676.00 on or about the 8th or 9th March 1970.
(2) Rs. 97,069.50 towards the end of March 1970.
(3) Rs. 91,818 towards the end of April 1970.
(4) Rs. 81,516 in the first week of May 1970.
(5) Rs. 1,00,672.50 in the middle of June 1970.
(6) Rs. 88,552.50 towards the end of July 1970.
(7) Rs. 83,925 towards the end of August, 1970.
(8) Rs. 1,18,254 towards the end of September 1970 – Probably on 28th September 1970.
(9) Rs. 58,631 in the first week of November 1970.
(10) Rs. 37,537.50 in the first week of December 1970.
(11) Rs. 33,042.50 in the first week of January 1971.
(12) Rs. 32,192 towards the end of January 1971.
(13) Rs. 27,991 towards the end of February 1971.
(14) Rs. 31,245.50 in the first week of April 1971.
(15) Rs. 29,958.50 towards the end of April 1971.
(16) Rs. 31,214 on or about the 25th May 1971.

(c) That S/Shri Karunanidhi and P.U. Shanmugham committed serious acts of impropriety in violation of the National Sugar Policy settled by the Government of India and the established norms of official procedure in as much as—

(i) they permitted the Mills to sell levy sugar in the free market even to bulk consumers such as *Halwais*, Restaurants, confectionery, factories, etc., without any restriction or scale, much to the determent of the weaker sections of society who were entitled to this sugar on ration scale;

(ii) that even the observance of the nominal conditions was not ensured; no attempt was made to see at what price sugar reached the consumer ultimately. No proper effort was made to ascertain how and to whom the sugar factories distributed stocks, much less how it was distributed further down the line. It is not even known whether any part of there levy sugar stocks were exported outside the state;

(iii) by giving up the government margin of Rs. 4.06 per quintal, monetary loss of approximately Rs. 13 lakhs was caused to the State Government and considerable pecuniary advantage was conferred on the sugar factories which facilitated their payment of illegal gratification to the extent of Rs. 13 lakhs, to the Ministers;

(iv) on a major policy issue of this nature, the Minister, Shri P.U. Shanmugham, took a decision straightaway without the usual examination by the secretariat;

(v) even though the State Government at one stage had indicated to the Government of India that sales of levy sugar to bulk consumers would be discontinued, the matter was peremptorily closed on the ground that the Government of India had not pursued the matter.

Allegation No. 18

There is a absolutely no substance in the allegation that Shri V.S.T. Mudaliar had 'swindled' or 'misappropriated' Rs. 2 crores of the funds of the Thanjavur Co-operative Marketing Federation. There was no recommendation either by the Chief Secretary or any other officer to prosecute him. The acts of omission and commission on the party of the Ministers, particularly the then Chief Minister Shri Karunanidhi, were not actuated by bad faith or with a motive of undue favour to Shri V.S.T. Mudaliar at the cost of the T.C.M.F. or the public interest. Although Shri V.S.T. Mudaliar was known to Shri Karunanidhi both being natives of the same village. Shri Karunanidhi at the discussion held in the State Guest House on 25th April 1970, did give a green signal to the Registrar and the other authorities to go ahead with the inquiry under Section 65 of the Tamil Nadu Co-operative Societies Act, 1961. If he was against any drastic action against Shri V.S.T. unless sufficient ground was disclosed by the inquiry, it was only a note of caution, which any fair-minded Chief Minister would have sounded in the circumstances of the case.

This allegation has, thus, not been substantiated.

Allegation No. 20

The contract for the construction of the Kodaikanal-Palani Road was given to M/s. Nagappattinam Import and Export Corporation and not to S. Ahmed and Co. The contract for the construction of the over-bridge at Coimbatore was given to Shri K. Rajagopalan and not to M/s. Ahmed and Co. In the circumstances, the question of giving huge sums of money as advances to S. Ahmed and Co. for either of the above two works does not arise. This allegation has, thus, not been substantiated.

Allegation No. 21

The following facts have been established:

(1) *The Madras D.M.K. Charitable Trust*

In collecting 'donations' for this Trust, in some cases, pressure tactics were used and arbitrary deductions made from the salaries of some Elementary School Teachers by the Chairman of the Panchayats in Central of such schools.

The source of an excess of Rs. 1,32,011.55 over and above the amounts shown as receipts in the income tax return, has not been explained.

It cannot be said beyond doubt that the sellers of the property, situated at No. 85, Mount Road, Madras, were coerced or pressurised to part with the property at a gross under-value. Granting exemption from Urban Land Tax with retrospective effect in respect of this property, was an act of impropriety or misuse of power.

The circumstances that the bulk of the Trust funds has been expended on the purchase of immovable property and no part the funds or corpus of the Trust has so far been applied towards the charitable purposes declared in the Trust Deed, does raise a suspicion that the professed objects and intention may not be the real object and intention in creating this Trust.

(2) *The Madurai District D.M.K. Charitable Trust*

There is no evidence to show that the valuable property in Madurai Town situated at 159, West Masi Street, was purchased by the Trust at a gross under-valuation.

The objects of the Trust as enumerated in the Trust Deed are public charitable objects but nothing has been expended towards any of these objects. This does raise a reasonable suspicion that the ostensible state of affairs, as contemplated by the Trust Deed, is not the real state of affairs.

The lack of proper accounts to the sources from which money flowed into the Trust, does raise a suspicion that some unaccounted money collected in a questionable manner from questionable sources might been ploughed into the Trust. There is, however, no positive proof for this.

In respect of this Trust as well as the D.M.K. Charitable Trust, Madras, the majority of Trustees are to be nominated by Shri Karunànidhi, who has been given absolute power to fill up permanent and non-permanent vacancies of Trustees. This amounts to concentration of all authority and control on his hands.

(3) *Navalar Nedunchezhian Educational Trust*

(a) This Trust is not a private Trust, but ostensibly, a public charitable trust and it has not been used to acquire personal or private properties by the Trustee.
(b) That a part of the Trust Funds has been expended towards the professed charitable objects of the Trust;
(c) That there has been a misuse of the official machinery and his position as Minister of Education, and as Chairman of the Tamil Nadu Text Book Society, by Shri Nedunchezhian, to induce by the exercise undue influence and pressure, the distributors/stockists of the Tamil Nadu Text Book Society to contribute to the Funds of the Trust;
(d) That a donation for the Trust was collected from a student's parent as consideration for securing his admission in a college.
(e) That Shri Nedunchezhian, the Education Minister unduly in-

duced and pressurised Amaravathy Sri Venkatesa Paper Mills to pay a donation of Rs. 5,000 to this Trust, as a condition precedent for his accepting the Mill's invitation to participate in the College Day Function of the women's college run by the said Mill — which conduct was not in keeping with the dignity of the high public office then held by him;

(f) That under pressure from Shri Nedunchezhian, the then Minister for Education Shri S.N. Chockalingam, then Managing Director of Tamil Nadu Text Book Society, caused Shri Devadasan, Sales Officer of the Society, to tour the Districts, primarily with the purpose of collecting contribution from the distributors/stockists of Text Books for the Trust and incidentally for checking the stocks and sale accounts of the Distributors, as a result of which, the Society had to incur unnecessary expense in the shape of T.A. and D.A. for those avoidable tours.

(4) *Perarignar Anna Arakkattalai*

Shri P.U. Shanmugham misused his official position and the official machinery to extract or collect funds for this Trust. There was also fraudulent diversion of Panchayat funds. It is clear that funds were originally collected for the personnel ends of Shri P.U. Shanmugham and it was only on the imposition of President's rule that he coverted those funds into the Trust's funds to escape liability.

(5) *Mandram Trust*

This Trust from its inception has remained still-born but only serves to contrast Shri Nedunchezhian inability to raise donations for this Trust, when not in power, with the manner in which he extracted funds for the Navalar Nedunchezhian Education Trust.

(6) *Rama Arangannal Arakkattalai*

Nothing particularly adverse was found about this Trust except that no proper accounts have been maintained for its funds.

(7) *Kalaignar Karunanidhi Charitable Trust*

No accounts books have been maintained with regard to the funds of this Trust. There is reason to suspect that the grant of Rs. 2,000 said to have sent to the Registrar, University of Madras, for creating a Scholarship to the evening class students in Thiagaraja College, Madras, has not been fully accounted.

(8) *Anna Trust*

It is a public Trust and expenditure is being incurred towards the professed charitable objects of the Trust.

The source of an excess deposit of Rs. 1,06,000 over the donations shown in the account books, is unexplained.

Five thousand rupees donated by one Shri Panju has not been brought to account.

Ten thousand rupees claimed as donation received from A.V.M. Charities is questionable, since the donor denied having any donation to this Trust.

(9) *Muthuvelar Arakkattalai*

Almost the entire collections have been spent over repair and remodelling of the building. All expenses have been arbitrarity incurred by Shri Amritham, nephew of Shri Karunanidhi, without any resolution of the board of Trustees.

Accounts have not been placed before the Board of Trustees. No vouchers are available to substantiate the genuineness of the expenditure.

Temple funds have been illegally diverted for the establishment of the library run by this Trust.

(10) *Dr. Vetrichelvi Anbazhagan Trust*

The only impropriety with regard to this Trust was that Shri Karunanidhi on receiving a donation of Rs. 40,000 for the Health Department from this Trust, directed that the Government Homeopathic College, Madras, be named after Dr. Vetrichelvi Anbazhagan. This decision was, however, revoked under the presidents rule and the donation refunded to the trust.

Allegation No. 23(i)

From the evidence discussed, the undernoted facts and circumstances appear to stand established, to a varying degree of probability.

(a) The very idea of forming these lift irrigation societies and raising loans in their names, was mooted by Shri S.B. Aditanar at a meeting held at his residence at Srivaikuntam on 28th January 1971 attended by Krishnakanthan, Murugan, Arichandran, Jayaraman, and others.

(b) While coming at Tirunelveli from 28th January 1971 to 31st January 1971 Shri S.B. Aditanar briefed, instructed and impressed upon Subbiah, Joint Registrar, Co-operative Societies, Pathiamuthu, Chairman of the Primary Land Development Bank and Hariharan, Extension Officer, Co-operation, to cause the registration of the West Thathankulam and East Thathankulam Lift Irrigation Societies. Due to his constant pressure exerted through Subbiah the officers of the Co-operation Department, registered the Societies post-haste, by passing even the basic formalities enjoyed by the Co-operative Societies Act and the Rules, and without observing the norms of discretion and duty. Keelaperumaneri and Serakulam Societies were registered on the very date of making the applications, Gandhidoss, sub-Registrar, registered them instantly, because, by then, he had come to know that Beemsingh, who has brought the applications for registration, was a man of Shri Aditanar (vide evidence of Subbiah, Hariharan, Gandhidoss, and Puthiamuthu—witnesses Nos. 1, 3 and 8 respectively, Puthiamuthu and A. Subbiah, vice-chairman of the Bank, have deposed that Shri Aditanar told them that the societies were formed by his man.)

(c) The respondent, Shri Aditanar, briefed and instructed Subbiah to get the loans sanctioned and disbursed to these Societies immediately. The respondent was phoning to Subbiah every 15 minutes to know the progress, and through him pressurising the Departmental Officials and the officials of the Bank of rush through the sanction and disbursement of the loans, without applying their mind and without complying with the requirements of prudence and the established procedure.

(d) Shri Aditanar instructed S. Ramakrishnan, Assistant Secretary, State Land Development Bank, Tirunelveli (through Shanmugham, Chairman of the Tamil Nadu State Land Development Bank) to sanction the loans and disburse their entire amounts in a lumpsum. These instructions were conveyed by Shri Aditanar, telephonically from Tirunelveli (vide evidence of Ramakrishnan, W. No. 14, Shanmugham, W.No. 19 T.A. Bills of Shri Aditanar Document No. 16 and Circuit House. House Trunk call registrar, Document No. 19).

(e) Shri Aditanar personally instructed Kumarasundaram (W.No.5), Acting Sub-Registrar, to Registrar the declarations and agreements and mortgage bonds executed by the West Thathankulam and East Thathankulam Societies, after office hours on 8th February 1971 (vide evidence of Kumarasundaram, who has stated that Krishnakanthan and Beemsingh had taken him to Srivaikuntam to meet the Minister).

(f) Shri Aditanar was also coming at Tirunelveli when the loan applications of Keelaperumaneri and Serakulam Societies were processed. He rang up Shri Shanmugham at Villupuram and directed him to instruct Sivasubramanian of the State Land Development Bank to get the loans disbursed immediately and report compliance to him on telephone. (vide evidence of Shanmugham and Sivasubramanian, W. No. 19 and 18 respectively Trunk call Register—Document No. 19 and note of Sivasubramanian in the file).

(g) Shri Aditanar requested Shanmugham on 3rd February 1971 over trunk telephone to get the second instalment disbursed, immediately, to the Keelaperumaneri and Serakulam Societies. Shanmugham then contacted Ramakrishnan, Secretary, State Land Development Bank, Tirunelveli. Shri Aditanar himself spoke to Sivasubramanian, who instructed Srinivasan, Legal Assistant, over the telephone is the matter (vide evidence of Shanmugham, W. No. 19, Ramakrishnan, W.No. 14, Sivasubramanian W.No. 18 and Srinivasan, W.No. 13, and entry in Trunk call Register and Note, dated 3rd March 1971 recorded by Sivasubramanian in the file).

(h) Shri Aditanar deputed Kuttalam to Tirunelveli, specifically, for the purpose of getting certain documents inserted in the loan files of the Primary Land Development Bank (vide evidence of Kuttalam, Kini and Puthiamuthu).

(i) Shri Aditanar himself dictated to Subbiah, the report, dated 15th May 1972 (Exhibit No. CW. 36/1) Subbiah could not have known except through Aditanar, the societies were going to supply Mestha to Sun Paper Mills (vide evidence of Subbiah, C.W. 36).

(j) The fair copy (Ex. CW. 44/15) of the reply sent by the chairman, State Land Development Bank to the Reserve Bank of India contains 'corrections' in ink made by Shri Aditanar himself (vide evidence of Natarajan, CW.44).

(k) Shri Aditanar directed Natarajan to give a highly inflated valuation of the development works executed on the project area of these societies (vide evidence of Kandasamy and Nargunam, W.No. 39 and Affidavit No. 102, respectively).

(m) Shri Aditanar took extraordinary interest in getting the loans sanctioned to the four societies by the Canara Bank (vide evidence of Kini, CW. 40, Belliappa, W.No. 32 and Gurumurthy, W.No. 33).

(n) The reply (Ex. CW. 36/3) to the Reserve Bank of India sent by Shri Shanmugam, Chairman of the State Land Development Bank was drafted by Shri Aditanar himself, and the original draft in his handwriting is still retained in the file (vide evidence of Subbiah, CW. 36 and opinion of handwriting expert – Document No. 67).

(o) From the account books and documents seized from Auditor Narayanan (Document No. 56), it appears that the supervisory staff who did the development works, had made trips to meet "Periya Ayya", meaning Shri S.B. Aditanar, and claimed batta (T.A.), for these trips from the societies. Narayanan claims to be an Auditor of these Societies. He, admittedly, has done tax representation work for Sun Paper Mills and Shri S.B. Aditanar was in a position to have dominion over him.

(p) (i) The "Sales" of lands in March 1970 by the Aditanar Educational Institution to the sponsoring members of the four Lift Irrigation Societies, in question were, at any rate at their inception, mere paper transactions. None of the ostensible vendees paid the sale consideration to the ostensible vendor for the purchase of these lands. None of them appeared before the sub-registrar at the time of registration or entered into possession or cultivation of the land ostensibly sold to him.

(ii) The cultivating possession of the lands (later covered by the project area of these four societies) even after these ostensible sales, continued with the Aditanar Educational Institution, and it was the Respondent's brother,

Shri S.D. Adityan, who hold a general power of attorney from Aditanar Educational Institution, who continued to be in actual management and control of these lands. Whatever was done, albeit belatedly, towards the reclamation, development and cultivation of these lands, was done under the direct, personal supervision of the said brother of the Respondent (vide W.No. 23, Navaneethakishnan, and W.No. 24, Muthukumarasamy).

(iii) The sponsoring "members" were not genuine "small farmers" but were either relatives of Shri Aditanar, or employees of one of the concerns, namely: "Malai Murasu", "Dina Thanthi" and Sun Paper Mills Limited, over the affairs and employees of which, in general, and the office-bearers of the Societies, in particular, who were employees of those concern, could exercise and in fact appears to have exercised — *de facto* influence and control through his close relatives on the managing bodies of these concerns. The employees of the aforesaid concerns, particularly those who are alleged to be office-bearers of these societies, use to call Shri S.B. Aditanar, out of reverence, as 'Periya Aiyah' and always complied with his wishes and instructions (vide witnesses Kandasamy, Murugan, Palvannan, Singamuthu, Nargunam and Jayaraman).

(iv) With the possible exception of the office-bearers, Krishnakanthan, Murugan, Arichandran and Thyagarajan, the other "members" of these societies were absolute figureheads. Most of those members have never been seen in the lands, much less they have been its cultivators.

(v) In view of (i) to (iv) above, I will not be unreasonable to infer that by and large these societies were bogus societies.

(q) Within six days of the disbursement of the loans, the societies, withdrew — apart from the withdrawals for payment of share capital — Rs. 17,40,000, being the bulk of the loan amount, from their accounts with the Bank, in February/March, 1970, as follows:

	Rs
West Thathankulam	3,51,000
East Thathankulam	3,34,000
Serakulam	4,22,000
Keelaperumaneri	6,33,000
	(vide the Bank accounts)

(r) The aforesaid sums withdrawn from the Bank, totalling Rs. 17,40,000 were handed over to Krishnakanthan, who claimed to be the common chairman of the group of these four societies. Although Murugan in his earlier five statements had said that the sums thus withdrawn were handed over either to Krishnakanthan or Shri S.B. Aditanar, he, in his belated affidavit, exculpated Shri S.B. Aditanar. Krishnakanthan has admitted the receipt of the amounts of these withdrawals. It cannot, therefore, be said beyond doubt, that any part of the sums withdrawn were actually handed over to Shri S.B. Aditanar.

(s) These withdrawals which have been made on the eve of elections to the Tamil Nadu Legislative Assembly, do raise a suspicion that possibly, they had some connection with the coming elections, but there is no evidence whatever to show that any part of money thus withdrawn was actually expanded on the elections or for a purpose extraneous to the reclamation and development of the lands for which the loans were taken.

(t) (i) It appears that at least for eight months, if not more, after the withdrawal of these amounts, no steps were taken for executing the works for which the loans had been taken.

(ii) The bulldozers were hired for clearing the jungle and juliflora from the lands in November 1971 which indicates that the reclamation work probably started in November 1971 only and in right earnest it was stepped up only after the visit of the Reserve Bank officials on 16th December 1971.

(iii) The Reserve Bank officials' team headed by Venkatanarayana, who visited the project area of these societies on December 16, 1971 found that hardly 80 acres of land had been reclaimed, while the rest of the area appeared to be a vast tract of barren land under thorny bushes.

They also fund only two newly dug wells in this area, though they also noticed some pump-sets and machinery lying there for installation. Taking the rates at which Natarajan had prepared his estimate, the amount expended till 6th December 1971 on the reclamation, digging of wells, or development of these lands would not exceed Rs. 22.32 lakhs.

(iv) Even if Natarajan's estimate of the cost of improvements of these lands, is taken as correct, then also up to 15 April 1972, Rs. 7.75 lakhs, and up to 28th July 1972, Rs. 14.57 lakhs only had been utilised for reclamations, sinking of wells, and executing other development works on the lands covered by these societies. The estimate of Rs. 14.57 lakhs includes an estimate of the cost of concrete-lined irrigation channels, fencing and sprinkler irrigation. Technically, expenditure on these two items was not covered by the sanction. This expenditure having been incurred without the prior sanction of the Registrar, was from the audit point of view, unauthorised. But this defect was not one of substance, because from a broad point of view, expenditure on these items could not be said to be alien to the purpose which the loans were taken.

(v) Thus, even if Natarajan's original valuation is taken at its face, value, then also, up to the repayment of the loans, the societies had expended about Rs. 14.57 lakhs only out of Rs. 17.40 lakhs withdrawn by them in February/ March, 1971. The balance of Rs. 3 lakhs approximately, still remained to be utilised. Development works costing Rs. 3 lakhs if any, executed, were executed only after the repayment of these loans to the Land Development Bank.

(u) (i) Krishnakanthan's story that he had after withdrawal of the loan amounts, totalling Rs. 17.40 lakhs from the Bank, had disbursed the same pro rata among the members of the societies, has not been proved, and it appears to be untrue.

(ii) No credible explanation is forthcoming as to what was done with this money amounting to Rs. 17.40 lakhs during the period of 8 months, commencing from its withdrawal in February/March 1971 till the commencement of the development works in November, 1971 on the project area covered by these societies.

(v) (i) The report sent in reply to the Reserve Bank's reference, at the dictation of Shri S.B. Aditanar, enclosing utilisation certificates dated 25th November 1971 from Mahadevan certifying full utilisation of the loans, and the Audit Report of Narayanan, were to put it at the lowest, factually incorrect. On the other hand, the finding of Mr. Venkatanarayana recorded in his inspection report, regarding the affairs of these societies and the utilisation of the loans taken by them, appear to be substantially correct.

(ii) It seems there was a close nexus between Shri Krishnakanthan and Shri S.B. Aditanar in the matter of withdrawal of these loans. Krishnakanthan was the Manager of "Dina Thanthi" office and retailed to Shri S.B. Aditanar. Shri Aditanar was in a position to exercise dominion and control over Krishnakanthan.

(w) The money for the repayment of the loans was supplied by the Sun Paper Mills at the behest of Shri S.B. Aditanar, whose anxiety it was to stave off the threatened second visit by the R.B.I. officials to these societies, by repayment of the loans — even before, the due date — to the Land Development Bank and stepping up development work on the project area of the societies.

(x) Attempts have been made to intimidate, suborn or tamper with witness who were summoned by the commission and were supposed to give evidence inculpating Shri S.B. Aditanar. It will, therefore, be not unreasonable to presume that the attempts were made by persons acting with the consent or under the direction of Shri S.B. Aditanar.

The facts and circumstances catalogued above, reveal deep, personal involvement of the then minister for co-operation, Shri S.B. Aditanar, in the affairs of the four Lift Irrigation Societies, in question. I was his powerful hand which was steering the whole show from behind the scenes, be it the formation or registration of these societies, the sanction and disbursement of the loans to them, or the arranging of money for repayment of those loans, or the cover-up action to defuse the censure or escape the consequences of the adverse report made by the Reserve Bank of India. The primary responsibility for the various irregularities and improprieties enumerated above, relating to the registration of these societies, the sanction and disbursement of loans to them, the furnishing of incorrect utilisation certificates and the like, committed by the public officials concerned, must squarely rest on the Respondent, because they were but the result of blind obedience by the officials concerned to the improper or illegal dictates of the respondent. It was his wip looming large and high at their back that sent them stampeding on an aberrant course for them. By making them do, what they would not have normally done in the due discharge of their public duty, the respondent had abused his power and position as minister.

On the basis of the evidence before the Commission, it cannot be said that a criminal case has been made out. At the same time, the possibility of an offence of criminal misappropriation of temporary embezzlement of Rs. 17.40 lakhs cannot be ruled out. Only further investigation in the criminal case which has already been registered against the office-bearers of the societies, might unravel if an offence has been committed and to what extent, the respondent, Shri S.B. Aditanar was concerned in the offence under investigation.

Allegation No. 23(2)

There is one Shri A. Rajamanickam who is an Advocate and belongs to the D.M.K. Party but there is no criminal case against him, nor is there any evidence of his involvement in any shady transaction. This allegation has thus not been substantiated.

Allegation No. 23(3)

It is true that Shri P. Manickavasagam, a member of the D.M.K. General Council had misappropriated about Rs. 2 lakhs while he was Chairman of the Tanjore Central Co-operative Marketing Bank. He was arrested, prosecuted and sentenced to two years rigorous imprisonment. The erstwhile D.M.K. Government thus allowed the law to take its course even against an influential member of their own party. This cannot, therefore, be held as an allegation against the

Ministers of the erstwhile D.M.K. Government.

Allegation No. 23(4)

It has been established that irregularities in the affairs of the Dharmapuri District Central Co-operative Bank were committed during the Presidentship of Shri Karuvangadam, who was a prominent member of the D.M.K party.

When these irregularities came to light, erstwhile D.M.K. Government got the Board of Management replaced, and nominated the District Collector as President and the Joint Registrar of Co-operative Societies as Secretary. Shri Karuvangadam himself was not proceeded against since there was no evidence of any criminal liability either against him or any other members of the Board of Management. His being re-nominated to the Board even after having mismanaged the affairs of the Bank, was a suspicious circumstance but there is no evidence to connect with it any Minister of the erstwhile D.M.K. Government.

Allegation No. 24(i)

The following circumstances have been firmly established:

(i) Soon after the establishment of the Separate Labour Wing of the D.M.K. party known as the "Thozhilalar Munnetra Sangh Peravai" (Progressive Labour Federation) in May 1970, the Chief Minister, Shri M. Karunanidhi, personally intervened in a dispute going on between the Union led by Shri Gurumurthy and the Management of the Simpson Group of Companies and asked Gurumurthy to accept Rs. 50 lakhs as interim bonus against the workers' demand of Rs. 110 lakhs. Gurumurthy and his group of workers spurned this offer.

(ii) The District Secretary of the D.M.K. party purporting to act after consultation with Shri Karunanidhi, advised workers of the D.M.K. to retaliate if they were assaulted by the workers belonging to the non-D.M.K. Union. D.M.K. workers led by Pratapchandran on 22nd April 1971 assaulted several non-D.M.K. workers. Sixteen of the 18 cases registered on that day were against D.M.K. workers. When Gurumurthy and other office-bearers of his union complained to Shri Karunanidhi about the acts of violence indulged in by the D.M.K. Group, they were humiliated and snubbed and accused of aggression against D.M.K. workers by Shri Karunanidhi. This forced Shri Gurumurthy to resign.

(iii) On 9th May 1971, Shri Karunanidhi addressing a meeting of the workers of the Simpson Group openly faliciated Kattur Gopal and announced his unanimous election as President of the Union.

(iv) Thereafter, Kattur Gopal entered into a agreement with the Management on the same terms suggested by Shri Karunanidhi to Gurumurthy and his associates.

The above circumstances indicate that the campaign of violence against non-D.M.K. workers was covertly and overtly encouraged by the D.M.K. Party and the D.M.K. Government headed by Shri Karunanidhi. Although there is no direct evidence that Shri Karunanidhi or his colleagues or agents planned and engineered the numerous assaults and acts of violence against non-D.M.K. workers, there was sufficient indication to the Police that the D.M.K. Government was on the side of the pro-D.M.K. workers, and this induced them to adopt an ineffective and passive attitude and to ignore, overlook and even condone the violent activities of the pro-D.M.K. workers, which fostered an impression that they could commit violence with impurity.

(v) The withdrawal of the few cases which were started against the miscreants, amounted to undue interference on the part of the State Government with the course of justice.

(vi) It was the failure of the D.M.K. Government to use its police machinery effectively against the militant D.M.K. workers that led to the murder of the D.M.K. worker, Pratap Chandran.

(vii) The chaotic conditions that prevailed for over a year in the Simpson Group of Companies were largely, the responsibility of the erstwhile D.M.K. Government under Shri Karunanidhi.

Allegation No. 24(ii)

The following facts have been established:

(1) Shri A.L. Srinivasan closed the studio unilaterally with a view to circumvent and defeat the claims of the recognised union

representing the majority of the workers. He contrived to got an agreement favourable to the management with the rival union representing the minority of the workers, much against the claims and protests of the recognised union and the objections of the officers of the Labour Department.

(2) The then Superintendent of Police, the Deputy Superintendent of Police and a large contingent of Armed Police openly sided with the management in harassing the workers of the majority union and removing them in police vehicles to far off places and leaving them stranded in wilderness. The police arrested the workers apparently on unsustainable charges of criminal trespass and charge-sheeted them in court but-subsequently withdrew the same.

(3) In adopting a partial attitude helpful to Shri Srinivasan, the Labour Department appear to have acted under pressure from the then Chief Minister, Shri M. Karunanidhi, who was a close friend of Shri Srinivasan.

It has been established that the D.M.K. Government extended full support to the D.M.K. controlled Accounts Subordinates Union and the Tamil Nadu Electricity Workers' Progressive Union and also directly and illegally pressurised the management of the Board to show favoured treatment to the members of these unions. This encouraged the members of these unions to indulge in assaults, coercion, go-slow and other acts of indiscipline which adversely affected the efficiency of the Board's working and caused loss of revenue, to the detriment of the public interest.

Allegation No. 25

(i) With regard to the demonstrations held before the office *Ananda Vikatan* on 24th June 1972 and 25th June 1972, the acts committed by the demonstrators who did not do any violence to person or property except the protest burning of copies of *Ananda Vikatan* and *Kalki* already possessed by them, *per se* would not come within the clutches of law. But, since these demonstrations were held in deliberate disobedience of a prohibitory order under Section 41(2) of the Madras City Police Act, 1888, they were unlawful. Although there are circumstances which do create a suspicion about Shri Karunanidhi's involvement in these demonstrations. There is nothing in evidence that Shri Karunanidhi, personally or through some specific messenger, asked Shri Balasubramanian, Editor of *Ananda Vikatan* to publish the apology, although it has been established that the apology was published under pressure of the demonstrators.

(ii) The evidence on record, beyond creating a suspicion, does not clearly establish that the attack on the office of *Kumudam* was made in pursuance of a plan hatched by Shri Karunanidhi or the members of his Government. Shri Karunanidhi, however, did indirectly encourage and rouse the feelings of hatred in the minds of D.M.K. leaders of "Murasoli" against *Kumudam* for its alleged lampooning and defaming the D.M.K. Administration and policies through published writings and cartoons. Shri Karunanidhi as Minister in-charge of the police department of the State failed to initiate any action against the police for their failure to investigate the cases properly for bringing the miscreants to justice. He thus, failed to discharge the responsibility for ensuring good and impartial administration, particularly of the police department.

The order of the State Government made on 22nd August 1975 for seizure and forfeiture of copies of *Kumudam* dated 28th August 1975, was illegal. The State Government, however, was labouring under a genuine misapprehension as to the correct legal position. The State censor added to this confusion by assuring that he would persuade the publisher of *Kumudam* to republish the copies after deleting the portion objected to by the State Government. There was thus, no lack of good faith on the part of Shri Karunanidhi when he directed forfeiture of the issues of *Kumudam* dated 28th August 1975.

(iii) The attacks made on *Alai Osai* and Shri Narayanan were made by some D.M.K. elements who were part of a crowd that had gathered at the residence of Pratapchandran on the day of his funeral. The object of the miscreants in mounting these attacks was to punish *Alai Osai* and its publishers, including Shri Velur Narayanan, for the policy which the paper adopted through news-items and editorials in supporting the cause of the anti-D.M.K. group of workers of M/s Simpson and Co., led by Kuchelar, and also in persistently criticising the D.M.K. administration and its labour policy.

These attacks on *Alai Osai* were not made in pursuance of a conspiracy or a pre-plan, conceived in concert with, or otherwise at the behest of Sri Karunanidhi or his colleagues in the government. Thus, the Gravamen of the charge against the respondent has not been established.

The police failed to take adequate preventive and investigating measures appropriate to, contemporaneous with, and subsequent to these events. The awareness on the part of the police that the miscreants were in all probability, members or sympathisers of workers of Simpson and Co., having the general support of the D.M.K. party and government, had introduced a psychological difference in them, undermining their capacity and will to deal effectively with the rowdy elements who attacked *Alai Osai.*

(iv) It has not been established that discriminatory power-cut was used a lever to bring pressure on the journals for political ends.

Allegation No. 26

It has been established that on the occasion of the D.M.K. Party conference at Rajapalayam on 12th and 13th February 1972, the Public Relations Department of the State Government prepared and displayed a banner showing the picture of Sheikh Mujibur Rehman and Shri Karunanidhi and the same conference a booklet was distributed containing a speech of Shri Karunanidhi, in which he had drawn a parallel between himself and Sheikh Mujibur Rehman. When State autonomy demand is made in a manner which equates it with an armed struggle for an Independent State successfully waged by a neighbouring country, it tends to assume an anti-national complexion. Although the officers of the Public Relations Department, S/Shri Karunanadam and Jeevakalaimani, were mainly responsible for this Shri Karunanidhi cannot escape vicarious responsibility since, however, all concerned with creation of this banner, and Shri Karunanidhi, also, seem to have realized their mistake and subsequently got it destroyed, their act of indiscretion or misdemeanour stands considerably mitigated.

It has not been established beyond doubt that electricity was directly tapped from the main lines with the full knowledge of the Electricity Department for consumption at the D.M.K. Conference at Madurai in April 1972.

Allegation No. 27

There is no ground to hold that the incident at Singambuneri in Ramanathapuram District on 27th August 1972 was an instance of misuse of police and government influence to crush opposition parties, on the part of the D.M.K. Government.

The allegation that in October 1971 the police entered the compound of St. Xavier's College, Palayamkallai and beat inmates without any cause or justification, is completely misconceived. The police entered the campus only on the request of the principal and they also used the minimum of force necessary to restore law and order.

The allegation that in September 1971 the police attacked, at the instance of the D.M.K. every house in village Kadayampatti near Bhavani in Coimbatore District other than those belonging to D.M.K. men, appears to be baseless.

The allegation that in November 1971 at *Karivalamvandhanallur* in Tirunelveli District a Harijan was done to death in the police-lock-up, is baseless. There was an inquiry into the police firing, following this incident by a senior I.A.S. officer of the rank of Members, Board of Revenue, who found it to be justified.

The police action against the striking workers of the Heavy Vehicles Factory at Avadi in January 1972 was not a pre-meditated or pre-planned attack on selected labour leaders. All the four unions including the D.M.K. union, participated in the strike. Labour leaders belonging to different unions received injuries in the police action. The cases started in respect of this incident were also withdrawn on the appeal of the joint action council representing all the four unions.

This allegation appears to be wholly misconceived. Shri Chinnappan who died in the police lock-up at Namakkal on 26th February 1972, was not a Harijan. His death was not due to beating up by the police but due to poisoning, which, in all probability, was self-committed. An inquiry by Revenue Divisional Officer and further inquiry by the crime branch of the C.I.D. was held in connection with this incident.

Although the local police did act in a partisan manner and were reluctant to take action he was a close friend of Shri Madhvan, then Minister for Law and Industries, there is no evidence to show that any ministerial influence was brought to fear on the police.

The police had to act in self-defence during various incidents which took place as part of the State-wide struggle launched by the farmers. Except, perhaps, at Peddanaikenpalayam where 8 lives were lost in the police firing, it cannot be said that the firing was excessive.

Senior Executive Magistrate held magisterial enquires and concluded that the firings were justified.

None of the incidents mentioned by Shri Kalyanasundaram in his memorial would justify the conclusion that the erstwhile D.M.K. Government "misused" the police force "to Crush the Opposition Parties".

Allegation 27 has thus not been substantiated.

Allegation No. 28

There is absolutely no substance in the allegation that provision had been made in the proposed L.A. Bill 38 for the payment of compensation of nearly Rs. 2 crores to the owner of Sakthi Pipes Limited and that this was a political design to siphon off funds from the public exchequer in the name of paying compensation to the owner to finance and further the political aims of the ruling party with the help of Thiru N. Mahalingam, who was an ardent supporter of the ruling party.

All that has been established is that they were financial irregularities from the audit point of view in advancing loans or rendering other financial assistance to the company without taking adequate steps for safeguarding the interests of the Government. But it has not been proved that these irregularities were actuated by dishonest motives or extraneous consideration on the part of the Chief Minister or any Minister of the then D.M.K. Government or its Departmental Officers.

General Observation

Very pertinent observations have been made in the reports of previous commissions of inquiry about the need for an independent, strong, straight and efficient secretariat as the *sine quo non* of good administration. Attempts have been made to indicate principles that should govern the relationship between a Civil Servant and a Minister.

Democracy is a system of Government in which decisions are not taken by any single individual according to his whims, but necessarily arise from a process of discussion and mutual deliberation. In democracy, Public Accountability is the essence of Public Administration. Requests from the public have, therefore, to be handled with full appreciation of the anxiety and the uncertainty which they may feel while their problems are being looked into. Care should be taken to explain the basis of the decision so that the public do not run away with the impression that it was not taken on merits, with due consideration of all the pros and cons of the matter.

The transaction of official business in all Departments of Government is, to a large extent, regulated by procedure prescribed by statutory rules or executive instructions. Such rules and instructions are, broadly, speaking, of two types. Of the first type are those, rules/instructions which are purely directory. Rules of this type are useful servants but dangerous masters. Therefore, substantial compliance with them, with due despatch and discretion is commended. This will mean less red-tapism, less delays, and less occasions for "speed money" for those black-sheep who become addicted to this "stimulant." Then, there is the other type or class of rules which are matters of policy and substance. Strict compliance with such rules is necessary, and their infraction injuries the public interest more than a contravention of the rules of the first category. Observance of rules/instruction of the mandatory type, operates as a safe-guard against interplay of favouritism and arbitrariness in executive decisions. No Government in a democratic system can afford to depart from the time-tested norms .of such rules, founded on well-considered principles of policy, without laying themselves open to the charge of maladministration. It is the responsibility of the senior civil servants to respectfully remind the minister he is also bound by such norms. The civil servant will be failing in his duty if he does not caution the minister whenever the latter shows an inclination to depart from them. He should politely remind the Minister of the harm which is likely to result from a departure of those norms to the interest of the public and the fair name of the administration. If the Minister still insists, the civil servant should insist on getting written orders. But once such orders are made by the minister, the civil servant must faithfully implement the same.

Our Constitution provides that without depriving the states of their right to form their own civil services, an All India Service, recruited on all India basis with common qualifications and uniform scales of pay, will also be created, members of which could be appointed to strategic posts, both at the Centre as well as in the States. In his address to the conference of Chief Ministers convened in 1946 to consider the question of setting up an All-India Administrative

Service, Sardar Patel said:

> "It is not only advisable but essential if we want to have an efficient service, to save a central administrative service, in which we fix the strength as the provinces would require them and we draw a certain number of officers at the Centre as we are doing at present. This will give experience to the personnel at the Centre leading to efficiency and administrative experience of the district, which will give them an opportunity to come in contact with the people. They will thus, keep in touch with the situation in the country and their practical experience will be most useful to them. Besides, their coming to the Centre will give them a different experience should make the service more efficient. They will also serve as a liaison between the provinces and the Government and introduce certain amount of freshness and vigour in the administration, both of the Centre and the provinces."

At this conference, the Chief Ministers unanimously decided in favour of having an All-India Administratives Service and one of the main considerations which weighed with them was that just action and independent advice could be more easily expected from the officers of an All-India Service than from those locally recruited and controlled.

Keeping in view the main objective of constituting an All-India Service, Government have given adequate protection to the members of the All India Service against any arbitrary action that might be taken against them while serving in connection with the affairs of a state. While the State Government is competent to institute disciplinary proceeding against a member of an All-India Service, the penalty of dismissal, removal or compulsory retirement, can be imposed on him only by an order of the Central Government. Even before imposing minor penalties such as censure, with holding of increments, etc., the State Government has to consult the Union Public Service Commission, and when there is difference of opinion between the State Government and the Union Public Service Commission, such matter has to be referred to the Central Government for its decision. A member of an All India Service has also the right of appeal to the Central Government against an order of suspension or an order imposing any minor penalty passed by a State Government or against an order of a State Government which desires or varies to his disadvantage, his pay, allowances or other conditions of service, or interprets to his disadvantage the wordings if any such rule or has the effect of superseding him in promotion to a selection post. A right of appeal to the Central Government is also provided against an order of the State Government. Stopping him at the efficiency bar or reverting him while officiating in a higher grade or post, to a lower grade or post otherwise than as a penalty. All this protection has been given to ensure that they do not remain tonguetied dummies, but express their views fearlessly and frankly. Sardar Patel himself in his speech in parliament, while introducing the All-India Services Act, said that he had a secretary who dared not tell him that he was in the wrong, he would immediately get him replaced.

The Senior Civil Servant is after all, an instrument and it ultimately depends on the minister as to how he would use this instrument. The knife which in the hands of a skilful surgeon, operates to save life, can in the hands of an assassin, put out life. The Minister should look upon the Senior Civil Servant as a companion, expert in administration, who is there to assist him and carry out his policy decisions and commands, but he should leave their implementation entirely to the civil servant. The Minister should not interfere with the day-to-day administration or over the head of his chief civil servant, ordinarily give directions to his subordinate office hands. Nor should be attempt to use the civil servant as a tool or agent for his personal aggrandisement, or subvert his loyalty to him for extraneous purposes.

Several distressing cases have come to the notice of this commission in this inquiry, where even senior officers of the I.A.S.—some of them otherwise having a clean record have committed deliberate dereliction of duty, knowing fully that they were acting wrongly. They have pleaded that they had no alternative but to carry out verbal orders of the Minister. They went to the extent of allowing themselves to be used as negotiators and even collectors of bribes for the minister.

It would be relevant in this connection to refer to Rule 3(3) of the All India Service Rules, 1968 which reads as follows:

"No member of the service shell, in the performance of his official duties or in the exercise of powers conferred on him:

(i) act otherwise than in his best judgement except when he acting under the direction of his official superior and he shall obtain such direction in writing wherever practicable, and where it is not practicable, he shall obtain written confirmation as soon thereoften as possible.

(ii) evade the responsibility devolving legitimately on him and seek instructions from or approval of, a superior authority, when such instruction or approval is not necessary in the scheme of distribution of powers and responsibility."

There is a history behind the insertion of this provision in the Conduct Rules. In the Mundra episode, which was inquired into by Mr. Justice Chagla, a Senior Civil Servant took the plea that he acted under the verbal orders of the Minister. The Minister, however, denied this and ultimately, the Senior Civil Servant had to leave in disgrace. This rule was subsequently inserted mainly with a view to protect the civil servants so that they could always resort to this rule whenever verbally ordered either by a Minister or a superior official to do something relating to their official duty. If a civil servant blindly carries out such verbal orders knowing fully well that they are against the rules or established norms, and without insisting on orders in writing or without at least getting confirmation in writing as soon as practicable after carrying out the orders, he not only violates the aforesaid Conduct Rule, but also makes himself vulnerable to the accusation that he was an accomplice in the act of misdemeanour committed by the Minister. A Minister should also welcome this role because there is always the possibility of an unscrupulous civil servant committing misconduct on his own and later claiming that he acted under verbal orders of the minister.

When this rule was specifically brought to the notice of some of the civil servants who appeared as witness before the Commission, they pleaded that it was not possible to insist on having orders in writing or getting confirmation in writing from the Minister in such cases without incurring the risk of losing their job or grievous injury to their service career. In support of this plea, they cited the examples of a chief secretary and an inspector-general of police who, they said, were victimised by the erstwhile D.M.K. Government simply because they refused to deflect from the path of administrative rectitude, to take the line of the minister concerned. What appears to have happened in these two cases was that the chief secretary and the Inspector-General were removed from the prestigious posts, they were occupying and transformed to relatively unprestigious posts, though of equivalent pay and rank, I think this is a small price to pay for adhering to ideals and principles of good administration, particularly when such transfers involve only incidental inconvenience and no monetary loss. So, the mere possibility of a transfer to another post or station, should not inhibit a Senior Civil Servant, particularly of an All India Service in stating his view fearlessly or in insisting on written orders whenever he is asked to act against his conscience. There are also cases were a civil servant adopts the line of least resistance and then later, to absolve himself, take the plea that he was pressurised by the minister. If there is no direct evidence to connect the minister with the alleged misdemeancur, it must be presumed that the civil servant in his anxiety to be more royalist than the king, went out of his way to carry favour with a minister. A supine and pusillanimous civil servant of this type demoralises the entire cadre, and deserves no sympathy.

On the question of how far a minister should accept blame for actions taken by a civil servant in his department, four propositions were enunciated in an authoritative statement made in the British House of Commons on July, 1954 by the then Home Secretary, Sir D.M. Fyfe which may usefully be extracted hereunder:

(1) In a case where there is an explicit order by a minister, the minister must protect the civil servant who has carried out his order. He takes the blame if necessary; or he defends it.

(2) Where the civil servant acts properly in accordance with the policy laid down by the minister, the minister must protect and defend him.

(3) Where an official makes or causes some delay, but not on an important issue of policy, and not where a claim to individual rights is seriously involved, the minister accepts the responsibility, although his not personally involved.

He will take corrective action is the department but should not expose the official to criticism.

(4) Where action has been taken by a civil servant, of which the minister has had no prior knowledge and the conduct of the official is reprehensible, then there is no obligation on the part of the minister to endorse what he believes to be wrong or to defend what are clearly shown to be errors of his officers.

Following proposition No. 4 referred to above, if a minister fails to take action against an official who has acted without his approval in a reprehensible manner, it may be presumed that the official acted with his prior knowledge or his approval was tact, if not explicit.

The most striking feature of the search for effective remedies for maladministration in the last 20 years in several countries has been the institution of the Ombudsman, or a Parliamentary Commissioner, to whom any citizen may send a complaint with regard to maladministration on the part of either a minister or an official and who would have the necessary authority to investigate fully and recommend an appropriate action. A modified institution of the Ombudsman type has already been set up in some states and a bill has been introduced in Parliament to appoint a Lokpal and Lokayukt at the Centre as well. The success of such an institution would depend on the capacity and integrity of the Ombudsman, as well as the political will of the government which sets him up, to accept and implement his advice promptly. In the words of whereas:

> "The success of an Ombudsman is likely to be greatest in the sort of political and constitutional community which needs him least. It is essentially the sort of institution which can only be effective where habits of constitutionalism are well established and are believed in. It is more likely to make a good government better than bad government good".

When an Ombudsman type of institution is set up, the civil servant who has acted under verbal orders of the minister and is not courageous enough to put it down in writing in the file itself, may make a contemporaneous record confidentially and send a copy of the same to the Ombudsman. But it is extremely unlikely that than officer who is not bold enough to insist on orders in writing as provided under the rules, would enough, courage to send a confidential report to the Ombudsman.

The only remedy seems to be that there should be a honest effort both on the part of the ministers as well as the civil servants to observe the Salutary Rule 3(3) of the conduct rules both in better and spirit.

There can be no doubt that while the civil servant proposes, it is the minister who disposes, and once having expressed his view frankly and faithfully, the civil servant should have no mental reservations about carrying out orders of the minister. It should, however, be remembered that while the minister has the privilege to reject a view without assigning any reason, he must also keep in view the larger public interests. Before assuming office as minister either at the centre or in a state, while taking his oath of allegiance to the constitution and will do right to all manner of people in accordance with the constitution and law, without fear or favour affection or ill-will. He is thus, in the capacity of a trustee and is answerable not merely to the legislature but also to the public. He should, therefore, have the courage to reduce his orders to writing. He should not allow himself to be driven to a situation where he has to compel a civil servant to act against his conscience, while he, without committing himself in writing, remains in the background.

3

RAILWAY ACCIDENT INVESTIGATION REPORT ON FIRE ON LEADING COACH NO. 7010 (MOTOR COACH) OF T-84 UP THANA – BOMBAY-VT LOCAL TRAIN AT ES 10/13-14 BETWEEN SION AND MATUNGA STATIONS OF BOMBAY DIVISION ON CENTRAL RAILWAY AT 15.00 HOURS ON 12TH FEBRUARY, 1976

February 12, 1976–May 2, 1976[1]

One Man Commission Shri D.G. Divgi, Additional Commissioner of Railway Safety, Central Circle, Bombay

Officers Present Shri Prem Sagar; Shri A.S. Agarwal; Shri K.P. Padiyar; Shri R. Ananthakrishnan

Appointment

The Commission was constituted under Rule 4 of the Statutory Investigation into Railway Accidents Rules, 1973 (notified by the Ministry of Tourism and Civil Aviation vide No. RS.13-T/(8)/71 dated 19th April, 1973).

Terms of Reference

To inquire into the fire on leading Coach No. 7010 (Motor Coach) of T-84 Up Thana-Bombay-VT Local Train at ES 10/13-14 between Sion and Matunga stations of Bombay Division on Central Railway at 15.00 hours on 12th February, 1976.

---

1. Ministry of Tourism and Civil Aviation, Commission of Railway Safety, Government of India, New Delhi, 1982, i + 21 p.

Conclusion

Cause

On full consideration of the factual, material and circumstantial evidence, I have come to the conclusion that the fire in the leading coach No. 7010 (Motor coach) of T-84 Up Thana-Bombay VT Local train at E.S. 10/14 between Sion and Matunga stations on the Thana-Bombay VT electrified quadruple line suburban section of Bombay Division of Central Railway at about 15.00 hours on 12th February, 1976, was caused by the ignition of an inflammable liquid, similar to turpentine in its burning quality, which was being carried by a passenger/passengers below the seat level in the right hand side rear end corner of the compartment.

The conflagration injuries and the fatalities would have most probably been avoided, if plywood – a fire escalating material – had not been used in the seats.

Responsibility

The passenger or passengers who carried the inflammable liquid, which is prohibited, is/are responsible for the accident.

Relief Measures

I am satisfied that medical aid was prompt as could be expected in the circumstances, and the care and attention adequate. The relief measures were satisfactory.

Recommendations

80. Plywood or any other flammable material should not be used in the seats or any other portion as it has a high fire escalating quality. This one measure alone seems to have the potential of eliminating serious consequences from fires even if started. This also applies to the Main Line coaching stock.

81. P.V.C. sheets should not be used anywhere in the coaches as when in contact with fire they emit acrid fumes which often result in fatalities.

82. The deficiency of steps at the doorway has been the cause of

many avoidable serious injuries deaths to the passengers and the practice of running coaches devoid of steps should be given up forthwith.

83. The feasibility of providing emergency doors in partitions to afford fire escape should be examined. Also window bars should be removed, as they prevent emergency exit in certain situations and serve hardly any other purpose in the suburban service.

84. Measures to prevent the carriage of inflammable materials by passengers should be tightened up, this step being next in importance to that in para 79.

Railway Board's Comments on Various Paras of the Report

Para 80: RDSO have advised the Railway that IInd class EMU seats should be of densified resin impregnated (compressed) plywood and that before assembly it should pass resistance to spread of flame tests as per IS: 2046-62; Ist class EMU seats have to be of latex foam and rexine conforming to IS: 1741-60 and IRS-LI-56 respectively. Though, intensive explorations have been made to find out suitable alternatives to foam rubber used in Ist class EMU seats, these efforts have not succeeded. Imparting fire-retarding properties on foam rubber cushions by suitable treatment has also not been possible. However, efforts in this connection are being continued in consultation with the manufacturers.

Para 81: Use of PVC sheets for ceiling has since been discontinued. Wherever required, as a fire-prevention measure, steel sheets have been provided.

Para 82: Similar recommendations made earlier were considered and it was not found practicable to provide steps at doorways in EMU coaches. In this connection, attention is invited to this Ministry's Office Memorandum No. 75/Elec (TRS)/113/7 dated 24-7-1976 conveying Railway Ministry's decision in this regard. However, RDSO is being asked to find a solution whereby the passengers have some alternative convenient means to get down in cases of emergency.

Para 83: (i) Emergency exist: In view of excessive overcrowding, provision of easily breakable/openable exits will not be possible. It is considered that provision of at least two doorways in each EMU compartment, wherever possible, should meet the need for having an emergency exit to a large extent.

Further, RDSO/ICF have been instructed to build one batch of 6 EMU rakes from out of the next order for manufacture of DC EMUs with a provision of vestibules on trial basis.

(ii) Removal of window bars: Window bars have been provided to ensure safety of the passengers during the run and security of the coaches when stabled. It is, therefore, considered that window bars should be retained as removal may cause accidents due to passengers peeping out.

Para 84: Instructions already exist vide Board's circular No. 74/TKT. Checking/54 dated 23rd April, 1975 that the Railways should exercise strict vigilance through the staff, particularly the ticket checking staff, to prevent carriage of inflammable and explosive materials, and also educate public through notices and public address system about the hazards of carrying such materials in their luggage. Smoking in suburban trains has been banned. It is seen that CRS has noted the action being taken by the Railway Administration.

4

RAILWAY ACCIDENT INVESTIGATION REPORT ON FIRE ON LEADING COACH NO 7069 OF G-2 UP GHATKOPAR–BOMBAY V.T. LOCAL TRAIN AT ES 15/17 ON UP LOCAL LINE BETWEEN VIDYAVIHAR AND KURLA STATIONS OF BOMBAY DIVISION OF CENTRAL RAILWAY ON 11TH APRIL, 1976

April 13, 1976–June 17, 1976[1]

One-Man Commission Shri J.Y. Marathe, Additional Commissioner of Railway Safety, Central Circle, Bombay

Officers Present Shri Prem Sagar; Shri A.S. Agarwal; Shri K.P. Padiyar; Shri R. Ananthakrishnan;

Appointment

The Commission was constituted under Rule 4 of the Statutory Investigation into Railway Accidents Rules, 1973 (notified by the Ministry of Tourism and Civil Aviation Vide No. RS.13-T(8)/71 dated 19th April, 1973).

Terms of Reference

To inquire into the fire on leading Coach No 7069 of G-2 Up Ghatkopar-Bombay V.T. Local Train at ES 15/17 on Up Local Line between Vidyavihar and Kurla Stations of Bombay Division of Central Railway on 11th April, 1976.

---

1. Ministry of Tourism and Civil Aviation, Commission of Railway Safety, Government of India, New Delhi, 1981, ii + 14 p.

Conclusions

On full consideration of the factual, material and circumstantial evidence, I have come to the conclusion that the fire on the leading motor coach No. 7069 of G-2 Up Ghatkopar-Bombay VT local train at ES. 15/17 on the Up local line between Vidyavihar and Kurla stations at 09.49 hours on 11-4-1976 was due to an electric short-circuit caused by stray wires (placed by birds or thrown by some persons using road or foot-over-bridge) between the 1500 volts overhead electric lines/pantograph and the roof of the coach.

Responsibility

No Railway staff are held responsible for the accident.

Relief Measures

I am satisfied that the medical aid was prompt and the care and attention adequate. The relief measures were satisfactory.

Recommendations

39. It is understood that RDSO have prepared or are preparing a manual of instructions for inspection and upkeep of the mechanical portion of the Electric Multiple Unit Stock but they have not so far undertaken preparation of such a manual for electrical portion of the stock. Some stenciled instructions have been supplied to the staff engaged on maintenance of Electrical Portion but they are not comprehensive. For instance they do not include instructions that in the fortnightly schedule any stray wires lodged between the false roof and the main roof and those fallen on the false roof should be looked for and removed. It is considered that RDSO should also prepare a proper manual of instructions for electrical portion also.

40. In a similar accident which took place on 10-8-1970, the Additional Commissioner of Railway Safety had recommended that to avoid stray pieces of wires remaining undetected between the main roof and the false roof, a megger test should be conducted between these roofs in the fortnightly inspection and this recommendation was accepted by the Board vide their letter No. 70-Elec-113-1 of 6-5-1971. It was, however, seen that these megger tests were not

being carried out in the fortnightly inspections. Effective steps should be taken to ensure that these tests are carried out.

41. As the base plates or brackets of the insulators between the main roof and the false roof are not insulated, any metallic substance lodged between these roofs and touching the base plate establishes an electrical connection between them. Similarly damaged insulation of the roof at isolated spots due to falling objects also makes those spots susceptible to carry electric currents. The mild steel supports of the cat walks are also not insulated. It may be examined whether the base metallic parts could be provided with some insulating paint or covered with some insulating material and any dents or cracks occurring in the roofing felt could be filled in by some insulating material. If so, provision for the same may be made in the Manual to be prepared.

42. The gap between the main roof and the false roof is very narrow varying from about 50 mm to 75 mm. Cleaning of any stray pieces of wire, cloth, rubbish, etc., lodged between these roofs is not possible by bare hands or by brooms and brushes. It is, therefore, suggested that such objects should be cleared from the gap by blowing compressed air through the gap. Provision for this may be made in the Manual to be made out.

43. Although the M.S. false roof is insulated on top by roofing felt, its end cross-sectional surface is not insulated. This surface should also be insulated for obvious reasons.

44. At present the false roof is made of M.S. sheets and requires to be properly insulated to make it effective. On the other hand, if the false roof is made of some non-conducting material such as Permali sheets pressed wood, or plain wooden planks, the same would be more effective. The false roof is, however, not level but is raised at ends under the porcelain insulators in same designs and, therefore, it may be difficult to manufacture pressed wood sheets of that shape. In that case the bigger portion of the roof which is level could be of pressed wood and the smaller raised portion of steel sheets. The possibility of making out such a false roof which would be more effective may be examined.

45. The RDSO in their letter No. MC/EMU/JSP/66/67 dated 29/30-9-1972 addressed to M/s. Jessop & Co. have stated that the rubberoid or bitumen felt at present used on the main roof or the false roof is not satisfactory and roofing felt to the revised specification given in their letter should be used in the manufacture of future

coaches. It is understood in the discussions with the RDSO that the roofing felt to this revised specification has been found satisfactory according to the laboratory tests but it is to be seen whether this is satisfactory in actual practice also. It is also understood that Western Railway is experimenting with other roofing materials such as Nitrile rubber, fibre glass laminate, etc. These experiments should be pursued with vigour and a proper and effective material found out for insulating the roof.

46. Normally, the ceiling in a coach consists of plywood sheeting with glass-wool and an aluminium foil on top of it. This does not prevent the molten metal due to fire to pierce and fall through it. Limpet asbestos (i.e., asbestos bonded with rubber) was tried for ceiling but with the molten metal falling, the rubber portion gives way and the ceiling collapses. Sprayed asbestos at the bottom of the main roof was tried but with the Weight of the molten metal, it collapses and the molten metal falls in the coach. Mill board (pure asbestos sheet) supported by hylam or ferrobestos was tried for ceiling and it was found that the molten metal does not penetrate the ceiling and fall in the compartment [para 12*(c)vi*]. It is, therefore, recommended that Mill board supported on some stiff sheeting may be used for ceiling under the pantograph portion.

47. The layout of motor coach No. 7069 was such that the pantograph was mounted on the small general compartment in the rear with the result that when the fire broke out and the molten metal started falling in the compartment, the panic striken passengers had no escape except through the two side doors (situated on either side of the falling molten metal) from which they had to jump out. It is considered that this General compartment be inter-connected with the long Ladies' compartment next to it and converted into a longer General compartment so that in the event of such an accident taking place, the passengers will have an escape to the rest of the long compartment where they can remain safe. In that case, Ladies' compartment may be shifted to the next trailer coach.

48. In the present accident it was found that the feeder from Kurla sub-station which was close-by tripped but the feeder from Vikhroli sub-station which was far away did not trip; as a result, the current continued to flow intensifying the fire and its resultant damage. It is considered that if by laying underground cables and connecting the two feeders, an arrangement could be made that if the nearer feeder trips the distant feeder should also trip, the same

would stop the fire instantly and not allow it to persist and spread an thus reduce the serious consequences. It is suggested that this arrangement if feasible, should be carried out as soon as possible in the interest of safety.

49. Provision should be made in the Traction Subsidiary Rules that when a buzzer is sounded, the Motorman should reduce the speed then look for fire on the roof and if there is fire, he should lower the pantograph first and then bring the train to a stop (Para 34).

50. Apropos para 35, various suggestions and recommendations have been made in the past, while investigating similar accidents. It is suggested that a Committee of Officers from RDSO, the Central and Western Railways and the Commission of Railway Safety should review the various suggestions and recommendations made from time to time and submit a report, listing feasible suggestions alongwith financial and other implications. Thereafter in respect of such of the suggestions which are accepted by the Board, there should be a time bound programme for their implementation.

Railway Board's Comments on Various Paras of the Report

Para 39: This recommendation is accepted. RDSO is being directed to prepare the Manual of Instructions for Inspection and Upkeep of Electrical Portion of EMU stock.

Para 40: Megger tests are being carried out by the Railways. However, instructions are being repeated to all the railways to ensure compliance.

Para 41: The draft Code on Practices for Prevention of Fires in EMU Stock being finalised by RDSO contains provision of insulation of main roof, false roof, cat walk, etc.

Para 42: Railways are being directed to ensure cleaning of gaps between the main roof and the false roof.

Para 43: RDSO have issued necessary drawings to the Railways for insulating pantograph platform. The drawings provide for inward folding of insulation on all edges of platform to the extent of not less than 75 mm.

Para 44: Instructions have also been issued to the Railways that as an interim measure the roof below the platform be covered with densomator fibreglass or nitrile rubber, extending from the end of the coach to a distance of 600 mm beyond the edge of the roof fuse box.

Similarly, the platform shall be insulated with available materials such as polyester impregnated fibreglass cloth, etc. Central Railway is also trying permali laminates bonded with fibreglass lining on roof below the pantograph.

Para 45: Railways have been asked to try insulation of pantograph platform and roof below the platform. A few coaches both on Central and Western Railways have been tried with roof insulation of (i) densomat, (ii) butadyne nitrile rubber and (iii) epoxy coated fibreglass. Central Railway proposes to try permali laminates bonded with fibreglass lining on the roof below the pantograph. Before the material can be standardised, field trials to check their non-ignitability and electrical insulation properties covering at least one summer and one monsoon season are essential. The trials are in advance stage and on completion of these trials and standardisation by RDSO, the Railways will be asked to process the work on top priority.

Para 46: Provision of asbestos mill board supported by hylam or ferrobestos supported by L.P. sheets to prevent falling of molten materials in the compartment is being tried on Western and Central Railways. RDSO has taken up the work of standardisation of material and finalisation of specifications.

Para 47: To deal with the same difficulty, as is sought to be dealt with, RDSO is trying to ensure as far as practicable at least 2 doorways on each side to facilitate escape.

Para 48: Feasibility of simultaneous tripping of feeders from either end, supplying current to faulty motor coach, is being studied by RDSO who have been asked to accelerate the work of development of equipment for the provision of inter-tripping arrangements.

Para 49: This recommendation as modified by CRS is accepted and necessary instructions are being issued to the Railways.

Para 50: Based on Commissioner of Railway Safety's recommendations and suggestions to prevent fires on EMU coaches given in various accident enquiry reports, a list of 25 items has been compiled by RDSO. This list was recently discussed at Calcutta and Bombay between officers of RDSO, Eastern, South Eastern, Central and Western Railways. RDSO is continuing discussion on problems concerning implementation and is aiming to try out a time bound programme for implementation.

CRs' Additional Remarks

Preliminary design work in connection with the relocation of a pantograph on DC EMU stock to a non-passenger-carrying portion of the coach has already been completed by RDSO and drawing issued to Central and Western Railways. They are making prototype coaches incorporating these modifications. Thereafter, the modifications will be finalised for implementation on rest of the coaches.

5

JOINT COMMITTEE FOR THE REORGANIZATION OF THE ASIATIC SOCIETY, BOMBAY AND THE CENTRAL LIBRARY, BOMBAY – REPORT July 5 – October 16, 1976[1]

Chairman Professor Niharranjan Ray

Members Shri Ajai Shankar; Shri D.M. Sukthankar; Shri K.D. Puranik; Shrimati Bansari K. Sheth; Shri S. Ranganathan

Convener Shri D.R. Kalia

Appointment

The Joint Committee was constituted by the Government of India in the Department of Culture by a letter bearing DO No. 17-11/75-CAI(II) Dated 23rd April, 1976.

Terms of Reference

To examine the needs and requirements of the Asiatic Society, Bombay and the Central Library, Town Hall, Bombay.

Contents

Section One: Introduction; Section Two: The Situation that Obtains; Section Three: Analysis of and Comments on the Situation; Section Four: Remedies and Recommendations; Appendices from I to IX

---

1. July—October, 1976, Bombay

SECTION ONE

Introduction

2. Evidently some time was lost in receiving the letters of consent and in making whatever other preparations were called for. In any case, the First Meeting of the Joint Committee was not summoned and convened before July 5, 1976, when some more information and further clarification in regard to the terms of reference were sought for from Shri Ajai Shankar, the Bureau Head of the Department of Culture of the Government of India. Shri Ajai Shankar stated that the Joint Committee expected to identify the problems and suggest remedial measures giving in detail the financial implications of each. He also mentioned *inter alia* that the Union Minister for Education had recently visited the Asiatic Society and the Central Library to get some idea of the problems involved and desired that an expert Committee should look into them comprehensively.

3. The Joint Committee held three meetings altogether as follows, all in Bombay, at the meeting room of the Asiatic Society:

(i) First Meeting on July 5, 6, and 7, 1976
(ii) Second Meeting on August 20 and 21, 1976
(iii) Third Meeting on October 15 and 16, 1976.

The detailed proceedings of these meetings will be found in Appendices I, II and III of this Report.

The First and Second Meetings took into account and discussed in considerable detail the statements made verbally and in writing by Shri D.M. Sukthankar and Shri K.D. Puranik respectively on behalf of the Government of Maharashtra and the Directorate of Libraries of the State of Maharashtra on the one hand and by Shrimati Bansari K. Sheth, on behalf of the Asiatic Society, Bombay on the other. The President of the Asiatic Society was gracious enough to make a courtesy call on the Chairman and members of the Joint Committee and to host a dinner for them.

The Third Meeting was held to consider in detail the draft of the Report which had already been circulated and to adopt it with whatever additions and/or alterations that were considered necessary. It was decided at this meeting that the Report as finally adopted, should be presented at the first instance to the Minister in charge of the Department of Culture of the Government of India who were responsible for the appointed of the Joint Committee.

4. In-between two sessions of the First Meeting itself of the Joint Committee, the Chairman, the Members and the Convener met Shri Ali Yavar Jung, the Governor of Maharashtra and the Patron of the Asiatic Society who took a great deal of interest in its affairs. The President of the Asiatic Society was also present. Shri Ali Yavar Jung was gracious enough to discuss with the Joint Committee the problems of the Society in considerable detail and give the Committee the benefit of his valuable advice. Later he followed it up by forwarding to the Committee a detailed Note summarising what he had told them, this Note will be found in Appendix IV.

The Joint Committee also met the same morning Shrimati Prabha Rao, Minister for Education, Government of Maharashtra. They had a very fruitful meeting with her and very graciously she assured them of her active sympathy and help in regard to the work before them.

5. The Committee records with thanks and appreciation the kind and willing help and cooperation extended to them by the staff of the Asiatic Society and by the Directorate of Libraries of the Government of Maharashtra.

SECTION TWO

The Situation that Obtains

1. The Asiatic Society of Bombay and the Central Library, Bombay are both housed in the Town Hall. The original occupant of this enormous and magnificent edifice was the Asiatic Society alone, but the sprawling main hall with its adjacent areas were allowed to be used for occasional public purposes. The accommodation of the Central Library was however effected much later, pursuant to a decision of the then Government of Bombay to raise a Central Library of their own. But at that time the State Government could neither manage to rear up the infrastructure of a Central Library nor could they find an accommodation for the purpose. There was thus no other alternative open to them than to entrust to the Asiatic Society, the Central Library and its projected functions. In 1950 therefore a Trust Deed was executed between the Asiatic Society on the one hand and the then Government of Bombay on the other, to the above

effect. As a part of this Deed, receipt of reading materials under the Press and Registration of Books Act of 1867, except that in Marathi, Gujarati and Kannada, by the Government of Bombay and their organization and management were entrusted to the Asiatic Society, evidently with the full concurrence of the latter.

The Trust Deed just referred to, seems to have called for a certain change in the higher to accepted "objects" of the Society, the Central Library having been incorporated in the Society itself. But this change does not seem to have been statutorily recorded before November 10, 1954, by which time one more change had taken place, namely the Society had decided to cut off its natal bond with the Royal Asiatic Society of Great Britain and Ireland. A few years later, in 1960, another change also took place; a major part of what was originally stated to Bombay that became the State of Maharashtra with Bombay as its Capital.

In July, 1950 the General Body of the Society decided as follows:

1. The name of the Society shall be the Asiatic Society of Bombay.
2. The objects of the Society shall be:

(a) to investigate and encourage Sciences, Literature and the Arts in relation to Asia in particular to India, and to promote research therein;
(b) to conduct a journal;
(c) to publish works embodying research; and
(d) to maintain a general library *which will also function as Central Library for the State of Maharashtra and which shall be known as 'the Library of the Asiatic Society of Bombay and the Central Library'*." (Underlines ours).

Obviously, the change relevant to this Report, is 2(d), which added a new function and a new responsibility to the Asiatic Society.

More than 12 years later, in 1967, the Government of Maharashtra enacted the Maharashtra Public Libraries Act which envisaged, among other things, the creation and maintenance of a State Central Library and the setting up of a Directorate of Libraries. The former has not yet come into being nor has any step yet been actually taken in this regard, but the Committee has been assured that the Government of Maharashtra is prepared to move in this direction as soon as possible; indeed, they are now awaiting the Committee's Report. The Directorate of Libraries has actually been set-up, with a Director at the head, who has his office and headquarters at the Town Hall itself, but neither the Director nor the Directorate has anything to do as yet with the Central Library which remains organizationally and administratively an integral part of the Asiatic Society's organization and administration.

Much earlier than 1967, indeed from 1956 onwards, the Central Library had been functioning as one of the three national deposit centres for books received under the Delivery of Books Act of the Government of India. While it certainly extended the book-resources of the Central Library, it also doubtless strained the organizational and administrative resources of the Asiatic Society which was in over-all charge.

2. Since the Asiatic Society and its Library, as well as the Central Library are all housed in the Town Hall which is a very old edifice, it is necessary to take a look at the physical condition of the Town Hall itself, the space available and its distribution as at present.

The architectural dignity and grace of the monumental Town Hall is indeed very impressive. Even in this age of functional architecture and of generalised shapes and forms one would like to preserve and conserve an edifice of this kind. We have been told and assured, old and hoary as it is, the building is still sturdy enough to last for two more generations provided it is thoroughly renovated and maintained regularly with proper care and attention.

But as it is today the entire edifice, inside and out, presents a depressing picture; evidently it has not been kept in adequate maintenance. The ill-lighted stairs, rooms, the halls and the corridors, the walls, balustrades and the ceilings, the alcoves and the book-stacks, all present a very shoddy appearance. There is nowhere an environment for the facilities for the quiet, concentrated reading even, nothing to speak of advanced study and research. The ceiling and the wooden flooring in the edifice are all in a state of slow and steady decay. During heavy monsoons of Bombay, the roof leaks in many places. The plaster too is falling off at several places.

The elevated main floor of the building, made of wooden planking, cannot bear much weight. Shelves of books therefore, stand along side the walls or on beams, thus keeping much of the valuable floor space vacant and practically unutilised. There is therefore, no alternative but to jampack the dark and somewhat damp and humid basement with books reaching up to the ceiling. The shelves are inadequate even when the books are stacked in double rows which are often they are. In the corners and along the gangways books and periodicals are piled high up on the floor here and there. The unavoidable dumping of books makes it difficult to retrieve a needed volume. It also exposes the books to the mercy of the elements and also to dust and pests despite periodical fumigation.

It should be mentioned in this context that the collection of the Asiatic Society itself (leaving out for the present, the volumes received under the Press and Registration Act and the Delivery of Books Act) is a priceless national treasure consisting of hundreds of manuscripts, rare and out-of-print books, back volumes of journals and serials which have long been defunct, old files of national and regional dailies and periodicals, and coins and other antiquities of great historical value.

Roughly speaking, a part of the centre and the entire right wing of the basement as well as of the main floor besides certain areas on the left side of the main floor, are being used by the Asiatic Society to accommodate its own holdings, offices, reading rooms and alcover, meeting room, bindery, processing rooms and the UNESCO Information Centre. The Central Library occupies, again roughly speaking, the entire left wing of the basement and of the main floor to accommodate, process and service the books, journals, periodicals etc., received under the two Acts already referred to. The stately, spacious central hall on the main floor is used almost exclusively as a news-paper reading area by a ceaseless crowd; the crowd is a swelling, surging one during the lunch recess. It is used once alone in the year by the Government of Maharashtra for their formal Independence Day "At Home" and occasionally by the Asiatic Society. On one side however of this spacious hall there are a few cubicle-like areas which provide room for those who come for reading and requisition books from the Library collection.

But the Asiatic Society and the Central Library are not the only occupants of the Town Hall. There are in addition at least three other organisations that have their accommodation in this edifice, covering considerable floor space. These are: (a) the office of the Directorate of Libraries of the Government of Maharashtra; (b) Office, stack-room and sales counter of Revenue Stamps of the Government of Maharashtra; and (c) Office of the Bombay Women's

Council.

3. The reference library of the Asiatic Society itself is used more or less regularly by a handful alone of scholars and experts, but its lending section seems to be more popular with its members who borrow books more for general reading than for any specialized reading for purpose of advanced study and research.

The Society publishes a technical research journal which is supposed to be issued twice every year. But it seems, its publication is irregular; indeed it is in arrears by more than a year.

The Society is supposed to have a publication programme for publication of research monographs, original texts (edited or/and translated) and catalogues of manuscripts, antiquities, etc., in the possession of the Society. But except one research monograph (An Illustrated Ms. of the Aranyakaparvan of the Mahabharata), no other publication seems to have been issued for a number of years.

Occasionally the Society holds meetings for lectures and/or reading of scholarly papers, but those seem to be few and far between. At any rate there is no regular fortnightly or monthly programme for the purpose.

An over-all view of the activities of the Society in the context of its declared "objects", seems to show a certain lack of scholastic and academic attention on the part of the authorities of the Society.

This is for understandable reasons, perhaps. It seems that much of the energy and attention of the Society is sucked up by the immediate demands in regard to the administration of the two Acts.

4. The budget of the Asiatic Society and the Central Library is an integrated one; income and expenditure on the two counts are not therefore shown separately.

The Asiatic Society has on its rolls as on April 1976 a little over 1500 members of which 874 are Resident Members, 149 Non-Resident members, 448 Resident Life members, 40 Non-Resident Life members and 8 Institutional Members. The Membership subscription has been on an average over the last three years Rs. 65,000 only. However, apart the income from Membership subscription, the Society has been receiving the following annual grants:–

(i) Rs. 1,15,000 from the Government of Maharashtra – Grant to the Press and Registration Section.

(ii) Rs. 1,50,000 approx. from the Government of Maharashtra on account of administration of the Delivery of Books Act.

(iii) Rs. 1,50,000 approximately from the Government of India on account of the administration of the Delivery of Books Act.

Besides the aforesaid annual grant, the Society was also receiving in the course of last three years an annual grant ranging from Rs. 50,000 to Rs. 85,000 from the Municipal Corporation of Greater Bombay.

The total annual revenue of the Society during 1975-76 thus came to Rs. 5,65,000 approximately against a total annual expenditure on all counts taken together, of about Rs. 6,00,000, leaving a deficit of about Rs. 35,000. For the last three years at any rate the Society has been on the red, obliging it to draw upon its endowed funds which are not very considerable.

The staff of the Asiatic Society and the Central Library are also shown on an integrated muster roll, and not following any clear-cut administrative chart. But it is not difficult to find out the specific job-content of each member of the staff and to allocate them to either the Asiatic Society or the Central Library in accordance with their respective duties and responsibilities.

SECTION THREE

Analysis of and Comments on the Situation

1. Even a casual analysis of the situation and circumstance that led to the Trust Deed which made the Central Library an integral part and an obligatory responsibility of the Asiatic Society, would make it clearly evident that the argument in favour of such an arrangement was just a contingent one dictated by immediate practical considerations rather than one based on good, well-reasoned out intellectual and cultural considerations.

The Asiatic Society of Bombay, by its historical antecedents or by its own traditions, in other words, and its declared "objects", was an institution devoted to advanced studies and research in Asian, particularly in Indian History and culture, language and literature, religion and philosophy, art and archaeology, ethnology and sociology, geography and science and technology. The activities of the Society in this regard were intended to be presented before the educated and sophisticated public in the shape and form of publications (journal, monographs and books) and through the media of lectures, reading of papers, demonstrations, exhibitions, etc.

These were indeed the activities of the Asiatic Society till about the beginning of the First World War, which imparted to this society an unique distinction in the academic and intellectual world. But, already by about that time the Society was falling off from that height of glory, and if one has to go by contemporary evidence as recorded in contemporary publications, lamentations were being voiced by knowledgeable people.

No serious attempt seems to have been made since then to regain for the Society the glory that the Society was for long in the past. Rather certain steps were taken which were ultimately responsible for shifting the main focus of the Society from scholastic, academic and high intellectual pursuits to the demands of a Central Library which was a general Public library intended for catering to the popular needs and requirements of the general reading public. This shifting of the main focus was worsened by the responsibility imposed on the Society, of organising and administering the large amount of reading materials received under the Press and Registration Act and later, under the Delivery of Books Act in addition, a very small percentage alone of which were books and periodicals for serious advanced study and research.

There seems to have been an opportunity to redeem the situation in 1967 when the establishment of a State Central Library was envisaged by the Maharashtra Public Libraries Act, an institution which could integrate the Central Library and take over the entire responsibility in regard to the two Central Acts referred to above. But this State Central Library remains as yet an idea along, one regrets to find; yet the idea has to be translated into reality, it seems, if one is to find a solution which will be good and healthy for the Asiatic Society as much for the Central Library.

A Central Library for a geographical area, by its very definition, is a public library for general reading purposes; its holdings of books, journals, periodicals, etc., and their servicing are all regulated and controlled by this basic but over-riding requirement. Socially, it is relatively more broad-based. The Asiatic Society, on the other hand, is relatively a much more selective, exclusive institution, intended for catering to the needs and requirements of advanced readers, scholars and experts in certain specified fields of study and research; its holdings of books and journals, etc., which are different, and their servicing are all regulated and conditioned by the very character of the institution. Indeed, the objectives of a Central or State Central Library and of an Asiatic Society of the are wide apart, altogether different. The integration of the Central Library and the Asiatic Society and its library was therefore from the very beginning, of the nature and character of an unholy wed-lock. It changed the character of the Asiatic Society for the worse, and it could not impact to the Central Library the character, appearance and function of a good and effective public library. One feels that the sooner this wed-lock is broken the better for both.

Once the two institutions become separate, it would be easier for both to gain or regain their own intrinsic character and personality. Such a separation can be effected by dividing the total holdings of reading materials in the Town Hall, minus the original collection of the Asiatic Society, between the Society itself and the Central Library, and by separating altogether the organisation and administration of the two. In doing so, the different objectives, needs and requirements of the two could be borne in mind.

Simultaneously with this separation, it will be convenient it seems, if the name of the present Central Library is changed to State Central Library and the Government of Maharashtra takes over its full share of responsibility, financial and otherwise, its organisational and administrative responsibility being taken over the Directorate of Libraries of the Government of Maharashtra, even from the very outset.

2. The question of the seat of the Asiatic Society and the Central Library is an important one and deserves full consideration.

The Town Hall which is today the seat of both the institutions, is already about 150 years old, and being of a monumental form and character, occupies a very wide area of land in a most important sector of the crowded metropolis of Bombay. One may argue that since this huge, heavy edifice is not likely to last long, it would be better to pull it down and replace it by one or more modern multistoreyed functional buildings which would accommodate not only the Asiatic Society with its library and Central or State Central Library but also one or more other Government or semi-Government cultural institutions of the city, for instance, the State Archives and the State Akademi. In fact, it was argued with some force that for historical and architectural reasons the grand flights of stairs at the entrance and the grander and magnificent colonnade could be preserved and maintained, and the rest of the sprawling building demolished and replaced by as many as three multistoreyed buildings of the same architectural form and design, all alongside at the back of the stately colonnade. These three buildings would accommodate the Asiatic Society in the middle, flanked by the State Central Library and the Directorate of Libraries on one side and the State Archives and Akademi on the other, so that the entire complex could provide a great cultural and intellectual centre to the City of Bombay.

This is certainly an attractive proposition, and one wishes the plan could be made real and effective. But the financial implications involved in the proposal are of such tremendous magnitude and this, in the face of many other more urgent and immediate needs and requirements of our people, as to sky and prejudice the State Government and the Centre against any consideration even of the proposal at this moment of our national life. Then there is also perhaps the question of finding accommodation for the two institutions during the interim period of demolition of the Town Hall and rearing up of at least one multistoreyed building to begin with. And finally one must take into consideration the question of the span of life of the Town Hall building as it is today. On this point the Committee has been assured by competent authorities (please see Appendix V) that the edifice is a very sturdy one still and it would last for at least another 40 years provided the basement and the main floor were thoroughly repaired and renovated and then the building was properly maintained at close and regular intervals.

One may therefore argue that it would be wiser in the situation that obtains, to follow the path of least resistance from any quarter and to proceed on the basis of the minimum that should be necessary. In other words one may argue that the Town Hall may be allowed to stand as it is, provided the edifice was repaired and renovated in a comprehensive manner and the Government of Maharashtra undertook to maintain it regularly and properly. Should one choose to decide accordingly, even in that case the expenditure on over-all and thorough renovation would be considerable, Rs. 4 to 5 lakhs on a rough and ready computation. But in the circumstance of the case, this seems to be the only realistic and practicable course to pursue.

3. Ideally speaking, the Asiatic Society, with its library, reading rooms, research cubicles, meeting room, office and processing rooms, auditorium, exhibition hall, bindery, photographic and retrieval section, etc., should be the sole occupant of the Town Hall,

which is consistent with the dignity and renown of the Town Hall as well as of an institution like that of the Asiatic Society. But before this ideal situation can be translated in real terms certain other things seem to call for immediate action, which are as follows:

(i) it is understood that the Bombay Women's Council have already their own premises in Bombay; they may be asked to vacate with immediate effect;

(ii) The Stamps Office with its stack-room and sales counter, is an anachronism in the context of the Asiatic Society and the Central Library. The Government of Maharashtra would therefore be well-advised, it seems, if they choose to remove this office from the Town Hall to some other area adjacent to the Bombay city courts; and

(iii) Ideally again, the Directorate of Libraries and the proposed State Central Library to the raising and maintenance of which the Government of Maharashtra is all but committed and which would be the legatee institution of the present Central Library, should have a building of their own, and a decision may be taken to this effect as early as possible. But even if it be done and planning work started, a new building cannot crop up overnight. Indeed, it would take at least 3 to 4 years for such a building to come up, and may be, in more than one phase. Till that time it would be necessary, one feels, for the Directorate of Libraries and the State Central Library to continue to remain where they are at the moment. But the sooner the new building comes up, these two organizations should shift themselves there and leave the Town Hall minus the Central Hall on the main floor, to the Asiatic Society alone, the Central Hall being ear-marked for the use of the Government of Maharashtra for their formal and ceremonial public functions as well as of the Asiatic Society for their exhibition purposes.

It is understood that the University of Bombay has agreed to make available a suitable plot on their new campus at Kalina to enable the Government of Maharashtra to raise a new and spacious building there for the accommodation of their State Central Library and Directorate of Libraries. This proposal is most welcome and may be accepted.

4. It is somewhat unfortunate that in recent decades the Asiatic Society has been lacking in active scholastic and academic interest in advanced studies and research which should have been the main justification of their existence. One feels that with the shedding off of the lead of the Central Library and the responsibilities in regard to the two Central Acts, it would be possible for them confine themselves to their declared main objectives. To that end it would be necessary to enlist the cooperation and support of intellectuals, research workers, scholars and academic people and have these interests reflected in the general membership of the Society as well as in its various executive and advisory bodies, at any rate in larger proportions than as at present. It would also be necessary for the Society to draw up and carry out regularly a research programme and revitalise their publication programme including editing and translation manuscripts belonging to their collection, and seeing them published. A closer liaison with the universities of Bombay and Pune, with institutions like the Bhandarkar Oriental Research Institute and the Deccan College, both of Pune, should be helpful towards projecting a better image of the Asiatic Society as a centre of advanced study and research in Oriental subjects.

5. If the divorce of the Central Library from the Asiatic Society is to be made effective as early as possible, apart from the legal and procedural formalities which may be necessary for the purpose, immediate exercises would have to be undertaken in regard to many items of work. These would include the following:

(a) Preparation of a blue-print of the aims and objects and of the scope and function of the proposed State Central Library which will be the legatee institution of the present Central Library.
(b) Preparation of a blue-print of the plan and design of the new building of the proposed Maharashtra State Central Library and the Maharashtra Directorate of Libraries at the site of the new campus of the University of Bombay.
(c) Preparation of an organizational and administrative chart for the State Central Library to provide guidance in regard to these two counts to the authorities concerned.
(d) Preparation of rough budget estimates for the State Central Library, for the remaining years of the Fifth Five Year Plan, year by year, showing anticipated expenditure under recurring

and non-recurring heads, keeping in view (b) and (c) above. These estimates should include the estimated expenditure on transfer of reading materials from the Asiatic Society to the State Central Library.

(e) Preparation by the State P.W.D. of a rough budget estimate for a thorough and over-all renovation of the basement and the main floor of the Town Hall.

(f) Preparation of an organizational and administrative chart for the re-organized set-up of the Asiatic Society and separation and allotment of the existing staff according to the requirements of the Asiatic Society and the proposed State Central Library.

(g) Preparation of rough budget estimates for the Asiatic Society, for the remaining years of the Fifth Five Year Plan, year by year, showing estimated income and expenditure, under recurring and non-recurring heads, keeping in view (f) above and the items of re-organization indicated above.

(h) A rough estimate of the extent of the total financial responsibilities to be borne by the Government of Maharashtra and that of the Government of India, in regard to the Asiatic Society and the proposed State Central Library, should also be prepared.

The remedies to be suggested and the recommendations to follow, would depend on the information furnished in regard to sub-items (a) to (h) referred to above. At any rate, these items of information should constitute the background material on which any recommendation could be made.

SECTION FOUR

Recommendations

From what has gone into Sections two and three basic remedies of the situation, are hopes, have already suggested themselves; indeed, these have been indicated in the comments. Besides, the decisions which the Committee was led to in course of their discussions, and which are recorded in the Proceedings of the First and Second Meetings, contain more than enough indication of the remedial measures that may and should be undertaken towards the reorganization of the

Asiatic Society and the setting up of the State Central Library. The following recommendations are being made on the basis of those suggestions, decisions and indications.

I. Structural and Organisational

It is recommended that —

1. The Central Library to divorced as early as possible, from the Asiatic Society and the latter be freed from the responsibility of receiving, processing, housing and servicing the reading materials deposited under the Press and Registration of Books Act and the Delivery of Books Act;
2. The Government of Maharashtra resolve to set-up as early as possible, the State Central Library as envisaged by the Maharashtra Public Libraries Act, and that the State Central Library, become the legatee of the present Central Library, entrusted with the responsibility, apart from other duties and functions, of receiving, processing, housing and servicing the reading materials deposited under the two Acts referred to above;
3. The Asiatic Society confine itself within the limits of its original aims and objects and develops itself as a centre of advanced study and research in the field of Oriental Studies with special reference to the sub-continent of India-Pakistan-Bangladesh, West and Central Asia and East and Southeast Asia, that the Society work out a regular programme of research and a publication programme and see to it that these programmes are carried out regularly and effectively, and that in their general membership as well as in their various advisory and executive bodies academic, scholarly and intellectual interests be represented in larger proportions than these are at present;
4. The Asiatic Society be requested to amend sub-clause (d) of the "objects" of their Memorandum of Association so as to read "(d) to maintain a general library for the above purposes," and that in view of the fact that the Government of India and the Government of Maharashtra would have to share deficit in the budget of the Asiatic Society and its Library, it was proper that the services of the Library should

be made available to all those who were engaged in advanced study and research, on an equal footing with the members of the Society, at any rate for reference purposes. For the privilege of borrowing books for home-reading by non-members, the Society might choose to ask for cash deposits, but for library services on the premises no discrimination should be made between members and non-members;

5. The Society initiates research activities by appointing, to begin with, at least 2 Research Fellows of their own at University Grants Commission terms and conditions, enlist the cooperation of other research bodies in the same field and raise some endowment funds towards the furtherance of their research activities;
6. The Society publishes at least 2 issues annually at regular intervals, of their journal, and established a Publication Unit with a Publication Officer in charge, at a monthly salary in the grade of Rs. 300-800, to look after the publication of the journal and other research monographs, books, etc., (on average, one research monograph and one edited or/and translated text of a Ms. from their holdings, or an annotated catalogue of the materials in their possession, should be published annually).
7. The Society transfers to the Central/State Central Library (a) all publications received under the two Acts from the very beginning, *except* those titles which are meant for advanced study and research; (b) all titles in modern Indian languages including back-files of periodicals *except* those which might be necessary for research purposes; (c) all materials which are meant for recreational reading; (d) all UNESCO publications; and (e) the UNESCO unit itself. The Government of Maharashtra should designate the State Central Library as the depository centre for all UNESCO publications;
8. The division of the stock of reading material referred to in 7 above, should commence with immediate effect; the authorities of the Asiatic Society and the Central Library might, if they chose, set up a small joint committee for the purpose;
9. Materials which have no academic, scholastic and high intellectual value should not be acquired by the Society, even through gifts, since eventually they mean locking up of much

valuable shelf space;

10. The Asiatic Society might re-organize their organisational set-up and the Central/State Central Library might initiate an organisational set-up for their respective administration in accordance with the respective administrative charts enclosed (see Appendices VI (a) and VI (b). These charts should be followed as closely as possible;
11. An analysis of the staff of the Asiatic Society be made immediately and the members of the staff be reallocated to the Asiatic Society on the one hand and the State Central Library on the other, to each according to their respective *basic, minimum immediate needs*. The services of those who should be allocated to the State Central Library might be transferred accordingly to the latter from the rolls of the Asiatic Society.

II. Building and Accommodation

It is recommended further that

12. Immediate steps be taken by the Government of Maharashtra to have the Town Hall rooms and other spaces occupied by the Bombay Women's Council and the Revenue Stamp authorities, vacated as soon as possible, since without such vacation no thorough and over-all renovation of the building should be possible. Besides, for several years to come all spaces available at the Town Hall, will be required by the Asiatic Society, the State Central Library and the Directorate of Libraries.
13. Considering the enormous cost involved even in the demolition of the main body of the Town Hall and then in the raising of even one multi-storeyed building on a part of the area, taking into consideration the sentiments in regard to the historic associations of the edifice and its dignified asthetic character and following the way of practicability and the path of least resistance, the Town Hall might be allowed to continue to provide accommodation to the Asiatic Society and its Library for another two generations, but it must be thoroughly strengthened, renovated and reconditioned and made suitable for the proper functioning of the Society. In this regard the renovation of the ceiling should be taken up by the State

P.W.D.

14. Considering the unlikelihood of availability of any standing building in the city and the extreme pressure on available land even within the limits of Greater Bombay, the Government of Maharashtra might immediately accept the offer of the University of Bombay of a 2.2 acre piece of land on their new Kalina campus and undertake as early as possible to raise a suitable building, for the present, with adequate floor-space for the accommodation of a well-provided for State Central Library and for the headquarters of the State Directorate of Libraries. The State Central Library should be developed in such a way as to serve as the apex of the State's library system, which should be the responsibility of the Directorate of Libraries of the Government of Maharashtra.
15. The establishment of the State Central Library should not await the construction of the new building referred to in para 14 above, since it may take at least 2 to 3 years' time. Indeed, the State Central Library should start functioning as soon as possible, as a separate organisation, in the Town Hall building itself, with whatever re-shuffling and re-allocation would not be possible without the Bombay Women's Council and the Stamp Office vacating the premises. The re-shuffling and re-allocation suggested, may be done by a small Joint Committee set-up for the purpose, if necessary, by the authorities of the Asiatic Society and the State Central Library. The re-shuffling and the re-allocation of the members of the staff as at present (see para 11 above), might also be done by the same Joint Committee.
16. As soon as the necessary funds could be raised by the Society for the purpose (the Committee was given to understand that this was within the bounds of possibility) through generous donations by individuals and private corporate bodies, the repair and renovation of the Town Hall (the basement first, followed by the main floor) should be taken up and completed as an urgent piece of work. (The Joint Committee felt that with judicious incentives extended by the Income Tax exemptions, such donations as referred to above, should be forthcoming without much difficulty. The Committee felt further that for a purpose like this, the incentive asked for, might be extended to prospective donors by the Ministry of Finance

of the Government of India).

17. The work of repair and renovation of the Town Hall might be done in 2 phases, within a period of not more than 2 years, and budget estimates might be prepared accordingly.

III. Financial

Further it is recommended that –

18. The estimated cost of repair and renovation of the Town Hall in its first phase, which will be about Rs. 4.00 lakhs (for the basement alone), be raised by the Asiatic Society through public donations, and that Shri Ali Yavar Jung, the Governor of Maharashtra and the Patron of the Society be requested to extend his gracious help and patronage in this regard.
19. Estimate of the cost of repairs and renovation of the Town Hall in its second phase (the main floor) should be prepared immediately and the drive for raising funds through public donation should be undertaken simultaneously with the first phase.
20. The payment of grant of Rs. 1,00,000 recommended by the Committee for Steel shelving to be paid to the Asiatic Society by the Central and State Governments in equal proportion for the year 1976-77, would be subject to the Asiatic Society agreeing to the bifurcation and its implementation by 31st March, 1977. Intimation to this effect should be sent to the Central and State Governments, so that action may be taken to release the grant.
21. The estimates of expenditure during the last 3 years of the Fifth Five Year Plan, namely 1976-77, 1977-78 and 1978-79 for the Asiatic Society of Bombay are given in Appendix VII. The estimates related only to recurring expenditure and took into account the income of the Society by way of subscription of about Rs. 75,000 and Bombay Municipal Corporation grant of about Rs. 85,000. The Central and State Government contribution would be confined to the recurring expenditure. Non-recurring expenditure would be met by the Asiatic Society of Bombay out of its own resources. The grants for the year 1977-78 of the Central and State Government would be paid to the Society only if bifurcation of the book-stock, furni-

ture and equipment, staff and the accommodation was completed before April, 1977 and intimation to this effect was sent to the State and Central Government before the commencement of the financial year 1977-78.

The Asiatic Society should submit the detailed budget for the year 1977-78 to the Central and State Governments not later than 15th November, 1976. The budget estimates amount should not exceed the amounts shown in Appendix VII.

22. The grant of Rs. 50,000 for the Central Government to State Government for the year 1976-77 would be payable only if the State Government takes immediate steps to establish the State Central Library in the Town Hall, Bombay. Intimation to this effect should be sent to Central Government by January 15, 1977 along with the statement of estimated expenditure for the year 1976-77, so that steps could be taken by the Central Government to release its share of 50 per cent of the estimated expenditure.
23. The estimates of the expenditure of the State Central Library were shown in Appendix VIII. Grant from the Central Government would be subject to the State Government agreeing to construct a building for the State Central Library at the Kalina Campus of the University of Bombay. The release of grants for the building would be subject to the State Government submitting the plans and estimates of the proposed building not later than July 15, 1977.
24. The Central Government grants towards the recurring expenditure of the State Central Library for the years 1977-78 and 1978-79 would be subject to the State Government submitting the statement of estimated expenditure for the years well in time. However, the State and Central Governments should make due provision in their respective budgets on the basis of the recommendations of the Committee.
25. The share of grants of the Central and State Governments arising out of the recommendations of the Committee were given in Appendix IX.

Conclusion

The Committee hopes that once their recommendations are implemented the Asiatic Society should find itself once more on the way towards achieving their main objectives of higher learning and research and the State Central Library should function as the apex of a State Library system which would do credit to the State. To that end it may be helpful to have the Central and State Governments represented on the executive of the Asiatic Society and the Central Government on the executive of the State Central Library, to keep themselves in close touch with the activities of the respective organisations. Finally the Committee feels that after five years there should be a review of the working of both the institutions.

APPENDIX I

Joint Union Government and Maharashtra Government Committee on the Asiatic Society and the Central Library, Bombay

Proceeding of the First Meeting
5th, 6th and 7th July, 1976

The first meeting of the Joint Committee set-up by the Department of Culture, Ministry of Education and Social Welfare of the Government of India and the Department of Education, Government of Maharashtra, to examine the needs and requirements of the Asiatic Society, Bombay and the Central Library, Bombay, was held at the Asiatic Society, Bombay on three consecutive days – 5, 6 and 7 July, 1976, in several consecutive sessions.

First Session : 5 July, 1976, 10 a.m.

The following members were present:

Members: : Professor Niharranjan Ray, in the *chair*; Shri Ajai Shankar, Deputy Secy., Department of Culture Government of India; Shri D.M. Sukthankar, Secretary, Department of Education and Youth Service, Government of Maharashtra; Shrimati Bansari K. Seth, Honorary Secretary, Asiatic Society, Bombay; Shri K.D. Puranik, Director of Libraries, Government of Maharashtra; Shri S. Ranganathan, Assistant Financial Adviser, Ministry of Finance, Government of India.

Convenor : Shri D.R. Kalia, Director, Central Secretariat Library, Government of India, New Delhi.

Before they took their seats in formal session the Chairman suggested that the Committee should go round all the rooms and halls of the Town which accommodated the Asiatic Society and the Central Library, see the stacks and shelves, the offices and the reading spaces, the general condition of the books, etc., with a view to forming a general idea of the over-all situation that obtained.

The Committee agreed and the members took a rapid round.

While the Committee felt very much impressed by the architectural dignity and grace of the monumental edifice and by its stateliness and solidity (the members were given to understand that the foundations of the edifice were still very strong, its thick walls still very secure and solid and the building had still a great load-bearing capacity along the walls and around its stately pillars), the members could not but feel that the entire edifice had not been kept under adequate maintenance for quite a long time, that its exterior offered a very shabby and shoddy appearance and that its interiors presented a very depressing sight and atmosphere all round – in the stacks and shelves as much as in the offices and reading halls and alcoves. There was indeed nowhere an atmosphere and environment nor the facilities for quite concentrated reading even, nothing to speak of advanced study and research.

Well-nigh a century and a half old, uncared for and unattended to for decades, the ceiling and the wooden flooring were throughout in a dilapidated condition. The roofs leaked in many places once there was a heavy monsoon shower. The plaster was falling off from the two giant-domed skylights, exposing the bamboo framework, and from one skylight rain water dripped continuously on to a marble statue, 50 ft. below. In a part of the research section used by the scholars, the plaster kept on falling into the sackcloth hung across the entire ceiling. As the elevated main wooden floor of the building could not bear much weight, shelves had been placed along the walls and over beams, thus keeping much of the valuable floor space vacant and unutilized. There was, therefore, no alternative but to jampack the basement with books almost reaching up to the false ceiling. The shelves were pitifully inadequate, even when the books were stacked in double rows. Consequently, books and periodicals were piled high up on the floor. The unavoidable dumping of books made it difficult, if not impossible, to retrieve a needed volume. It also exposed the books to the mercy of the elements and also to dust and pest. Moisture seeped through the floor. A high percentage of humidity in the city throughout the year had an adverse effect on the books too. Some of the old books and manuscripts would crumble at a touch. As the shelves and floors and were crammed with books, the once-a-month fumigation was unable to extirpate white ants, other termites and the silverfish playing havoc with the stock.

Yet, even the hurried cursory look the Committee took, showed that the collection of the Asiatic Society was a priceless national treasure consisting of hundreds of manuscripts, rare and out of-print books and back volumes of journals and serials which have long been defunct, besides old files of national and regional dailies and periodicals.

The Committee also found out that, roughly speaking, the left wing of the basement of the main floor were taken up by the stock and the processing section of the Central Library which was supposed to accommodate and make use of intake of the books, periodicals and journals, etc., received under the Registration and Delivery of Books Act of the Union Government while, again roughly speaking, part of the centre and the entire right wing of the basement and of the main floor, besides certain areas on the left side were being used by the Asiatic Society to accommodate its own holdings, offices, reading rooms and alcoves, meeting room, bindery, processing rooms, etc. The big, stately hall on the main floor was being used as a newspaper reading area by a ceaseless crowd of unemployed or under-employed people and by a lunch-hour inundation of ordinary why collard office-employees of all sorts. This hall, used only once in the year, by the Maharashtra Government for their Republic Day meeting presented indeed the spectacle of a veritable small town market placed only less noisy but equally dirty, drab, disorganised, shabby and shoddy.

The Committee also found out that the Asiatic Society and the Central Library were not the only occupants of the building. There were at least three other organisations that had occupancy rights on the premises, covering considerable floor area. These were (a) the Office of the Directorate of Libraries, (b) Office, Stock-room and Sales Counter at Court Stamps of the Maharashtra Government, and (c) a Women's Organisation (Bombay Women Council).

The preliminary survey-tour of the building over, the Committee met in formal session at 11 a.m.

The Chairman called the meeting to business and welcomed all the members, hoping that their deliberations would help identification of the problems before them and suggestions of remedial measures.

To begin with the requested Shri Ajai Shankar who represented the Department of Culture of the Government of India, on the Committee, to explain the terms of reference of the Committee since the Chairman felt that the letters of the Governments of India and Maharashtra which he had received, were not clear and exhaustive enough.

Shri Ajai Shankar stated that the Committee was supposed to identify the problems and suggest remedial measures giving in detail the financial implications of each. He also mentioned that the Union Minister of Education and recently visited the Library to acquaint himself with the problems of the Library and desired a Committee to look into them in detail.

The Chairman then called upon Shri D.M. Sukthankar, Secretary, Department of Education and Youth Services, Government of Maharashtra, to present the thinking of his Government in this regard.

Shri Sukthankar said that the overwhelming problem was of space in the Town Hall where the Asiatic Society's Library was located. He described the circumstances leading to the transfer responsibility of the Maharashtra Government to establish and maintain the State Central Library, to the Asiatic Society. He said that in 1950 when the functions of the State Central Library were entrusted to the Asiatic Society, no separate Director of Public Libraries existed in the then State of Bombay nor was there any library-legislation. At that time there was no other alternative open to the State Government than to entrust the Central Library functions to the Asiatic Society. As a part of the Trust Deed executed between the Government of Bombay and the Society in 1950 receipt of reading materials under the Press and Registration of Books Act, 1867 was entrusted to the Society. Shri Sukthankar, further stated that the Maharashtra Public Libraries Act of 1967 provided for the establishment of a State Central Library by the Government of Maharashtra, and as such the Government of Maharashtra proposed to establish the State Central Library as a separate Institution. He observed that the Asiatic Society had not been able to do full justice to either or its responsibility as a research institution or as a Central Library, primarily because of lack of adequate accommodation and financial resources. According to him there was no legal bar to the Maharashtra State Government establishing the State Central Library so long as an amicable settlement was reached with the Asiatic Society, despite the Trust Deed of 1950. He read out, in this connection, Section 50-A of the Bombay Public Trusts Act, 1950. It laid down that the Charity Commissioner could modify a trust deed of a Society for better functioning of a Society. He said that once the question of bifurcation of the Asiatic Society's functions took place and it was divested of the responsibility of maintaining the Central Library, arrangement could be made to divide the present holdings of the Asiatic Society between the Asiatic Society's Library and the proposed State Central Library. He said that in most cases, two copies of a title were available in the Asiatic Society received under the Press and Registration of Books Act and the Delivery of Books Act, and one copy of each could be spared for the State Central Library even if the Society wanted to retain a copy for its Library.

The Chairman then called upon Mrs. Bansari K. Sheth, Secretary of the Asiatic Society of Bombay, to present her points of view which were relevant in this regard.

Smt. Sheth stated that the Asiatic Society was burdened with new responsibilities by the declaration of its Library as a Depository under the Press and Registration of Books Act and the Delivery of Books Act, without placing adequate resources at the disposal of the Society. According to her, lack of adequate accommodation and finances were the primary problems. She stated that whatever reserves the Society had, had been eaten up in meeting its recurring routine expenditure. She complained that the grants-in-aid from the Government of Maharashtra and the Central Government were not made available in time which further aggravated the Society's financial problems. She had no objection to the Government of Maharashtra establishing the State Central Library with goodwill on both sides. She did not envisage any difficulty in transferring duplicate copies of books received under the Depository Acts. She further state that there was fire hazard and the Society was not in a position to meet the cost of installing fire-fighting equipment. The Society was neither in a position to provide air-conditioning which was absolutely necessary for better preservation of manuscripts and rare books. Recurring cost of maintaining the air-conditioning units was beyond the means of the Society.

The Chairman then called upon Shri K.D. Puranik, the Director of Libraries, Government of Maharashtra to present his views.

Shri Puranik stated that negotiations had been going on between the Government of Maharashtra and the Asiatic Society during the last 10 years or so to sort out the problems arising out of the Trust Deed of December 1950. The State Government had been trying to acquired a suitable site for the State Central Library. Recently, the Government had received an offer from the Bombay University, of a plot measuring eight acres on the new Campus of the University. He did not envisage any serious problems in bifurcating the two institutions, namely, the Asiatic Society Library and the State Central Library. Once the State Central Library was established, it would receive the material under the Press and Registration of Books Act and the Delivery of Books Act.

The Chairman then requested Mr. Kalia to state his views in regard to what was being discussed.

Shri D.R. Kalia stated that no problem was intractable so long as there was determination to meet it. There seem to be lack of determination on the part of the authorities concerned, to meet the situation. If it has been there, funds cold have been found. It was necessary, therefore, for the State Government to accord high priority to the establishment of the State Central Library.

Second Session : 5th July, 1976, 3 p.m.

(All members were present except Shri D.M. Sukthankar)

Meeting after lunch-break the Chairman observed that from what the members said and from what he had gathered on his own as background material, his idea was that the Asiatic Society of Bombay, like all other Asiatic Societies elsewhere in the world, was originally founded as a centre of activities in the higher learning and research in the field of what was once known as Oriental Studies, and this with special reference to the Indian sub-continent. Since its inception the Bombay Society despite its ups and downs, has been carrying on its work faithfully and true to aims and objectives. Indeed, it was able to establish a creditable record of its own by its publications and its accommodation of scholars and intellectuals of repute, though already from the early decades of this century it has been experiencing somewhat of an ebb-tide of its activities. Yet, one may not forget that it was under its roofs that Mr. P.V. Kane worked out his monumental work on the *History of the Dharmasastra* in several volumes.

But in 1950, as a result of a Trust Deed executed between the Society and the Government of Maharashtra, the Society became the receipt-centre of all printed materials received by Government under the Press and Registration of Books Act of 1867. The Chairman failed to understand why this was done and why the Society undertook this task and responsibility — one which was not even remotely connected with its legitimate activities under its original character. But this was not the end of the creation of an anomalous situation. A few years later when the Delivery Books Act came into operation (1954), again the Asiatic Society was made the deposit station for all printed materials received under this Act. Then in 1967 the Government of Maharashtra promulgated their Public Libraries Act which provided for the establishment of a State Central Library which was proposed to be set-up as a separate, independent institution. But since there was as yet no Directorate of Libraries, this institution was not established as an independent unit. What was done was to ask the Asiatic Society to house and administer the State Central Library, to which the Society seems to have agreed, and to receive the contents (books, periodicals, etc.) under the two acts. It was thus that the Asiatic Society and the Central Library was made to enter into a wed-lock and share the same household the habit at of which was the Town Hall.

The Chairman felt that it was a most unholy wed-lock which was destined to be harmful for both the partners. The Asiatic Society designed and evolved as a centre of higher learning and research and its library was meant to serve the aims and pursuits of advanced students and scholars working mainly in the wide field of Oriental Studies. The State Central Library was intended to be a public library meant for general readers, for pleasure or for gaining general knowledge, information and enrichment. The aims, objectives and character of the two institutions were thus altogether different; hence their clientele, their process and procedures of work, their needs and requirements, their programmes, etc., were also very different. Maladjustments were thus inherent in the very situation itself, and over the years this had been made more than manifest. The Asiatic Society has lost its character, very largely if not altogether, it has not been functioning properly for long; its legitimate duties and obligations have been thrown into the background and it finds itself burdened, physically, financially and intellectually, with an obligation which strains all its nerves and organs. The State Central Library too, seems to exist but in name; it does not function as a central public library should, and hence it falls very much short of fulfilling any meaningful social and intellectual obligation. The Directorate of Libraries the office of which is located in the premises, has nothing to do with the State Central Library except the Director acting as a co-ordinator, or whatever it may mean. The State Central Library also plays no role in the library system of the Maharashtra State.

The contents of the library too, are very much under-utilised because of the lack of readers' facilities and of space. Thus the State Central Library too, has hardly evolved any character of its own as a public library which is supposed to be at apex of the State Library system.

The Chairman therefore felt that no worthwhile improvement of the present situation was possible without effecting a separation of the two partners, for the good of both, which meant that there should be a structural change, to begin with. This was the first issue to be discussed seriously by the Committee and to be decided upon. Once a decision was taken in this regard, further details in regard to the act of separation ways and means of re-organisation of the Asiatic Society and the setting up of the State Library as a separate, independent union, etc., could be more fruitfully discussed and decisions arrived at. He, therefore, requested the members to give him the benefit of their thinking on the first issue first, followed by other issued that were associated with the main issue.

To one other issue the Chairman invited the attention of the members; it was to the physical condition of the Town Hall building itself. Srimati Sheth, the Honorary Secretary of the Asiatic Society, had assured the members of the Committee, while on their round, of the soundness of the building from the engineering point of view, that its foundations and walls were so strong that it could yet last for two more generations. Assuming for the moment that it was so, it could be argued that these mid-nineteenth century monumental buildings, architecturally so magnificent and dignified, were most unsuited to serve the purposes of either the Asiatic Society or of the State Central Library and that there was considerable wastage of vertical and horizontal spaces. Besides, the fact remained that the edifice was more than 142 years old, and even in the best of situations it could not last for very long and that the annual cost of maintenance of such an old building in proper condition would be enormous. One may therefore argue that this monumental structure be pulled down while retaining its majestic colonnade and the grand staircase as examples of past glory and magnificence, and that atleast a couple of multi-stcreyed modern buildings be raised in its place, the colonnade serving as the facade for both, one for the Asiatic Society and the other for the State Central Library.

Or, alternatively, considering the difficult situation of our economy and of Government finances at the Centre and the States, one might argue that it would be better to retain the Town Hall as it was, in its pristine purity of form, not only because it was architecturally magnificent and historically meaningful but also because it would save the authorities in the State and at the Centre, a very huge, sizeable amount of money that should be needed to raise two multistoried buildings. Instead, the Town Hall could be thoroughly renovated, strengthened wherever necessary, alternations carried out and painted all over; a re-wiring of all electric lines, provision for fire-fighting equipments and installation of air-conditioning plant for a part of the building at any rate, should also be included in this total renovation of the building.

The Chairman also wanted the members to express their opinions in regard to the accommodation of the State Central Library. Did they want it to be located, even after separated at the Town Hall itself alongside of the Asiatic Society, or were they in favour of a separate building somewhere else in the city? If the latter, was such a building available? If a new building was to be set-up, was land available for the purpose; if so, where?

The Chairman's observations were immediate followed a long discussion on all the main issues, in which all the members participated one by one. Ideas were freely given vent opinions were expressed equally freely and suggestions thrown out. At the end of the season the general consensus reached on the various issues, was as follows:

(a) It was generally agreed that the State Central Library should be taken away from the organisational and administrative control of the Asiatic Society and the latter should be divested of the responsibility or receiving, processing and housing the materials under the Press and Registration of Books Act and the delivery of Books Act. The Maharashtra Government may, if they choose, had over this responsibility to the State Central Library which should be established as a separate institution, by the Maharashtra Government as early as possible. This was an obligation laid on the Government of Maharashtra by their Maharashtra Public Libraries Act.

(b) The Asiatic Society may confine itself within the limits of its original aims, objectives and functions and develop itself as a centre of advanced study and Research in the field of Oriental

Studies with special reference to the sub-continent of India, West Asia, Southeast Asia, Central Asia and East Asia. It may also work out a regular Research Programme and a Publication Programmes and see to it that these programmes are carried out.

(c) The Town Hall building should be placed in its entirety at the disposal of the Asiatic Society, if it has to function properly and maintain its invaluable treasures in a proper and healthy manner. Steps should be taken as early as possible to move the office of the Director of Libraries of Maharashtra Government, the Stamp Office of the same Government and the offices of the Bombay Women's Council, out of the Town Hall and have them shifted elsewhere.

(d) Considering the enormous cost involved in the demolition of even the main body of the Town Hall and in the raising of even one multi-storied building in its place, taking into consideration the sentiments, the historic and the aesthetic associations of the edifice and following the path of least resistance, the Committee felt that the present Town Hall may be allowed to continue as habitat of the Asiatic Society, but it should be thoroughly renovated, strengthened, re-conditioned and made suitable for the proper functioning of the Asiatic Society.

(e) Considering the unlikelihood of availability of any existing building in the city and extreme pressure on available land even with the limits of Greater Bombay, it was thought advisable that the Government of Maharashtra should accept the offer of the University of Bombay of an eight acre piece of land on their new Kalina campus of the University, and raise on this plot a three-storied building for the present with adequate space for the State Central Library and for the headquarters of the State Directorate of Libraries. The State Central Library should be developed as the apex of the State's library system which should be the responsibility of the Director of Libraries of the Government of Maharashtra.

(f) Regarding the division of the present holdings of the Central Library owned, managed and controlled by the Asiatic Society, it was generally agreed that all materials received by the Asiatic Society under the provisions of the Delivery of Books Act since its inception should be handed over to the

State Central Library. Of material received by the Asiatic Society under the Registration of Books Act, all duplicates and material which are not meant for advanced study and research, should be handed over to the State Central Library.

Before the Second Session was drawn to a close, the Chairman suggested that arrangements should be made for the members of the Committee to meet the Governor of Maharashtra who happened to be the patron of the Asiatic Society and took a great deal of interest in the institution, and the Minister in charge of Education of the Maharashtra Government, with a view to soliciting their valuable opinion on matters that have been engaging the Committee's attention.

Both the meetings were arranged to be held the next morning, at 9.30 and 10.30 respectively.

Third Session: 6th July, 1976, 12 noon

Before the Committee met in formal session the members of the Committee and the President of the Asiatic Society called on the Governor of Maharashtra at 9.30 a.m.

The Chairman solicited the views of the Governor on the functioning of the Asiatic Society. The Governor emphatically stated that the Asiatic Society was the victim of certain decisions which burdened it with responsibilities which did not legitimately belong to it. The society was made a depository under the Press and Registration of Books Act and the Delivery of Books Act. These additional responsibilities relegated the real functions of the Society to the background and made it almost a Society meant for running the Central Library.

He wanted the Society to be relieved of these responsibilities so that it could resume its real functions of promoting Oriental Studies and Research. The general readers should not admitted into the Library. It should be opened only to serious readers and researchers. He suggested that the State Archives be moved into the Town Hall building and the offices other than those of the Society and its library, should be moved out of the building. He desired that the estimate of cost involved in renovating the building be worked out without any further delay. According to him it was the responsibility of the Maharashtra Government to establish the State Central Library and entrust to it the depository functions under the two Acts. He believed that the Central Government should finance the cost of receiving processing and maintenance of the reading material received under the Delivery of Books Act which was a legislation of the Parliament. He did not envisage any difficulty in raising necessary funds through voluntary efforts, for the renovation of the Town Hall.

After meeting the Governor, the members of the Committee called on Mrs. Prabha Rao, Education Minister of Maharashtra, at her residence.

She expressed her willingness to establish the State Central Library and asked the Education Secretary, Mr. D.M. Sukthankar to work out the cost involved. She entirely agreed with the Committee that the Asiatic Society should function only as a research organisation, and the Society should concentrate on the promotion of Oriental Studies with special reference to India.

When on their return, the members of the Committee, except Shri D.M. Sukthankar, sat in formal session, they expressed their satisfaction at the general support extended to their tentative main decisions, by the Governor and the Education Minister.

The general consensus already arrived at, at the Second Session, were gone over once again and members were asked, individually and collectively, if they had any objections to any of them or any fresh suggestions to make. There was none, but since Shri D.M. Sukthankar was not present, the decisions were not finalised as recommendations. It was decided to be done in the after-lunch session when Shri Sukthankar was due to be present.

Meanwhile, after a short discussion, it was decided that–

(a) the Director of Libraries of the Government of Maharashtra may get ready a rough sketch of the State Central Library and Directorate of Libraries headquarters and a rough estimate of cost involved in the construction of the building, phased out over the remaining period of the Fifth Five Year Plan;

(b) the Director of Libraries may draw up a list of his requirements for the above purposes, in terms of staff, equipments, shelving and furniture, etc., along with financial estimates, both in terms of capital expenditure and annual recurring expenditure;

(c) the Director of Libraries may also draw up a blue-print of the aims and objectives and of the functions of the State Central

Library;

(d) the Honorary Secretary of the Asiatic Society may work out the cost of total renovation of the Town Hall and of providing the Society's offices, reading rooms and alcoves and the Library with additional lighting, fans, fire-fighting equipment and air-conditioning plant, etc., for atleast a part of the basement, for holding rare books and manuscripts;

(e) the Honorary Secretary of the Asiatic Society may also draw up a list of additional items which should be necessary for the re-organisation and revitalisation of the Society, in terms of staff, equipments, new programmes of research and publication, etc., alongwith a financial estimate of annual recurring expenditure involved in this re-organised set-up;

(f) the Honorary Secretary of the Asiatic Society and the Director of Libraries both may keep their requirements and their financial estimates at their barest minimum;

(g) in principles as well as in practice the financial responsibility of capital expenditure as well as of recurring annual expenditure on the State Central Libraries, should be borne in its entirety by the Government of Maharashtra, the Government of India sharing this responsibility to the extent of the expenditure involved in the receipt and processing of materials under the two Central Acts alone, referred to above;

(h) in regard to the Asiatic Society, a good part of the capital expenditure involved in the renovation of the Town Hall and reorganisation of the physical side of the Society, should be raised through voluntary donations and benefications, the remainder being met by the Government of India and the Government of Maharashtra, on a half and half basis respectively. The responsibility for the recurring annual expenditure should also be equally shared by the two Governments, considering that the Society occupied an all-India national status in the field of higher learning and research, a national institution which was located. in the capital city of the State of Maharashtra.

Fourth Session: 6th July, 1976, 3 p.m.

(All members including Shri Sukthankar were presents)

Since Shri Sukthankar was not present, the tentative findings an decisions which were arrived at the *Third and Fourth Sessions* were read out to him and explained wherever it was necessary. Shri Sukthankar considered these, one by one, and extended his approval to all of them.

These findings and decisions were then placed formally before the meeting and eventually adopted unanimously, following a short discussion.

The Chairman then requested the Convener to incorporate these findings and decisions in the final report of the Joint Committee.

It was decided to meet next morning at 10.30 a.m. for the Fifth and final session of the present meeting of the Committee.

Fifth Session: 7th July, 1976, 10.30 a.m.

(All members were present)

1. To begin with, the Committee, with a view to eliciting more information and inviting fresh suggestions, met the following members of the staff of the Asiatic Society:

Shri P.D. Chakradco, Librarian
Shri A.V. Gharse, Deputy Librarian
Shri S.A. Agaskar, Assistant Librarian.

2. The Committee also met Shri A.K. Banerjee, one of the Vice-Presidents of the Society.

3. The Chairman handed over to the Honorary Secretary of the Asiatic Society and to the Director of Libraries of Maharashtra Government, two separate lists, one to each, of items in regard to which adequate information and materials were sought for by the Committee for their further consideration in their next meeting, in order to enable them to work out the financial implications and responsibilities. They were both requested to send these materials to the Convener by not later than 10 August, 1976.

4. It was decided that the next meeting of the Committee would be held in Bombay at the Asiatic Society, on 20th and 21st August, 1976.

5. It was tentatively decided that the final report of the Committee should be in the hands of the Governments of India and Maharashtra, but not later than 30th September, to enable them judi-

cious apportionment of funds in their revised budget estimate. For this purpose a third meeting of the Committee might be necessary, again in Bombay, for the finalisation of the report by about the middle or third week of September, 1976.

30th July, 1976.
Approved by
Niharranjan Ray,
Chairman

D.R. KALIA
Convener

APPENDIX II

Joint Union Government and Maharashtra Government Committee for the Re-organisation of the Asiatic Society, Bombay and the State Central Library, Bombay

Proceedings of the Second Meeting 20th and 21st August, 1976

The Second Meeting of the Joint Committee was set-up by the Department of Culture, Ministry of Education and Social Welfare of the Government of India and the Department of Education of the Government of Maharashtra, to examine the needs and requirements of the Asiatic Society, Bombay and the State Central Library, Bombay, was held at the Asiatic Society, Bombay, on two consecutive days, 20th and 21st August, 1976, in three consecutive sessions.

First Session: 20th August, 1976, 1.00 a.m.

The following members were present:

Members : Prof. Niharranjan Ray, *in the Chair*; Smt. Bansari K. Seth, Honorary Secretary, Asiatic Society, Bombay; Shri K.D. Puranik, Director of Libraries, Government of Maharashtra; Shri S.R. Ranganathan, Assistant Financial Adviser, Ministry of Finance, Government of India.

Convener : Shri D.R. Kalia, Director, Central Secretariat Library, Government of India.

Dy. Secy. : Shri Ajai Shankar, Department of Culture, Government of India, regretted his inability to be present because of indisposition.

1. The proceedings of the First Meeting of the Committee held in Bombay on 5th, 6th and 7th July, 1976, which had already been circulated to the members, were confirmed with the following verbal changes:

(a) On page 1, para 2, line 15, the words "Republic Day meeting" be changed to "Independence Day meeting"; and

(b) On page 21, para (g), last line, the words "two Central Acts" be changed to "the Central Act."

2. The Chairman reported that Shri Ali Yavar Jung, the Governor of Maharashtra had very graciously addressed a communication to him under date July 26, 1976, enclosing a note summarising the discussion the Joint Committee had will him at the Raj Bhavan on July 6, 1976, and giving his valuable suggestions. He had also added that the same note had also been sent to the President of the Asiatic Society, Bombay and to the Secretary, Education Department, Government of Maharashtra.

The Chairman said that the Joint Committee even at their First Meeting, had already taken into full consideration the suggestions so graciously made by the Governor and that they Committee was greatly benefited by the discussion they had with him. They could not, however, take into consideration his suggestions in regard to the State Archives and their housing since the matter lay outside their terms of reference.

The Chairman placed on record the appreciation and gratitude of the Committee for the keen personal interest-taken by the Governor in the re-organisation of the Asiatic Society and its Library.

3. The Chairman requested Mr. D.R. Kalia, the Convener of the Joint Committee to offer his comments, first, on the proposals and estimates of cost, etc., submitted to the Committee by Mrs. Bansari Sheth, Hony. Secretary of the Asiatic Society.

Shri Kalia presented the following comments before the Committee:

(i) The number of books, etc., which the society's Library was likely to retain on their shelves, consequent on the bifurcation of the current stock of books, would be about 2 lakhs, and not 2.5 lakhs as estimated by the Society. The stacking area for 2 lakh volumes would work out to 13,333 sq.ft. at the usual rate of 15 vols. per square foot, against the Society's estimate of 12,500 sq.ft.

(ii) The number of volumes likely to be added over the next 10/15 years, namely 3 lakhs as estimate by the Society, was a gross over-estimation. At the most, the Society was likely to add more than 4000 volumes a year (2000 by purchase and another

2000 by exchange and gift), once it was divested of the responsibility of operating the Depository Acts. The additional space needed over the next 10/15 years, would therefore work out to 4000 sq.ft. (at the rate of 15 vols. per sq.ft.) only, and not 15000 sq.ft. as estimated by the Society.

(iii) The estimates presented for the accommodation of the different sections and divisions of the Library and other departments, were also very much on the higher side, judged by national and international standards. These estimates called for discussion and revision.

(iv) The Society had not submitted any estimate of cost in regard to the renovation of the Town Hall which was their habitat. From a letter addressed and the Executive Engineer, Presidency Division, Bombay, to Shri K.D. Puranik, Director of Libraries, Government of Maharashtra, dated 11.8.1976 it appeared that this monumental and historic edifice might last for another 40 years or so, if alone thorough renovation of it was done and after renovation it was properly maintained on a regular basis. An estimate of cost for thorough renovation was therefore necessary and such an estimate should take into account the cost of electric installation, lights, fans, etc.

According to Shri Kalia the work of renovation could be undertaken in two phases, the basement in the first and the first floor in the second. He calculated that the renovation of the basement which had a floor area of 22,000 sq.ft., would cost about rupees four lakhs.

(v) The estimate of cost of furniture and fittings, as given by the Society, was also very much on the high side and therefore called for reconsideration and revision.

(vi) The requirements of staff estimated by the Society were also similarly much in excess of actual needs in relation to the proposed reorganisation of the Society and its Library.

Responding to Shri Kalia's comments Shrimati Bansari Sheth said that all their estimates were prepared keeping in view what an ideal and full-fledged institution for advanced study and research and its library should be like, as it was intended to be, and that the estimates of requirements and costs were prepared by an expert committee set-up by the Society for respective purpose, experts who were supposed to have certain acceptable standards to go by.

This was followed by some discussion which mainly centred round national and international standards as to measurement of space for specific purposes and the Society's needs and requirements in terms of the aims and objectives of the Society and their scope of work.

While having the fullest sympathy for any institution of higher study and research, particularly in the field of Oriental history and civilization, the Chairman felt that the estimates presented by the Society were idealistic, that the Society and its Library were in such a state of disarray and out of focus that given the best of good will and of material wherewithal it would take quite some time to recapture the ideal situation of their glorious days. Besides, the financial situation in the Centre and in the State of Maharashtra was not very rosy; indeed, the constraints were much too felt very strongly that in revising the estimates, etc., the Committee should be barest minimum in the context of the current Fifth Plan period. Once this first phase was worked out realistically and efficiently there should enough scope, financially and otherwise, to advance towards an ideally desired situation step by step, phase by phase.

He felt that besides divesting itself of the responsibility in regard to the two Depository Acts and the Central Library, there should still be further scope for giving up obligations which did not fall within the orbit of society's activities, the UNESCO Unit, for instance. He drew the attention of the Committee to the aims and objective of the Society as laid down in the Memorandum of Association. These were as follows:

(a) To investigate and encourage Sciences, Literature, and the Arts in relation to Asia and in particular to India, and to promote research therein;
(b) To publish a journal;
(c) To publish works embodying research; and
(d) To maintain a general library which will also function as a Central Library for the State of Maharashtra and which shall be known as "the Library of the Asiatic Society of Bombay and the Central Library."

The Chairman felt sure that clause (d) was not a part of the original Memorandum, but was a later amendment consequent on the Society becoming the depository of books under the two Depository Acts and taking up the responsibility of the Central

Library. He felt that this after-thought and action pushed the Society out of focus to a very great extent. He therefore, asked the Committee to consider if the Society should not be requested to re-amend sub-clause (d) of their aims and objectives so as to read: "(d) To maintain a general library for the above purposes."

The estimate of needs and requirements of the Society should therefore be re-drawn up under the following four broad heads which defined the parameter of the activities of the Society:

(i) Research activities
(ii) Publication of a Journal
(iii) A Publication Unit for research publications
(iv) Maintenance of a Library

After further discussion the following decisions were taken:

(i) The Asiatic Society be requested to amend sub-clause (d) of the aims and objectives of their Memorandum of Association, so as to read "(d) To maintain a general library for the above purposes."
(ii) The Society should initiate research activities by appointing, to begin with, 2 Research Fellows of their own to carry on research on approved subjects, at the rate of Rs. 600 per month for each single Fellowship, and by enlisting the co-operation of the University of Bombay towards having their scholars registered with the Society for research for purpose of research degrees. The Society should also try to raise some endowment funds to enable them create more Fellowships. A research programme should in this regard be drawn up by the Society.
(iii) The Society should see to it that at least two issues of their Journal were published annually at regular intervals.
(iv) That a Publication Unit should be set-up by the Society, with a Publication Officer placed in charge, at a monthly salary in the grade of Rs. 300-800.
(v) That at least one piece of research work should be published annually. Steps should also be taken towards editing and translating selected manuscript texts in the holdings of the Society.
(vi) The Society should transfer to the State Central Library (a) all

publications received under the two Depository Acts from the very beginning, *except* those titles which are intended for advanced study and for research; (b) all titles in modern Indian languages including back-files of periodicals *except* those which might be necessary for research; (c) all materials which are meant for recreational reading; and (d) all UNESCO publications, the UNESCO Unit of the Society to be transferred to the State Library which should be designated by the Government of Maharashtra as the deposition of all UNESCO publications.

(vii) The bifurcation of the stock of books, etc., should commence with immediate effect, and the authorities of the Society and the Central Library should set-up a small joint committee for the purpose.

(viii) The Society should not accept gifts of books, etc., indiscriminately; materials which were of no research value should not be accepted.

(ix) The establishment of the State Central Library should not await the construction of the new building proposed for the purpose, which is likely to take 2 to 3 years' time for completion of even the first phase of the building. Indeed, the State Central Library should start functioning as soon as possible, as a separate organisation, in the Town Hall building itself with whatever re-allocation of space that should be necessary. This re-allocation may be done by a small joint committee set for the purpose by the authorities of the Asiatic Society the State Central Library.

(x) The work of renovation of the basement should be taken up as soon as necessary funds could be raised by the Society, the Committee was given to understand, through generous donations by individuals and private corporate bodies. The Committee was also given to understand that with judicious incentives extended by the Income Tax authorities towards Income Tax exemptions, such donations should be forthcoming without much difficulty. The Committee felt that for purposes like this, the incentives asked for should be extended to prospective donors by the Ministry of Finance of the Government of India.

As desired by Shri Ali Yavar Jung, the Governor, the Secretary, Buildings and Communication Department, might be requested to prepare the estimates of cost of renovation, separately, of the basement and of the main floor, as early as possible.

(xi) The Committee requested Shri Kalia to review the estimates of the Society in the light of the above decisions and place his revised estimates before the committee at their afternoon or last session of of the Second Meeting on 21st August, 1976.

Second Session: 20th August, 1976, 3.00 p.m.

Besides those who were present at the First Session, was also present Shri D.M. Sukthankar, Secretary, Department of Education, Government of Maharashtra

1. For the benefit of Shri Sukthankar who could not be present at the First Session, the Chairman gave a brief resume of discussion held and the decisions arrived at the First Session of the Second Meeting of the Committee.

Shri Sukthankar articulated his general agreement with the discussions and his acceptance of the decisions arrived at by the Committee.

2. The Chairman requested Shri D.R. Kalia to offer his comments on the proposals presented to the Committee by Shri K.D. Puranik, Director of Libraries, Government of Maharashtra, in regard to the re-organisation of the State Central Library.

Shri Kalia presented the following comments:

(i) The requirements in regard to accommodation of the State Central Library, worked out on the basis of well-known national and international norms, were found to be quite reasonable. Shri Kalia suggested, however, that the proposed new building at the Bombay University Campus at Kalina, should be phased out in two equals parts, the first phase to be completed by the end of 1979-80, at a cost of Rs. 25.175 lakhs spread over a period of three years as follows:

1977-78	– Rs. 4 lakhs
1978-79	– Rs. 9.175 lakhs
1979-80	– Rs. 12 lakhs
Total	Rs. 25.175 lakhs

The total cost involved would, however, be Rs. 50.35 lakhs for 62,625 square feet at the Rs. 80 per sq.ft.

The work of preparing the architectural and engineering design and plan of the building should be undertaken immediately.

(ii) The revised organisational structure of the State Central Library as eventually presented by Shri Puranik, were considered to have been in order, *except* a few very minor changes here and there.

According to the estimates presented before the Committee, the non-recurring annual cost, excluding the cost of construction of the building, would amount to Rs.* The recurring annual expenditure works out at Rs.*, the details where of appear in revised note received by the Committee from Shri Puranik.

(iii) Since it had been decided at the First Session, that the State Central Library should start functioning in the Town Hall itself and that as early as possible, separate budget estimates for the remaining three years of the Firth Five-Year Plan, namely, for 1976-77, 1977-78 and 1978-79 consideration as well as for that of the Government of Maharashtra.

The Committee discussed these observations and then took the following decisions:

(i) The estimate of cost of raising the building of the State Central Library and its phasing, as presented Shri Kalia, might be accepted.

(ii) The recurring and non-recurring expenditure on the Library, once it was moved in the new building, should take effect from 1980-81 (2nd year of the Sixth Five-Year Plan) till the end of the 6th Plan, that is, 1983-84. The estimates as presented by Shri Puranik might, therefore, be recast accordingly.

(iii) The entire recurring and non-recurring expenditure of the State Central Library should be shared by the Central and State Governments on 50:50 basis instead of, as at present, 50 p.c. in the case of recurring expenditure on non-recurring, used exclusively for the Delivery of Books Act operations. The Committee felt that in the case of the State Central Library it was difficult to identify in exact terms the actual recurring and non-recurring costs of Delivery of Books Act operations. It

---

* Figures will be supplied later on.

would be convenient, therefore, if the total cost was shared equally by the two Governments as the financial contribution of each was not likely to be very different in either case.

(iv) Shri Kalia was requested to prepare the budget estimates for the Central Library for the remaining-three years of the Fifth Five-Year Plan in consultation with Shri Puranik, and report to the Committee by the afternoon the 21st August, 1976.

Third Session: 21st August, 1976, 2.00 p.m.

All members except Shri Ajai Shankar were present.

1. The Chairman requested Shri D.R. Kalia to report to the Committee the revised estimates which he was requested to prepare, of the Asiatic Society and its Library and of the State Central Library, one by one.

The Asiatic Society and its Library

(a) The Society estimated an income and expenditure of Rs. 6,36,220 on the assumption that they would receive the usual grant-in-aid of Rs. 1,15,000 from the State of Government, Rs. 85,000 from the Municipal Corporation of Bombay and Rs. 2,81,500 in equal proportion from the Central and State Governments (Annexure 2). Shri Kalia suggested that the estimates might be accepted since it was too late to alter them, half the financial year having run out already.

(b) The disbursement of salaries to the Delivery of Books Act staff of the Central Library should continue to be made by the Society during the current financial year, to avoid any dislocation in the present arrangements.

(c) The expenditure on the staff of the Society numbering 44 persons, came to about Rs. 2.5 lakhs, and the establishment charges of the D.B.A. staff membering 43, worked out at Rs. 2.5 lakhs. The organisational chart as proposed by Shri Kalia, for the Asiatic Society Library was given in Annexure 3; it was suggested that actual organisation of the Society and its Library should strictly follow this chart.

(d) The total collection of books, etc., in charge of the Society is at present as follows:

D.B.A.	2,60,000 vols.
P.&R.B. Act	1,68,000 vols.
Society	2,06,000 vols.
Total	6,34,000 vols.

Out of this stock about 2 lakhs of volumes were estimated to be retained by the Society and the remaining 4.34 lakhs of volumes to be transferred to the State Central Library, subject to necessary adjustments, on the principle that the Society should retain all advanced study and research materials irrespective of their original source of acquisition.

(e) The wooden stands installed in the basement should be retained and utilised by the Society for shelving the back-files of newspapers and journals. The old imported steel racks should be repaired and then utilised for back-files of journals. All the steel shelves purchased out of D.B.A. grant received from the State and Central Governments should be transferred to the State Central Library. Steel shelves purchased by the Society out of its own funds should be retained by the Society. Once these adjustments are made the Society would be short of shelves by 15 units of 18 feet each, costing about Rs. 1 lakh. This amount should be made available on 50:50 basis by the Central and State Governments.

(f) During the current financial year the Central and State contribution should, therefore, be as follows:

Central Government	Rs. 1.50 lakhs - Usual grant
	Rs. 0.50 lakhs - Steel shelves
	Rs. 2.00 lakhs
State Government	Rs. 1.15 lakh - Usual grant
	Rs. 1.50 lakh - D.B.A. Grant
	Rs. 0.50 lakh - Steel shelves
	Rs. 3.15 lakhs

(g) The Society should submit to the Committee by 30th September, 1976, their budget estimates for the year 1977-78 and 1978-79 without including any expenditure on D.B.A. and P. and B.R. Act Sections. The total expenditure should not exceed Rs. 5.00 lakhs for the year 1977-78 and Rs. 5.25 lakhs for the year 1978-79. On the income side, Society should contribute at atleast Rs. 75,000 each year and the Bombay Municipal grant of Rs. 85,000 should be shown separately, would be shared equally between the State and Central Governments.

(h) The Society had a membership of 1511 persons on 1st April, 1976. Statistics show that these members borrow for home reading about 125 books only per day, despite each member being entitled to borrow 15 books at a time. About 100 books from the Society's Library stock the consulted on the premises. This is obviously a small operation for which not more than 500 sq.ft. space on the first floor should be needed, taking into full consideration the need for elbow room and further expansion.

(i) Nor more than 20 research scholars seemed to make use of the remaining facilities on the premises. By accepted standards the total reading room area should not therefore, exceed 3000 sq.ft., leaving enough margin for further intake.

(j) The Society's Library remained open from 10 a.m. to 7 p.m. which involved staffing in two shifts. It has been taken care of in the allocation of staff shown in Annexure 3.

(k) The Central and State Governments financing the deficit of the Asiatic Society and its Library, the services of the Library should be made available to all those engaged in serious study or research on equal footing with the members of the Society, for reference purposes, at any rate. For the privilege of borrowing books by non-members the Society might choose to ask for cash deposits. But for library services on the spot in the premises no discrimination whatsoever should be made between members and non-members.

(l) The Society's budget was in the red during the year 1975-76; the situation was going to be the same in 1976-77. Shri Kalia suggested that on the basis of the actual expenditure incurred on D.B.A. operation for these two years, the Central and State Governments should reimburse the deficit, if any.

The estimates presented and comments made by Shri Kalia were endorsed by the Committee after some discussion.

State Central Library

Shri Kalia made the following comments on the budget estimates presented by Shri Puranik, for the remaining three years of the Fifth Five-Year Plan, for State Central Library which was to start functioning as possible, in the Town Hall building itself, to begin with, till the proposed building was ready.

(a) The total expenditure over the remaining three years of the Fifth Five-Year Plan, was estimated to be as follows:

1976-77	Rs. 1.00 lakh
1977-78	Rs. 7.50 lakh
1978-79	Rs. 8.00 lakh
	Rs. 16.50 lakhs

(b) On the basis of 50 : 50 shared between the Central and State Governments, the contribution of each was estimated to be as follows:

(Rs. in lakhs)

Year	Central Government	State Government
1976-77	0.50	0.50
1977-78	3.75	3.75
1978-79	4.00	4.00

The details of expenditure were given in Annexure 4 along with the Organisational Chart under 4-A.

(c) The Committee accepted the above estimates subject to confirmation in the next meeting.

2. It was decided that the next meeting of the Committee should be held in Bombay on Friday the 15th and Saturday the 16th October, 1976.

The meeting ended with the vote of thanks to the Chair.

Encl: 14A Appendices.

Sd/-

D.R. Kalia
CONVENER

Niharranjan Ray
CHAIRMAN

APPENDIX III

Joint Union Government and Maharashtra Government Committee on the Asiatic Society and the Central Library, Bombay

Proceedings of the Third Meeting 15th and 16th October, 1976.

The third meeting of the Joint Committee set-up by the Department of Culture, Ministry of Education and Social Welfare of the Government of India and the Department of Education, Government of Maharashtra, to examine the needs and requirements of the Asiatic Society, Bombay and the Central Library, Bombay was held at the Asiatic Society, Bombay on two consecutive days — 15th and 16th October 1976.

The following members were present:

Members Prof. Niharranjan Ray, *in the Chair*; Shri D.M. Sukthankar, Secretary, Department of Education and Youth Service, Government of Maharashtra; Smt. Bansari K. Sheth, Honorary Secretary, Asiatic Society of Bombay, Bombay; Shri K.D. Puranik, Director of Libraries, Government of Maharashtra; Shri S. Ranganathan, Assistant Financial Adviser, Ministry of Finance, Government of India.

Convener Shri D.R. Kalia, Director, Central Secretariat Library, Government of India, New Delhi.

Dy. Secy. Shri Ajai Shankar, Department of Culture, Government of India, regretted his inability to be present because of indispostion.

1. The proceedings of the Second meeting of the Committee held in Bombay on 20th and 21st August, 1976, which had already been circulated to the members, were placed before the meeting.

Resolved that the proceedings be confirmed.

2. The draft report of the Joint Committee which had already been circulated to the members was taken up for scrutiny.

The report was gone through paragraph by paragraph in three consecutive Sessions and was eventually adopted unanimously with certain modifications.

3. The report was then signed by all the members present.

Sd/ D.R. Kalia
16-10-1976

Sd/ Niharranjan Ray
16-10-1976

APPENDIX IV

No. 751/APS/G/76

Raj Bhavan
Bombay 400035
23/26 July 1976

Dear Professor Ray,

It was a great pleasure meeting you and finding ourselves on common ground in discussing the question of the Asiatic Society's Library and the future of the Central Library and the Depository Library. In the meanwhile, I thought it would be desirable if, as far as I am concerned, I dictated a note on the discussions we held and the conclusions we reached, and although the note would naturally be subject to your own impressions of the discussions and any comments that you may have to make, I am sending a copy to you as well as to ex-Justice Desai and the Education Secretary for the same purpose. An extra copy is being sent to you for the representatives who accompanied you of the Government of India.

Yours Sincerely,

Sd/-
(Ali Yavar Jung)

Prof. Nihar Ranjan Ray,
C/17, Green Park Extension,
New Delhi 110016.

Text of the Minutes of Meeting

The following came to see me on 6 July at Raj Bhavan, Bombay:

1. Prof. Nihar Ranjan Ray
2. Shri K.T. Desai
3. Shri M.D. Sukthankar
4. Shri Ajai Shankar
5. Shri Kalia
6. Shri Ranganathan
7. Shri K.D. Puranik
8. Shrimati B. Sheth

2. The subject to the meeting was consideration of the future of the Asiatic Society and the question of its relationship with the Bombay Central Library and the Central Depository Library.

3. A note on the subject presented to me earlier by ex-Justice Desai is attached for reference and, as I had mentioned to him earlier and also to two other members of the Society and, above all, to the Union Minister of Education and Social Welfare. (I said that) the main problem was the anomalous nature of the present combination which was quite incompatible with each other in as much as the kind of readers, the nature of the books and their maintenance and upkeep as well as the equipment required was different in each case. In my view, which I had held for a long time, the Central Library and the Central Depository Library ought to be dealt with separately from the Asiatic Society's Library. This would not involve one building housing all the three, because the non-compatibility of the combination would then still persist, but a smaller building, which would also be cheaper, only for the Central Library and the Central Depository Library. The space saved could be used for shifting the State Archives from its present location in Elphinstone College to the present building of the Asiatic Society where the nature of the two and the type of research students attending either or both would be more or less the same. Prof. Ray, who knows the State Archives well, strongly supported this idea and had come to a similar conclusion although, with regard to the State Archives, he had not given detailed thought to it but he considered the suggestion practicable and agreed that it would both solve the problem of the State Archives and the

question of space for Elphinstone College.

4. It was stated at the meeting that the question was being looked into about the durability of the present Asiatic Society's building and the capacity of its first floor to hold weight. This would be particularly important if the State Archives were shifted there. I was told that a Committee of engineers had been appointed under the P.W.D. Secretary to report on this matter, though not in the context of the State Archives, and I asked the Governor's Secretary of the State Archives, and I asked the Governor's Secretary to enquire how far the matter had gone as I would like to see the report. In the meanwhile, I said I would call the Director or State Archives and elicit his opinion as well which I did the same afternoon and found that he liked the idea of moving out of the Elphinstone College and into the society's building.

5. All depends now, therefore, on the state of the Asiatic Society's building and its capacity to hold the load as everyone seems to be agreed on the separation of the present combination and the inevitability of a separate building for the Central Library and the Central Depository Library, the cost of construction of the latter to the extent of the part devoted to the Central Depositor Library having to be borne by the Centre. One of the Central representatives thought that, for the present we need not bring in the question of the State Archives as it might complicate the solution, but I do not agree with that view as I see no reason for any complication so long as the building can hold and accommodate the Archives which it should be able to do once that part of it is vacated which today houses the Central Library and the Central Depository Library.

6. I shall now submit the report from the P.W.D. Secretary of the Committee set-up by him, and should be obliged if the Governor's Secretary would pursue the matter actively. As far as the Union Minister is concerned Mr. Ray will not doubt acquaint him with the view stated by me on the occasion which, I am aware, the Education Minister would agree, I may add that, in the course of my talk with the Chief Minister that same morning, the Chief Minister in principle also agreed with my ideas though I spoke to him about them quite informally.

Governor
15.7.1976

Governor's Secretary

The Asiatic Society of Bombay
Brief Note for his Excellency

Two most urgent problems the Society is facing are:

(I) Lack of accommodation, (II) Want of finances.

I. Accommodation

The ideal solution to the accommodation problem is to erect a new building which is specially designed for a Library. Construction of a new building, when it does become possible, will take at least five to ten years. In the meantime, it is absolutely necessary to provide an interim plan to provide proper air-conditioning space for the preservation of the Society's valuable books and manuscripts. A project has been prepared for this purpose and its outline is annexed and marked 'A'.

II. Financial needs

(1) *Recurring Expenses for Maintenance*

The day to day expenses of running the Asiatic Society's Library and the Central Library are rising everyday. Hence it is necessary that the State Government should increase its grants but at least Rs. 2,00,000.

(2) *Books*

The amount now spent for purchase of books is Rs. 30,000 per year. Due to phenomenal rise in book prices this amount is grossly inadequate. Society has started permanent Book Fund with contributions received from its members. Appeals to Charitable and other institutions will be made for donations in order to meet Society's target for a Book Fund of Rs. 5 lacs. Appeals will be made to the Central and State Governments for recurring grants for books and periodicals to the tune of Rs. 1 lacs per year.

(3) *The Society's Learned Activities*

The Society's learned activities such as promotion of research in

Indology, publication of a Journal and of Works embodying research and its efforts to investigate and encourage Sciences, Literature and Arts in relation to Asia, etc., are all languishing for want of funds. For these activities as well as for purchase of valuable books and manuscripts, an endowment fund should be set-up with a target of Rs. 2,00,000.

(4) *Catalogue*

The General Catalogue of the Library in two volumes is now out of date. Printing on up to date Catalogue will cost Rs. 75,000 at a very moderate estimate.

(5) *Reference and Bibliographical Service*

This may be called the cream of any Library service. The present reference section is used by members of the public from all walks of life. With the fund of information available in the D.B.A. Section, an excellent reference section can be built up. This will be possible with (i) modern Abstracting and Cataloguing services by a competent staff of at least six, (ii) Purchase of additional reference books. A detailed project for the Reference Section up-to-date is under preparation.

(6) *Preservation*

It is imperative that immediate steps should be taken to preserve the Society's invaluable collection of books and manuscripts. An adequate space should be provided to guard these treasures against pests, dust, humidity and fire. As already stated, the Society has a plan for converting its basement into an air-conditioned area for preservation. This project must be implemented immediately.

The Society has decided to appoint a Committee for "Preservation of the Society's Invaluable Heritage". The scope of this Committee will be to assist and advice the Society on the following activities:

(i) To raise funds immediately for implementing the project marked 'A' for air-conditioning the basement in the Town Hall.

(ii) To create a Permanent Endowment Fund and Book Fund.

(iii) To prepare a project for constructing a permanent building.

His Excellency be requested to be the President of the "Preservation of the Society's Invaluable Heritage Committee". Some of the leading industrialists and other eminent persons who are members of the Society will be requested to join this Committee. The proposed names are as follows:

1. Mr. H.T. Parikh
2. Mr. R.D. Choksi
3. Mr. R.G. Saraiya
4. Mr. S.M. Dahanukar
5. Dr. (Mrs.) Sharayu Doshi
6. Mrs. Gool Shavaksha
7. Mrs. Asha Sheth
8. Mr. Ramu Pandit
9. Mr. Pratap Bhogilal
10. Mr. Arvind Mahtlal
11. Mr. S.P. Godrej
12. Mr. S.V. Somaiya
13. Mr. Vijaypat Singhania
14. Mr. J.G. Bodhe
15. Mr. Gerson Da Cunha
16. Mr. Kanti Kumar Poddar
17. Mr. Chatrabhuj Narsee
18. Mr. B.K. Daphtary.

It is proposed that this Committee jointly with the Cultural Committee of the Society hold an Exhibition of some of the valuable books and Manuscripts in the near future in order to publicise the Society's activities and to make its needs felt by the public. For this Exhibition, a Souvenir can be brought out which will help towards collection of funds.

At the inauguration of the Exhibition, the Education Minister of the Maharashtra State will be requested to formally release the Society's publication—"An Illustrated Aranyaka Parvan in the Asiatic Society of Bombay". At this function, His Excellency be requested to present the Campbell Memorial and other Medals.

ANNEXURE 'A'

Outline of the Project for the Preservation of the Society's Valuable Books and Manuscripts

The Society has about 2,000 manuscripts fully catalogued and about 1000 Manuscripts still to be catalogued. The Society also possesses old Newspapers and Periodicals about 1000 years old. Besides this, there is a large collection of rare and valuable old books on all subjects collected since the inception of the Society. In the opinion of some experts consulted, the first and most important step for preservation of old books and Manuscripts is to provide an air-conditioned space which is free of dust and humidity. The second step for preservation is to microfilm the valuable books, etc., so that physical handling of the original is not necessary or becomes very restricted. Microfilming also will preserve the contents of the books, etc., should the original be lost.

A Committee consisting of Librarians of three of Bombay's leading Libraries, one Architect, one Engineer, one air-conditioning expert and three of our Society's Committee members examined the various alternatives for providing air-conditioning space for storage of valuable books and have concluded that the best Project is to convert the basement of the Town Hall into a 'Preservation' area. The Project briefly comprises of —

(a) Air-conditioning the basement area;
(b) Providing fire preventive equipment;
(c) Microfilming of valuable books and Manuscripts; and
(d) Providing Microfilm Reader which will be housed in the basement.

The above Project has several distinct advantages:

(i) It will required negligible structural alternations as the walls of the basement are very strong and will provide an atmosphere free from dust;
(ii) It will provide safety in the preservation area as the basement is isolated; and
(iii) By re-arranging the stack of books and providing more shelves

and cupboards, extra storage space for at least 20 to 30 thousand books can be created.

M/s. Gherzi Eastern Ltd., Consulting Engineers, Industrial Consultants and Architects, Bombay, have been good enough to prepare a Project (free of cost) for converting the basement into the air-conditioned area. A summary of this Project together with an estimated cost is annexed.

Capital Cost	Rs.
The total estimated cost of both the Air-conditioning and fire preventive equipment	6,00,000.00
Cost of microfilming will be approx	2,50,000.00
Cost of Microfilm Reader	40,000.00
Cost of 2 Vacuum Cleaners	10,000.00
	9,00,000.00

Recurring Cost (per annum)	Rs.
Cost of Maintenance will be approximately	90,000.00
Cost of additional staff and other services will be	40,000.00
	1,30,000.00

Copy

N.D. GADGIL
G.D. ARCH., A.I.I.A.

15, Manjri Niwas, S.V. Road,
Goregaon (West), Bombay 400062
3rd March 1976

Asiatic Society Library,
Town Hall, Bombay.

A valuable collection of books, periodicals and rare manuscripts is stored in the basement of the Town Hall. At the present these books are restored in open teak wood racks and are not protected against decay and fire.

It is proposed to improve the storage conditions and ensure long life to this valuable collection of the books. Of the several steps to be taken towards this objective the air conditioning and fire protection are the most important. Some renovation of the existing windows on the east face and closure of openings leading into the other offices in the basement are required to be carried out.

It is felt necessary to improve lighting conditions as well. It is proposed to house microfilming and reading room in the basement. This will be housed in the area now used for book binding purposes.

It will be necessary to rearrange the storage racks in such a manner that 6 nos. of package units for air conditioning can be accommodated on the floor.

A statement of estimated cost is enclosed.

Sd/-

Asiatic Society Library
Town Hall, Bombay

3rd March 1976

Estimate of Cost

(For the works to be carried out in the basement — approx. area 11200 sq. ft).

1. Brick walls and teak wood partitions	25,000
2. New windows on east face	15,000
3. Lighting installation	20,000
4. Painting	15,000
5. Air conditioning (49 tonnes of refrigeration)	4,50,000
6. System of fire protection to the book storage area	75,000
Total	6,00,000

7. Cost of maintenance of lighting and air conditioning systems per month (12 hours working per day power consumption estimated 50 KV) 7,500 per month.

Sd/-

APPENDIX V

No. PB/SPO/T.Hall/7753
Office of the Executive Engineer
Presidency Division
Old P.W.D. Secretariat
Opp. C.T.O. Fort, Bombay 1.
(Tel. 270042) Dt. 11.8.1976.

To

The Director of Libraries
Town Hall,
Bombay-1

Sub :- Repairs to Town Hall and the life of the same.
Ref :- Your letter No.E/1/Misc/8/8489-90, dt. 2.8.1976

With reference to the above referred letter, it is stated that the present Town Hall building will remain for another 40 years after renovation and required funds as per norms for maintenance is available.

The present cost of construction prevailing in Bombay per sq. ft. Rs. 80 per sq. ft.

Executive Engineer
Presidency Division

Copy submitted to superintending Engineer, Bombay Circle Bombay for favour of information.

APPENDIX VI A

Asiatic Society and Central Library

President, Managing Committee, Secretary, Librarian — Rs. 650-1200

Technical Services Section	Readers Section including Reference & Bibliographical Service	Publication and Sales	Administrative Services	Research Section
Assistant Librarian (1) Rs. 240-500 Sr. Assistant (1) Rs. 200-350 Clerk (2) Rs. 115-215 Havildar (1) Rs. 90-120 Peon (1) Rs. 75-100 Total—6	Dy. Librarian (1) Rs. 380-1000 Sr. Clerk (1) Rs. 150-300 Clerks (Issue) (2) Rs. 115-215 Sorters (2) Rs. 100-150 Havildar (1) Rs. 90-120 Peons (Cleaners) (8) Rs. 75-100 Sorters (3) Shelving Sorters (2) Rs. 100-150 Peons (2) Rs. 75-100 Total—22	Publication Officer (1) Rs. 300-800 Clerk (1) Rs. 115-215 Total—2	Accountant (1) Rs. 240-500 P.A. to Secretary (1) Rs. 240-500 Sr. Clerk (1) Rs. 150-300 Accounts Clerk (1) Rs. 115-215 Clerks (2) Rs. 115-215 Havildar (1) Rs. 90-120 Peons (2) Rs. 75-100 Head Binder (1) Rs. 110-175 Asstt. Binder (2) Rs. 110-175 Jr. Binder (3) Rs. 75-100 Total—14	Research Fellows (2) Rs. 600 fixed. Total—2
	GRAND TOTAL 47 (Existing Posts : 44) (New Posts : 3)			

APPENDIX VI B

State Central Library, Maharashtra Organisational Chart

(Showing Divisions and Sections)

Technical Services Division I	For Staff Allocation See
1. Indian Language Section	Enclosure 1
2. English Language Section	Enclosure 1
3. Official Documents Section	Enclosure 1
4. Maharashtrian Section	Enclosure 1
5. Maps and Prints Section	Enclosure 1
6. Legal Deposit Unit.	Enclosure 1

Technical Services Division II	For Staff Allocation See
1. Rare Books and Manuscripts Section	Enclosure 2
2. Bibliographic Section	Enclosure 2
3. Documentation Section	Enclosure 2
4. Technical Guidance to other Libraries Section	Enclosure 2

Reader's Services Division	For Staff Allocation See
1. Stack Maintenance Section	Enclosure 3
2. Inter-Library Loan Section	Enclosure 4
3. Book Preservation Section (including Laboratory and Bindery)	Enclosure 5
4. Information and Reference Section (including Reading-room)	Enclosure 6

Administrative Services Division	For Staff Allocation See
1. Personnel Section	Enclosure 7
2. Finance Section	Enclosure 8
3. Supply Section	Enclosure 9
4. Maintenance (Building, Furniture, transport, etc.) Section	Enclosure 10
5. Reprography Section	Enclosure 11

APPENDIX 4 A Encl. 1

State Central Library, Maharashtra

Organisational Chart
(Showing Staff Allocation)

State/Librarian/Director (1800-2000)

Technical Services Division I Deputy Librarian (410-1200)	Assistant Librarian (300-625)	Technical Assistant (220-350)	Shelf Attendant (85-120)
1. Indian Languages Section			
Hindi	1	5	3
Gujarathi	1	4	2
Marathi	1	4	2
Kannada	1	3	1
Bengali	1	3	1
Tamil	1	2	1
Telugu	1	2	1
Malayalam	1	2	1
Punjabi	1	1	1
Assamese	1	1	1
Oriya	1	1	1
Urdu	1	2	1
Sanskrit	1	—	1
Sindhi	1	—	1
Kashmiri	—	—	—
2. English Language Section	1	5	3
3. Official Documents Section	1	3	4
4. Maharashtrian Section	1	1	1
5. Maps and Prints Section	1	—	1

	Head Clerk (200-350)	Senior Clerk (150-300)	Junior Clerk (115-215)	Self Attendant (85-120)
6. Legal Deposit Unit	1	2	6	3

APPENDIX 4 A Encl. 2

Technical Services Division III Deputy Librarian (410-1200)	Assistant Librarian (300-625)	Technical Assistant (200-350)	Senior Clerk (150-300)	Junior Clerk (115-215)	Shelf Attendant (85-120)
1. Rare Books and Manuscripts Section	1	1	1	1	1
2. Bibliographic Section	1	1	—	1	—
3. Documentation Section	1	—	—	1	—
4. Technical Assistance to other Libraries.	1	1	—	1	—

APPENDIX 4 A Encl. 3

Readers Services Division Deputy Librarian (410-1200)	Stack Supervisor (150-300)	Shelf Attendant (85-120)	Hamals (75-100)
1. Stack Maintenance Section	1	8	14

APPENDIX 4 A Encl. 4

Readers Services Division	Assistant Librarian (300-625)	Senior Clerk (150-300)	Junior Clerk (115-215)	Shelf Attendant (85-120)
2. Inter-Library Loan Section	1	1	2	1

APPENDIX 4 A Encl. 5

Reader Services Division	Head Binder (110-175)	Assistant Binder (100-150)	Junior Binder (75-100)
Book Preservation Section	1	2	3

APPENDIX 4 A Encl. 6

Readers Services Division	Assistant Librarian (300-625)	Technical Assistant (200-350)	Issue Assistant (150-300)	Clerk-Typist (115-215)
Information and Reference Section	1	2	6	1

APPENDIX 4 A Encl 7

Administrative Services Division
Senior Deputy Librarian
(650-1200)

1. Personnel Section	Superintendent (260-430)	1
	Stenographer (180-400)	1
	Head Clerk (200-350)	1
	Senior Clerk (150-300)	4
	Typist (115-215)	2
	Peon (75-100)	3

APPENDIX 4 A Encl 8

Administrative Services Division

2. Finance Section	Accounts Officer (340-830)	1
	Accounts Assistant (150-300)	1
	Senior Clerk (150-300)	2
	Junior Clerk (115-215)	1
	Typist (115-215)	2
	Peon (75-100)	3

APPENDIX 4 A Encl 9

Administrative Services Division

3. Supplies Section	Senior Clerk (150-300)	1
	Junior Clerk (115-215)	1
	Typist (115-215)	1
	Peon (75-100)	2
	Driver (110-150)	1

APPENDIX 4 A Encl. 10

Administrative Services Division

4. Maintenance Section		
	Senior Clerk (150-300)	1
	Peon (75-100)	2
	Watchman (75-100)	2
	Gardener (75-105)	2

APPENDIX 4 A Encl. 11

Administrative Services Division

5. Reprography Section	Chief Photographer (600-1100)	1
	Photographer (450-900)	1
	Dark Room Assistant (150-300)	1
	Shelf Attendant (85-120)	1

APPENDIX - VII

Asiatic Society of Bombay
Budget Estimates

(in lakhs)

Year	Society's Contribution	Bombay Munl. Corp. Grant	Central Govt. Grant	State Govt. Grant	Total
1976-77	Rs. 0.75	Rs. 0.85	Rs. 1.50 (D.B. Act) Rs. 0.50 (for steel shelving) ——— Rs. 2.00	Rs. 1.15 (Maintenance grant) Rs. 1.50 (D.B. Act) Rs. 0.50 (Steel shelving) ——— Rs. 3.15	Rs. 6.75
1977-78	Rs. 0.75	Rs. 0.85	Rs. 1.70	Rs. 1.70	Rs. 5.00
1978-79	Rs. 0.75	Rs. 0.85	Rs. 1.85	Rs. 185	Rs. 5.30
	Rs. 2.25	Rs. 2.55	Rs. 5.55	Rs. 6.70	Rs. 17.05

APPENDIX VIII

State Central Library

Year	Recurring	Non-recurring	Total	State Govt. Share			Central Govt. Share		
				Recurring-	Non-recurring	Total	Recurring	Non-recurring	Total
1976-77	1.00	—	1.00	0.50	—	0.50	0.50	—	0.50
1977-78	7.50	4.00	11.50	3.75	2.00	5.75	3.75	2.00	5.75
1978-79	8.00	9.20	17.20	4.00	4.60	8.60	4.00	4.60	8.60
	16.50	13.20	29.70	8.25	6.60	14.85	8.25	6.60	14.85

* *Figure in lakhs.*

APPENDIX IX

State Showing the Share of Grants from the Central and State Governments

(Rs. in lakhs)

Year	Central Government			Govt. of Maharashtra		
	Asiatic Society	State Central Library	Total	Asiatic Society	State Central Library	Total
1976-77	2.00	0.50	2.50	3.15	0.50	3.65
1977-78	1.70	5.75	7.45	1.70	5.75	7.45
1978-79	1.85	8.60	10.45	1.85	8.60	10.45
	5.55	14.85	20.40	6.70	14.85	21.55

6

COMMITTEE ON DRUG ABUSE IN INDIA, 1976 – REPORT[1]

Chairman Dr. C. Gopalan

Members Shri A. Shankar; Dr. M. Adiseshiah; Prof. R.C. Mehrotra; Shri J.P. Naik; Dr. M.C. Gore; Dr. Davinder Mohan; Shri K.R. Ramachandran; Dr. K. Bhaskaran; (replaced by Dr. A. Venkoba Rao); Shri K.K. Puri; Shri D.P. Anand

M. Secy. Dr. S.S. Gothoskar

Appointment

The reported increase in the use of intoxicating drugs, particularly by students, has been causing concern to the Government of India for some time. It has accordingly been decided to constitute a committee to inquire into the extent of drug addiction in the country and to submit their recommendations.

The committee was constituted under Resolution No. X.11029/1/76—D&MS of the Ministry of Health and Family Planning (Department of Health), Government of India, dated June 2, 1976.

Terms of Reference

(a) To enquire into the extent of addiction to drugs in the country, particularly amongst the student community;

(b) To determine the motivation for drug addiction;

(c) To identify the types of drugs that are misused and the steps that are to be taken to prevent the misuse of the drugs; and

(d) To recommend suitable de-addiction and rehabilitation programmes that should be initiated in the country.

---

1. New Delhi, Ministry of Health and Family Planning, 1978, 82 p.

Contents

Recommendations

In this concluding chapter, we shall give a summary of our main findings and recommendations for ready references.

Dependence Producing Drugs: The focus of this report is on the following dependence producing drugs and other substances that are commonly misused in India:

(1) Cannabis and its products (e.g., *Bhang, Ganja* and *Charas*)
(2) Hallucinogens (e.g., L.S.D)
(3) Tranquillisers, hypuoties and sedatives (e.g., meprobamate, diazepam, methaqualone and chloral hydrate.
(4) Barbiturates (e.g., phenobarbital and secobarbital)
(5) Amphetamines (e.g., dexteo-amphetamine and methyl-amphetamine)
(6) Tobacco.
(7) Other narcotic drugs (e.g., opium, pethidine, morphine, heroin, and cocaine); and
(8) Alcohol.

The report, however, does not deal explicitly either with tobacco or alcohol.

Current Prevalence of Drug Abuse: The existing studies on the subject do not cover all the different regions of the country. Even the few studies available, whether on the general population or on students, are mostly cross-sectional and not representative of the population, they have several methodological flaws and the investigators have used definitions and parameters which are not strictly comparable However, there seems to be fairly good evidence to draw the follov ing tentative conclusions:

1. **General Population:** The drug problem exists in the population as a whole. The drugs most frequently misused are a

cohol, tobacco, opium and cannabis, while the psychotropic drugs are just making their entry. The proportion of non-users is very large, but it is admitted that there is a small hardcore of addicts, many of whom become mentally ill and source of whom are treated in our psychiatric units and mental hospitals or by private practitioners. Within this hard-core, the alcohol addicts are obviously the most numerous and psychotropic addicts, the smallest group. Addition is also more common among men than among women.

2. **Students:** The prevalence of drug abuse among students is limited although it constitutes a complex and difficult issue that cannot be ignored–

   (a) Drug misuse among students exists at the secondary school stage also but becomes more pronounced at the university stage. It is perhaps a little larger than among the general population,

   (b) The drug abuse is more common among boys than among girls,

   (c) The drugs most commonly misused are alcohol and tobacco. Psychotropic drugs are more frequently used by students than by the general population whilst opium and cannabis are less used than in the general population,

   (d) The most common form of abuse is experimental, occasional and situational as at the time of examinations. Regular users are few and addicts, still fewer, and

   (e) As in the general population, one is impressed by the larger total abstinence rate among the students as well.

3. The prevalence of drug abuse is likely to show an increasingly trend.

All things considered, it appears that the extent of the drug problem is limited at present, except for alcohol and tobacco. However, in the opinion of the Committee, there are disturbing signs which show that the situation in our country is likely to worsen and get out of hand if adequate measures are not adopted to curb the evil. We, therefore, recommend that planned, comprehensive and sustained measures should be taken without delay to prevent and control drug abuse in the total population in general, and among the students in particular.

Research and Statistics: It is necessary to organize systematic studies on the prevalence of drug abuse for all regions of the country, separately for students and general population, and to repeat these studies to get longitudinal data. It is also essential to organise systematic research on different aspects of the problem on a continuing basis. The secondary data available on the subject can be improved to give a better picture of the situation.

Drug-individual-society reaction: Drug abuse is a behaviour whose manifestation depends upon the complex drug-individual-society relationship.

1. Drugs vary in their capacity to produce dependence. The risk of dependence is related to the amount of drug and intake route. Other facts which affect dependence are quality, form availability and price. Substitution of drugs is often possible and multiple drug use is fairly common. The effects produced by drugs are variable and often subjective.
2. Individuals use drugs because they meet some specific needs as perceived by them. It has not been possible to identify any specific personality factor(s) that make an individual prove to drug abuse which cannot also be explained fully in terms of the psychodynamic or learning theories. A view is therefore gaining ground that drug abuse is a behaviour acquired within a social context.
3. The social factors in drug are extremely important. Some social groups are more vulnerable to the evil than others. Caste-religion and local customs play a significant role in drug abuse. There are also religious variations in the prevalence of drug abuse which affects both rich and poor, although for different reasons. The social acceptability of drugs seems to be determined arbitrarily and has little relationship to their harmfulness. In the Indian context, drug control has developed an unhealthy relationship with revenue raising.

Theoretical framework for prevention and control: While adopting measures for the prevention and control of drug abuse, the following points will have to be kept in view:

1. drugs cannot be eliminated, but their abuse can be controlled

and minimized;
2. preventive and control measures should be directed at all strategic points and not concentrated at any one point, however, significant;
3. drug abuse cannot be treated in isolation from other forms of deviant behaviour;
4. instead of creating new, isolated and large structures for prevention and control of drug abuse, it would be more economical and efficient to develop the programme as an integral part of the existing administrative machinery; and
5. all drugs form a continuum and the drug problem must therefore be treated in its entirety.

Against the background of·the complex drug-individual-society relationship indicated, the framework for prevention and control of drug abuse will be as fallows:

1. Legal and penal measures which try to keep the drug away from man;
2. Educational measures which try to keep man away from the drug; and
3. Social action which tries to remove conditions which necessitate drug use of to develop alternatives for drug use.

Legal and penal measures policy: We should create at the Central level, an integrated machinery for the formulation of a comprehensive and balanced national drug contral policy. From this point of view, we recommend that a National Advisory Board on Drug Control should be established immediately. The Minister of Health and Family Welfare should be its chairman and a senior officer of the Ministry should be its Member-Secretary. It should have representatives of the Ministry of Finance, Ministry of Education, Ministry of Information and Broadcasting, the State Governments, and of the Department of Social Welfare, Central of Bureau of Investigation, Indian Council of Social Science Research, Indian Association of Chemists and Druggists and Association of Drug Manufacturers. The Health Secretary, the chairman, Central Board of Excise and Customs, the Narcotics Commissioner of India, and the Drugs Controller (India) should be its ex-officio members. It should also include a few eminent non-officials (psychiatrists, educationists, journalists, politicians, etc.) interested in the problem. The Board as a whole should meet once a year. But there should be a small standing committee which should meet more frequently, say, once a quarter.

The National Advisory Board on Drug Control shall:

a. reviewing periodically the situation of drug abuse in the country;
b. sponsors research, on a continuing basis, on different aspects of the drug problem;
c. call for compile, and publish all the relevant statistics on the drug problems;
d. submit an annual report to the Government of India on the status of the drug problem in the country, and
e. advise the Government of India and the State Governments on all aspects of the national drug control policy and its implementation.

1. There should be a special unit in the Ministry of Health and Family Welfare to function as the secretary of the Board and necessary funds for the Board, its programmes and staff should be provided on a priority basis.
2. The National Advisory Board on Drug Control should be established immediately so that it is able to take action on several of the important recommendations.

Legal and penal measures legislation: We are of the view that it would be an advantage to have a single law which would deal with the prevention and control of abuse of drugs whether narcotic or psychotropic.

1. The proposed law should deal with the dependence producing drugs and other harmful substances which should be classified into three categories, viz., prohibited drugs, controlled drugs (Category A); and controlled drugs (Category B). The severity of control would be in a descending order, the maximum severity beings on the category of prohibited drugs.
2. This law should deal comprehensively with the export, import, production, possession, transport, distribution and sale of all prohibited and controlled drugs. Its provisions should also be brought in line with our national commitments under the In-

ternational conventions to which we are or may become a party. Since this law cannot cover alcohol (which is a State subject) the Government of India, should, on the advice of the National Drug Control Board, lay down a coordinated national policy for prevention, regulation and control of drug abuse.

3. The punishment at present prescribed in our relevant laws for illicit import and export of narcotic drugs can hardly be considered effective. The position regarding illicit import and export of psychotropic drugs is still more unsatisfactory as there is no specific law to deal with such illicit export and import except the general provision of the Import and Export (Control) Act. As there is a real danger that the smuggling of drugs in the country will increase in the years, ahead, it is necessary to prescribe deterrent and heavy punishments for illicit export and import of drugs as a matter of urgency on a priority basis. It may also be emphasised that many of the other punishments provided under the present legislation are also too small to prove effective. The position needs to be examined in detail and the punishments made more deterrent where necessary.
4. In case of regular users of drugs, it becomes essential to maintain supplies of the concerned drug on medical grounds. There should, therefore, be adequate provisions in the law for notifying approved centres where regular addicts can register themselves and on production of prescribed medical certificates obtain the supplies of the drug required in prescribed quantities. There should be a regular system of registering opium addicts as its absence merely tends to encourage, illicit movement of opium to satisfy the requirements of addicts who have not been registered. We, therefore, recommend that such approved centres should be opened immediately, in both urban and rural areas, for users of all dependence producing substances.
5. In the treatment of drug addicts, it is often necessary for the psychiatrist to have regular supplies of drugs with which the usual dosage of the patient is gradually reduced. It is, therefore, necessary to provide that approved psychiatrists or other prescribing authorities may obtain all the supplies of controlled and prohibited drugs needed for treatment purposes.
6. The most despicable person is the pusher or drugs peddler

> who, for personal gain, is prepared to ruin the lives of young persons by enticing or encouraging them to drug abuse. The proposed law should therefore provide severe and deterrent punishments for pushers or drug peddlers. In this context the recommendation 4 made above is very important as it will reduce the dependence of drug addicts on pushers and peddlers. Similarly, adequate action will have to be taken against medical practitioners who are found to over-prescribe or to encourage surreptitions drug abuse so well as against chemists and druggists who abet the leakage of drugs into the market.

Legal and penal measures implementation: Legislation will not have its desired effect unless the implementation is satisfactory, i.e., unless the average law breaker realizes that he does not have an adequate chance of escape. From this point of view, we recommend (a) that the existing loopholes and inadequacies in the laws should be carefully studied and duly plugged and remedied in the proposed legislation, (b) that the implementing machinery should be strengthened to the extent possible, especially by creation of special squads at crucial points and in important areas, and (c) that every effort should be made to secure better coordination between the Central officials and the State police.

From Abstinence of Addiction

An individual passes from the stage of abstinence to addiction, generally through the interim stages of experimentation, casual or occasional use, and regular use without any serious adverse effects. The reasons why some persons become addicts and others stop at various earlier points are not clearly known. But two action points are indicated: (1) We have a strong tradition of abstinence which must be preserved and strengthened; and (2) educational and social measures along with medical treatment can be of use at every earliest stage to prevent addiction.

Educational measures: We attach great importance to the education of all social groups especially the elite, regarding continuous awareness of the drug problem. Drug education should be a part of health education activity at all levels of the society.

Carefully designed factually correct and scientifically evaluative programmes should be designed for specific target groups which impart information on drug abuse. Such groups may, for example, be students, persons engaged in operation of machinery or vehicles, rural labour, non-student youth and adults.

1. Educational programmes for students should be concentrated more at prevention or discouraging the use of socially acceptable drugs such as alcohol and tobacco rather than the total ranges of drugs. It is much easier to correlate the use of these drugs with general health education, especially because total abstainers pass to addiction and to the use of more dangerous drugs via the use of alcohol and tobacco which are readily available and have large social acceptance.
2. Student counselling and guidance services (which need to be generalized on strong educational grounds) should included drug use within the area of their activity.
3. Programmes of non-formal education on drug use should be developed for out-of-school youth and adults.
4. The mass media have obviously an important role to play and act as catalyst for social change. We would like mass media in general to play a more objective role in coverage and reporting of issues related to drug abuse rather than making it sensational. All India Radio, Doordarshan and Film Division have a special and major responsibility in formulating and presenting worth while programmes and films in consultation with experts.

The Departments of Social Welfare, Education and Mass Communication in consultation with Department of Health should develop such programmes and set-up a machinery to evaluate and advise other voluntary agencies who wish to participate in such programme.

Social action: The basic assumption underlying this approach is that the misuse of drugs is not a disease in itself, but the symptom of some social mal-functioning and the emphasis is placed not so much on treating the symptom, as on removing the causes of drug abuse through programmes of social reform. These are not quick to easy solutions. But in the long run, they alone can provide the genuine and lasting remedies, not only to the drug problem, but to several other illnesses that the society suffers from. This social action will include:

1. measures to create an enlightened and rational social opinion and the subject.
2. helping the adolescent and youth to grow, smoothly to adulthood and maturity.
3. strengthening of poor groups and using them meaningfully for individual and social development;
4. involving youth in meaningful and challenging programmes of adventure, risk-taking, physical education, games and sports, social service, and literary and recreational activities.
5. eliminating vested interests in drug abuse; and
6. transforming society on egalitarian lines and abolishing poverty.

Treatment of Drugs Addicts

At present, there are no specially organised facilities for the treatment of drug addicts in the country. Most of the drug dependent individuals are treated at Psychiatry Departments, wherever they exist, if they are referred to these departments. As these facilities are obviously limited, it is presumed that some drug addicts would be treated by general physicians and other wealth professionals, while quite a large number of them may not be receiving any treatment at all. Mental hospitals and in-patients units of Psychiatry Departments do provide admission on facilities for such patients. Some of the teaching and training institutions are also in the process of developing small addiction units. In the context of inadequate facilities for dealing with healthy problems, it is not desirable to provide specific and separate treatment facilities for drug addicts.

We make the following recommendations for future development of services for the treatment of drug addicts:

1. It would be both economic and efficient if the treatment of drug addicts is developed as apart of the general health services of the country.
2. There is a paucity of beds in hospital services in all the areas; hence the creation of special residential treatment facilities for drug dependence would not be a feasible proposition as a general method of treatment. The international trend now is to move away from the residential to the out-patient department or ambulatory treatment. We should also adopt the same policy.

3. It would be desirable to provide these services within the framework of Psychiatry Departments wherever they exist or develop.

   As in interim measure, these facilities could also be developed in medical specialities.
4. In urban areas where the current prevalence of drug abuse is large and is expanding into the student body we suggest that de-addiction centres should be established for the provision of comprehensive services. Such services should cover all dependence producing drugs and should also have in-patients and out-patients services, with accent on the latter. They should also be free to experiment with various treatment modalities on a time-bound basis with built-in-evaluations, so as to determine the best possible, techniques for the Indian setting. These centres should also be charged with maintaining and evaluation the legal registration systems and act as foci for training other health professionals for similar work within the country.
5. Between four to six such centres should be initially set-up with central finance in the country. Subsequently each state should set-up at least one centre during the Sixth Plan period. At the state level, encouragement should be given to all medical colleges to set-up such units in medical/psychiatric units.

Registration of Drug Addicts

We attach great significance to the programme of registering a regular users and drug addicts and saving them from the clutches of unscrupulous peddlers by establishing approval centres where they can have their needed quota of drugs at standard prices on production of medical certificates issued by prescribed authorities. The scheme should be introduced for all dependence producing drugs whose control has been advocated.

Rehabilitation

The rehabilitation of a drug dependent individual should continue to remain the main responsibility of his family and the social group and the de-addiction service should at best become a support and supplement. Efforts should, however, be made to involve the voluntary agencies in the programme.

7

RASHTRIYA BARH AYOG (National Commission on Floods), 1976 – REPORT (in two volumes)[1]

Chairman Shri Jaisukh Lal Hathi
Members Shri D.B. Anand; Shri N. Sanyal in place of Shri R.C. Prasad who died; Dr. N. Patnaik; Dr. Kamta Prasad; Shri A.N. Harkauli (replaced by Shri Pritam Singh); Shri R. Ghosh; Shri H. Gohain
M. Secy. Shri K. Ramesh Rao (replaced by Shri S. Babington)

Appointment

The increasing trend in flood damages in recent years and the need for taking up effective measures for reducing the annual loss, the Government of India, in the Ministry of Agriculture and Irrigation, constituted the Rashtriya Barh Ayog by their Resolution No. FC-52 (1)/76 dated the 2nd July, 1976. The Resolution *inter alia* reads as follows:

> "Sizeable progress has been made in the flood protection measures since 1954, when the National Flood Control Programme was launched for the first time, in the country. Since then, nearly one-third of the flood prone area has been afforded reasonable protection. During this period of two decades, considerable experience has been gained in planning, implementation and performance of the flood protection and control measures. Advancement in technology has taken place not only in India but also in foreign countries. Therefore, it has become necessary to conduct a study in depth of our approach and programmes of

1. New Delhi, Ministry of Energy and Irrigation, Department of Irrigation, March 1980, 370 p.

flood control measures. Formulation of a flood control policy would require detailed study of various problems concerned with flood control measures and also, aspects like soil conservation and afforestation. The Government of India have, therefore, decided to set up the Rashtriya Barh Ayog so as to evolve a coordinated, integrated and scientific approach to the flood control problem and draw out a national plan, fixing priorities which could be implemented in the near future.

Terms of Reference

(1) To review the flood protection measures undertaken since 1954 and to make an evaluation of the benefits and effectiveness of the measures undertaken so far with special reference to embankments in reducing the damage.

(2) To identify the areas where a large number of Zamindari and/or unauthorised embankments, bunds and spurs, etc., exist; to assess the effect of such constructions on the flood problem; and suggest remedial measures.

(3) To identify the areas where construction of roads, highways, railways, etc., and other encroachments into drains have aggravated flood problems and to suggest measures for improvements including legislative action, if any.

(4) To analyse the damages caused by floods in recent years and to identify areas requiring immediate flood protection measures.

(5) To evolve a comprehensive approach to the problem of floods in the country keeping in view the need for optimum and multi-purpose utilisation of water resources as also the role of soil conservation and afforestation in flood control.

(6) To make an analysis of the cost and benefits of flood protection measures.

(7) To suggest criteria for taking up flood protection measures and means of mobilising resources therefor.

(8) To recommend proper landuse in the flood plains with a view to minimise damage and to ensure overall increase in agriculture production.

(9) To examine the existing arrangements for maintenance of flood protection works and recommend measures for improving the same.

(10) To review the existing administrative and organisational set

up for flood control at the Centre and in the States and suggest improvements where necessary, flood control to include flood forecasting and warning, flood fighting, formulation and implementation of flood protection measures.

(11) To examine the present procedure of assessing flood damage and suggest improvements.

(12) To examine any other matter related to floods and flood control and make suitable recommendations."

Contents

Volume I: Introduction; Rivers of India; Floods — Incidence and Extent; Analysis of Available Data on Flood Damages; Methods of Flood Management; Past Approach and Achievements; Zamindari Embankments; Effect of Development Works and Encroachments; Methodology of Flood Damage Assessment; Areas Needing Urgent Attention; Landuse and Regulation; Costs and Benefits; Criteria; Future Approach; Planning and Implementation; Financing; Maintenance; Organisation; Legislation on Flood Control; Collection and Publication of Data; Research Education and Training; Cyclones and Sea Erosion; Summary of Recommendations. *Volume II*: Appendices from I to IX.

Recommendations

Floods – Incidence and Extent

1. The aggregate of different areas flooded at any one time during the period of record within the geographical limits of a State should be considered as the areas "liable" to floods.

2. Detailed figures of flood damages, should, as far as feasible, be collected under the various sub-heads listed.

3. The degree of protection may be adopted according to the criteria decided for protection of various types of areas. The totals of such areas should be considered the "protectable" area.

The extent of "protectable" area will undergo change from time to time, and, should be periodically reviewed.

Past Approach and Achievements

4. For the purpose of evaluation of the performance of the ex-

isting and future flood control works, data have to be collected in an effective manner so as to provide quantitative and dependable information on their long-term performance and their impact on various socio-economic factors.

Zamindari Embankments

5. The States should make a review of the utility of zamindari/test relief embankments depending on the importance of the areas protected.

6. Embankments which are considered useful should be incorporated in the overall flood control plan of the State.

7. Embankments which are not considered useful should not be retained but may be demolished or allowed to languish/disintegrate/disappear in course of time.

8. Embankments which are retained should be properly maintained.

In cases where realigning is necessary, the possibility of utilising the old embankment as the first line of defence or as a local ring bund may also be examined.

9. No new test relief embankments should be constructed as far as possible except where they are part of the flood plan. Relief may be provided by raising and strengthening existing embankments where necessary.

Effect of Developmental Works and Encroachments

10. There is need for closer coordination amongst concerned agencies like the Railways, National Highways, State Irrigation/Flood Control Departments so as to ensure that structures like bridges, roads, railways, etc., do not aggravate flood problems.

11. Prior consultation by National Highway authorities, State P.W.Ds, and Railways with the State Irrigation/Flood Control Departments should be made obligatory. To facilitate an expeditious check, the Government of India should evolve a guideline/checklist for the purpose of vetting of waterways by the State Irrigation/Flood Control Departments.

12. It should be mandatory that assessment of adequacy of existing waterways should be made by the State Committee of Engineers or some other Technical Board and the waterways for bridges to be

constructed in the future should be vetted by the State Irrigation/ Flood Control Department.

These Committees should be set-up in States where they do not exist at present.

13. The Standing Committee for settling disputes on waterways and sharing of costs, headed by the Chairman, Central Water Commission, should be vested with statutory powers for implementation of its decisions.

14. The State should undertake legislation to prevent unauthorised river bed cultivation and encroachments into drains, etc., and where such laws already exist, the enforcement agencies should be strengthened.

Cultivation of crops like water-melons, vegetables, etc., in river beds and berms, may however, be allowed with caution.

The practice of cultivation in the abandoned beds of Dhars which discharge into main rivers should be stopped.

15. Where suitable legislation with a penal clause for unauthorised crossings over drains has not been enacted, the same should be done and enforced.

Methodology of Flood Damage Assessment

16. The final estimate of crop damage in areas where they are completely destroyed but resown/replanted should be made in terms of loss of inputs.

17. Information on (i) stage of the crop at the time of food, (ii) crops completely destroyed, and (iii) crops damaged but replanted/resown should be collected.

18. Crop losses in terms of money should be estimated by using farm harvest prices.

19. Crop yield rates should be derived from crop cutting experiments.

20. The collection of crop damage statistics should be integrated with that of agricultural statistics.

21. Wherever possible, contour maps along with gauge data should be used by the Flood Control Department to derive estimate of area flooded.

22. Remote sensing techniques operated through artificial satellite(s) may be used in selected areas to provide a sample check on the extent of area and cropped area affected by floods.

23. State Government should take measures for collection of data on damages to household goods. As a first step, they should aid and sponsor research and set up economic cells for conducting suitably designed economic surveys in this respect.

24. The monetary value of the cattle lost should be estimated. With regard to loss of human life, only that due to floods should be taken into account.

25. In the case of public utilities, double counting of unrepaired damages of earlier years should be avoided.

26. The estimates of damages to properties of the Central Government should also be included in the consolidated figures of damages at the State, national and other levels.

27. Departments dealing with flood control at the Centre and in the States should arrange for exploratory studies and sample surveys for throwing more light on the significance or indirect damages due to floods and for indicating norms for including them in the future.

28. Flood damage may be repeated separately for the following three categories of areas:

(i) Unprotected areas;
(ii) Protected areas; and
(iii) Areas situated between the embankments and the river.

29. The extent of area affected by drainage congestion should be compiled separately for protected areas and unprotected areas.

30. Damage data should be compiled basin and sub-basinwise also.

31. The district statistical office should supervise the work of damage data collection at the village and block levels and prepare estimates.

32. At the State level the work of compilation and processing should be undertaken by the Directorate of Eçonomics and Statistics.

33. At the national level, damage data should be compiled by the Central Water Commission with an Economics units added to it. It should publish data at the national level.

34. Time schedules for submission of reports at various levels should be specified and adhered to.

35. At the State and national levels, there should be a periodical review of the methodology of data collection, compilation and publication.

36. The Central Water Commission should aid and encourage research in the methodology of flood damage assessment.

37. Finalisation of annual plans of States for flood control should be made contingent on their submitting final figures of flood damages.

Land Use and Regulation

38. For estimating flood discharge from the watersheds a more refined and scientific approach should be increasingly adopted instead of empirical formulae.

39. Large scale reclamation of alkali soils in the Indo-Gangetic plains should be taken up to reduce drainage congestion in alkali areas.

40. Hydrological studies in experimental water-sheds should be intensified by the agricultural and forestry research organisations and similar studies in representative watersheds undertaken by the engineering research organisations.

41. Integrated action plan on soil conservation and watershed management should be prepared, implemented and maintained in the flood prone basins/sub-basins. The implementation agencies should be adequately strengthened with trained personnel. People's participation should be mobilised.

42. More and more forest areas should be declared as reserve forests.

43. The present programme for the control of shifting cultivation should be intensified and the concept of growth or urban centres in the fertile valleys developed on a pilot scale.

44. Urgent action should be taken to rationalise forest gazing.

45. Special attention should be paid to the problem of forest fires in the inaccessible areas of the Himalayan coniferous belt and the deciduous forest region of Central India.

46. Stabilising mine spoils should be made obligatory on the lessees.

47. In the Himalayan region, steps should be taken to stabilise roadside land slides and arrangements should be made to monitor the effects of land slides.

48. The highly eroded hill slopes, especially in the Himalayan region should generally be closed to grazing and suitable measures taken to develop them as grasslands.

49. Flood plain management measures should be undertaken wherever necessary legislation exists and suitable legislation enacted in other States.

50. A Central Land Use Commission should be set-up and entrusted with the responsibility of bringing about uniformity in the existing land use regulation, for enforcement in Inter-State basins.

51. Restructuring of cropping programme during the flood free months should be undertaken and suitable programme for irrigation should be launched.

52. State Government should construct community grain stores and undertake research to evolve improved design specifications.

53. Special flood-prone area programme similar to the Drought Prone Area Programme or Tribal Area Development Programme should be launched for rapid development of *diara* land, along with appropriate research and development support.

54. Terracing for cultivation on steep slopes should be enforced as a general rule.

55. The State Governments of Assam, West Bengal, Bihar and Uttar Pradesh may consider the extensive areas under *tals*, *chaurs*, *beels*, etc., as exclusively fishery resources under their land and water utilisation policy.

Costs and Benefits

56. Cost-benefit analysis should be conducted for a complete range of viable alternatives.

57. Measures should be taken for progressive adoption of social benefit-cost analysis. To begin with, high priority may be given to sponsor and encourage research in this field and economic cells created at the Centre and State levels.

58. Indirect benefits of a project to the extent they can be quantified should also be included.

59. Up to date norms for costs usually estimated as percentages of capital works should be determined.

60. Costs likely to be incurred in future on embankment protection works like spurs and revetments should be taken into account while working out the benefit-cost ratio.

61. A construction schedule with year-wise costs should be included in the project.

62. Estimates of cost and benefit figures of future years should

be made on the basis of current prices.

63. The method of separable cost remaining benefits may also be taken into account for allocating cost of multipurpose projects having flood control as one of the components.

64. Area to be benefited from a flood control project should be estimated with the help of contour maps or with reference to the area flooded in some specific flood years in the past.

65. Flood damage data should be used for an assessment of benefits in monetary terms in States not following this practice.

66. Average annual damage should be derived from 15 to 20 years data after these are suitably adjusted for past changes in prices and productivity.

67. The cost of relief, rehabilitation, loans and remission of land revenue should not be taken into account in additional to direct losses for working out benefit-cost ratio.

68. The benefits on account of increased area being made available for cultivation and other purposes should also be taken into account.

69. Wherever applicable, the benefits of silt and inundation should be determined as the difference between yields of representative samples of flood affected farms and similar farms situated nearby in the flood free area.

70. Damages that may continue to occur even after the construction of flood control works should also be dealt with in project formulation, and especially examined during scrutiny and sanction.

71. Care should be taken to obviate multiple counting of benefits in the cases of projects which are inter-related or undertaken at the same time.

While preparing a master plan/comprehensive plan, some idea of overall benefits and costs in a broad sense may be given.

72. Sensitivity analysis should be conducted for projects costing more than Rs. 50 crores.

73. Benefits and costs should be discounted at the prescribed interest rate.

74. The Planning Commission and State Planning Department should get some of the projects examined by independent outside agencies and draw the attention of the executive agencies towards discrepancies, if any.

Criteria

75. Selection of projects should be made with respect to criteria which should be objective, well-defined and expressed preferably in quantitative terms.

76. The criterion of benefit-cost ratio be maintained. Projects showing benefit-cost ratio exceeding unity should be deemed as qualifying for selection.

In case of additions to existing works, the benefit-cost ratio criterion should be interpreted as the incremental benefit-cost ratio.

77. The benefit cost criterion may be dispensed with only in special cases where benefits cannot be quantified in monetary terms. Instead, the criterion of cost effectiveness may be followed; and among the various feasible methods, the alternative of relocating settlements or installations should also be considered.

78. In the case of embankments, the design of a project should be determined for the time being on flood frequencies suggested. Meanwhile necessary steps be taken for the eventual application of benefit-cost criterion for fixing the design flood.

79. Flood storage in reservoirs should be fixed taking into account different flood frequencies, safe channel capacity and the B.C. ratio.

80. The *inter se* priorities among flood control projects generally from amongst those included in the master plan should be fixed in the light of the following factors:–

(i) Benefit-cost ratio;
(ii) employment potential;
(iii) effects on environment and ecology; and
(iv) density of population in the flood affected areas as well as per capita expenditure on flood control in the project area.

Future Approach

81. The comprehensive approach to the problem of floods must form part of the overall comprehensive approach for the best possible utilisation of our land and water resources for optimum production on a sustained long-term basis.

The approach to the flood problem should remain dynamic and flexible, so as to accommodate future improvements in policy, if called for, taking into account the state of our economy, our social conditions, and the availability of resources.

82. Various alternative measures, physical or otherwise should be considered for flood management and the optimum combination of the measures available in a given situation, selected.

83. There is a need for storage in various forms, which would even out the flow, and also conserve water for use during the dry period.

84. Afforestation and soil conservation measures are recommended as a useful complement to other measures, and should be taken up specially in the watersheds of rivers with heavy silt charge.

85. Reservoirs, to the extent technically and economically, feasible, must be considered as an important component in any package of measures for flood management.

86. Where conditions permit, storage of natural detention basins should be brought into use for flood moderation during abnormal floods.

87. Research and development regarding groundwater recharge should be carried out.

88. While considering the use of embankments the associated problems and side effects should be kept in view, and minimised to the extent possible.

89. Because of high initial and maintenance costs, channel improvement measures should be considered with due caution.

90. Anti-erosion works should normally be taken up only protection of towns, industrial areas, groups of thickly populated village abadis, railway lines and roads, where relocation is not possible on techno-economic grounds. These works should not be taken up for agricultural areas, where the assets protected may not justify the cost.

91. Measures for drainage improvement should be planned and executed in a coordinated manner. Measures for irrigation and drainage should be integrated.

92. Measures to modify the susceptibility of life and property to flood damage should be adopted to much more increasing degree than heretofore.

93. Measures for modification of the loss burden like disaster relief, remission of taxes and *taccavi* loans, etc., should be continued.

There is need to conduct research, and if possible, take up pilot projects of flood insurance.

Planning and Implementation

94. Floods should find a place in the comprehensive planning for water resources development. The first choice should therefore, be to undertake comprehensive water resources development in a river.

95. It would not be advisable to hold over flood plans pending the preparation of comprehensive water plans.

96. Flood space should be provided in reservoirs after examining the need and feasibility.

97. Unless flood control/moderation by a reservoir is visualised within the next 10 years, its contribution should not figure in the solution of a flood problem.

98. Flood Master Plans should not in any way vitiate or conflict with future comprehensive plans for water resources development.

99. A river basin is the most suitable and proper unit for preparation of water and flood plans.

100. It is advisable to visualise flood works which may be needed for different reaches of the river and take account of their interaction.

101. Soil conservation and afforestation measures be stepped up.

102. Local factors may be taken into account and standards for planning and design of surface drains fixed by areas/regions in each State.

103. Drainage schemes undertaken in irrigated areas and for the purpose of land reclamation should not form a part of "flood" sector.

These schemes should however, be discussed in the Technical Advisory Committees of the State Flood Control Boards.

104. Due attention should be paid to the environmental changes likely to be brought about by a flood and/or a water resources development project.

105. The recommendation, that the work of preparation of contour maps in flood prone areas be taken up by the Centre, is supported.

106. Where the work-load justifies, the investigations and planning of flood schemes may be independent, but designs of both flood and irrigation schemes should be entrusted to a unified Design Organisation in a unified Department.

107. The staff employed for investigation, planning and design should be adequate in calibre and strength.

108. Investigations of extensive and complicated projects should be carried out under a special "Investigations" estimate.

109. Benefit-cost ratio should be worked out for all schemes.

110. Consultations and coordination be effected with departments likely to be concerned with/effected by projects.

111. Planning of inter-State rivers should be done basinwise by Basin Authorities.

112. Negotiations should be expedited between Nepal and India with regard to the construction of storages and development of water resources.

113. Unless adequate maintenance is assured, it is unwise to undertake new construction.

114. It is important not only to bring more area under watershed management and soil conservation treatment, but also to take measures to stop damage to further areas as also to maintain areas that are treated.

115. Barring exceptional cases, priorities fixed in the Master Plans should be strictly followed.

116. Completion of continuing schemes should receive priority in allocation of funds, to the extent necessary, by and large, not less than 60 per cent of Plan and Annual allocations.

117. Attempts should be made to obtain public participation.

Financing

118. Some resources should be mobilised from beneficiaries of flood control schemes.

119. The amount collected from the beneficiaries should be set apart for the maintenance of flood control schemes.

120. The flood cess should be collected along with existing taxes.

121. To start with, a cess of one per cent and three per cent of the capital cost of flood protection and drainage works respectively should be recovered. In the case of river bank erosion projects, allocable costs should be recovered from the beneficiaries.

122. Flood control sector be given preferential treatment while making allocations from funds meant for special problems.

123. Funds for specific schemes in the flood control sector should be earmarked. However, some flexibility should be provided to take care of special situations.

124. The Central Government should do the earmarking in the

case of inter-State projects and large projects costing more than Rs. 2 crore each and those in advanced stages of construction.

125. The outlay on flood control in States having a large backlog of continuing schemes should be increased and a greater proportion of the outlay be set apart for such schemes.

126. Schemes at locations, where emergent situations have been met during floods, should be undertaken only according to priorities fixed in the overall context.

Maintenance

127. For the maintenance of structural measures in soil conservation and watershed management during the first 3-4 years a provision of 4-5 per cent of the cost of works should be provided in the original estimates. Thereafter, maintenance should be the responsibility of the beneficiaries.

128. The methods and procedures detailed in the Embankment Manual and the Manual of Flood Operations compiled by the erstwhile CW&PC are adequate and should be normally followed.

129. The actual requirements of work, men and materials required for maintenance should be fixed for each location/State.

130. Instructions for watershed management and land treatment measures should be circulated.

131. Charging "maintenance" to "capital" under various forms should be discouraged.

132. Adequate funds for maintenance should be assured. Amounts for maintenance suggested for various types of works may be taken as a guide. These should be reviewed by the State officers on the basis of actual needs, and, norms fixed. These norms should be reviewed periodically.

133. In order to deal with emergent situations, emergency financial powers and discretionary grants should be given to specified officers.

134. The Planning Commission should, before, granting Annual Plan funds for new and continuing flood schemes, ensure that the State is making adequate provision for maintenance of existing works. A record of failure of control/protection works should be maintained and details supplied to CWC/GFCC, as also a resume to the Planning Commission.

135. Suitable checks of levels and cross-sections of works such as

embankments, drains, drainage channels, etc., should be exercised by higher officers.

136. In areas of high rainfall, some kind of surfacing should be provided on earthen embankments.

137. Arrangements should be made for connecting by telecommunication links, all points of important flood and drainage works to the headquarters of superior engineering officers and the control room of State headquarters.

138. All drains, whether dug of natural, should be properly maintained up to their outfalls.

139. Wherever sub-standard installations like ex-zamindari embankments, and test relief works are handed over to the Flood Control Department, funds should be provided to upgrade them to proper standards.

140. Additional funds should be allocated wherever embankments are used as public highways.

141. In emergent situations, the engineer-in-charge should take control of all operations. All Departments should render necessary assistance to him. Voluntary organisations of the locality should also be involved in works during such emergencies.

142. Proper training in maintenance of flood works should be imparted to the concerned persons such as unskilled labour, Government officers, Home Guards, local people, etc.

Organisations

143. River Basin Authorities should be set-up for preparing plans by basins/sub-basins of inter-State rivers.

144. For development of basins/sub-basins of inter-State rivers, the personnel for River Basin Authorities should be drawn from multi-disciplines.

145. A Central Authority may be constituted in due course of time with the Prime Minister as the Chairman and should be assisted by a strong technical body.

146. Non-recurring and recurring costs of Basin Authorities should be fully met by the Centre.

147. Pending constitution of the Central Authority, the State Irrigation Minister's Conference may carry out its duties.

148. The organisation giving technical assistance to the State Irrigation Minister's Conference may be strengthened in order to

discharge additional functions.

149. River Basin Authorities should be constituted as statutory authorities.

150. It would be preferable to have unified Irrigation and Flood Control Departments in the States.

151. Cells should be constituted for specialised items.

Legislation on Flood Control

152. The Central Government should assume the powers conferred on it by the Constitution under entry 56 of the Union List and enact suitable legislations for the regulation and development of inter-State rivers.

153. The States should enact legislation so as to amend Section 17(ii) of Land Acquisition Act with a view to make the existing provisions for emergent situations, at present applicable to Railways, also applicable for flood control works.

154. The Central Government should prepare a Model Bill dealing with all aspects of flood control to serve as a guide for the State Governments.

Collection and Publication of Data

155. The present coverage of rainfall stations in hilly stations should be strengthened.

156. The minimum density of self-recording raingauge network should be increased to 20 per cent.

157. A special Task Force should be appointed for finalising the hydrological network and a time schedule should be laid down for implementation.

158. The Central Government should exercise technical direction to ensure uniformity and continuity in the collection of hydrological and other data.

159. The hydrological, data collection of all inter-State and other important rivers should continue to be undertaken by the CWC, till the formation of River Basin Authorities, when the matter could be reviewed.

160. Contour surveys and preparation of maps of flood prone basins should be taken up immediately.

161. Using modern technology, land resources surveys for the

catchments of the flood-prone rivers should be taken up on a priority basis.

162. Use of advanced methods such as telemetering devices, radar, etc., should be intensified.

163. The CWC should review and standardise the existing forms and procedures in respect of hydrological data collection in the context of modern developments in this field. The finalised forms should be brought into use throughout the country within a time bound schedule.

164. The CWC through their regional centres should be entrusted with the responsibility of co-ordinating the data collection programme in the regions, as well as evaluation of the results of the completed projects in the light of benefits assumed.

165. A Central Data Bank should be established in the CWC where all data collected should be stored. It should have computer facilities for storing as well as retrieval. Suitable software for specific needs should be developed for processing of data for supply to different users.

166. The States should take immediate steps to publish the available data. Similarly the Central Water Commission should make up the time lag in the publication of Water Year Books.

Research, Education and Training

167. More emphasis should be laid on research, education and training as relevant to water resources development, river science and control of floods.

168. Central and State research organisations concerned with water resources development and water problems should increasingly participate in international programmes.

169. Early steps should be taken to establish the Documentation Centre on modern lines at the Central Water and Power Research Station, Pune.

170. Current research and development efforts should be geared to achieve automatic use of radar information for hydrological work.

171. Further studies should be carried out to improve the existing watershed models for using remotely sensed information in order to predict flood flow under inadequate or no data situations.

172. Pilot studies on the use of remote sensed data for a few subbasins in a couple of inter-State flood-prone rivers should be under-

taken.

173. Usefulness of scanner survey for flood plain mapping should be assessed.

174. Appropriate research studies on proto-type performance of hydraulic structures of check dams, small detention reservoirs, etc., should be undertaken in order to evolve technical manuals for adoption in different soil-climatic regions.

175. Scientific plans of research projects on hydrological studies should be drawn up carefully after identifying suitable watershed to represent major soil-climatic zones. In the first phase, planned studies in a few experimental and representative watersheds of the major flood-prone rivers should be implemented.

176. The existing research organisations should intensify their research investigations to obtain scientific information on river morphology and river response to various hydraulic structures and encroachments.

177. Scientific research should be taken up to determine the value of hydraulic conductivity, rate of water-table fluctuations and intake rates under different soil conditions, self cleaning velocities in drains and drainage indices for different regions of the country and to obtain information on the crop response to different depths, turbidity, and soluble salt content, both under stagnant and flowing water conditions.

178. Efforts should be intensified to evolve more and more mathematical model and use them to remove empiricism and introduce better rationality in decision-making processes.

179. Scientific surveys and investigations to determine the contribution of snow and glacier melt to annual floods in the Himalayan rivers should be intensified.

180. Research should be intensified to determine the effects of industrial pollution on structural materials and to evolve methods to maintain water quality.

181. Studies on sedimentation of reservoirs should be intensified.

182. Suitable research should be taken up to determine the effects of aquatic weeds on the loss of water in storage and interference with the flow conditions.

183. Intensive studies should be undertaken not only to identify suitable recharge areas for flood water absorption and recharging the ground aquifers but also an efficient methodology to execute such recharging programmes in the field on an operational scale.

184. Intensification of research is recommended on newer items of construction material like reinforced earth, fibre, reinforced concrete, etc., for use in river training works, etc.

185. Suitable pilot operational projects should be taken up to establish the economic feasibility of the proposed 'Range-Feedlot' system of cattle management.

186. Techno-economic research should be sponsored in order to develop new technology for flood control and methodology for quantifying indirect damages and indirect benefits.

187. A review of the adequacy of the present research organisations concerned with water resources development and water problems should be carried out. Pending this review, intensification of the current research efforts should be effected.

188. Regional Research Institutes under the National Institute of Hydrology should be established.

189. 'Barh Vigyan Kendras' should be established where training of land users and young students should be taken up.

Cyclones and Sea Erosion

190. The recommendations contained in the project report prepared by the IMD for better forecasting and warning are endorsed.

191. Human activities should be restricted in areas which are exposed to cyclones.

192. Disaster prevention policies should be encouraged.

193. The general range of land use regulation recommended for flood-prone areas may be applied for cyclone hit areas.

194. Casuarina and other plantations, wherever feasible, should be established as windbreakers for a width of about two km along the sea coast.

195. Shelter buildings, especially designed for cyclone conditions should be constructed in the coastal areas.

196. Future coastal embankment projects in deltaic areas should be planned in conjunction with other development projects such as highways, harbour and reclamation projects.

197. A National Council for mitigating disaster should be formed.

198. Adequate network of operational communication facilities connecting the warning service to all concerned and to one another for consultation and co-ordination should be established.

199. Planning and organisation of disaster preparedness should be kept under constant review.

200. Rehabilitation should aim to improve, rather than merely restore accustomed living standards and social conditions.

Resettlement should ensure that temporary settlements would become permanent only if they are suitable.

201. Financing of engineering works like coastal embankments and permanent shelters as protection measures should follow the practice as for flood control schemes.

202. The Beach Erosion Board should meet more often and in any case not less than once in six months. Sub-committees in respect of different States may meet as required and their. Reports considered by the Board during its meetings.

203. Erosion problems should not be considered in isolation nor on an *ad hoc* basis except in cases where protection cannot be postponed. Permanent solutions should be found by examining schemes of stretches of the coast between river mouths, high lands, or embankments, and, an overall plan prepared for the entire coast in a State.

204. Data collection should continue on the basis of recommendations made by experts.

The Coastal Research Engineering Centre, CWPRS, Pune should periodically evaluate the usefulness and reliability of the data collected and give appropriate guidance where required.

205. Works interfering with the coastal processes should be avoided as far as possible and the shore movements watched over a period of years before launching protection works.

206. Remedial measures should be undertaken for adequately safeguarding the interests of the people in the areas affected by the construction of coastal works like ports and harbours.

207. Government should review the sea erosion problem of various coastal States from the angle of rendering financial assistance to them.

ANNEXURE

STATEMENT REGARDING FLOODS IN THE COUNTRY, LAID ON THE TABLES OF BOTH HOUSES OF PARLIAMENT, BY SHRI GULZARILAL NANDA, MINISTER FOR PLANNING AND IRRIGATION AND POWER ON SEPTEMBER 3, 1954

I. The Problem of Floods

1. To study the situation created by the Floods in the North-Eastern regions of the country, I flew over the affected areas and took the opportunity of discussing the various aspects of the problem with the Chief Ministers and Officials of the States concerned, namely, U.P., Bihar, West Bengal and Assam. I was accompanied by the Technical experts of the Central Government.

2. Vast stretches of land submerged under water, numerous habitations nearly buried under silt, roads, bridges and railway lines torn to pieces — this was the spectacle of devastation which the eyes encountered for hours together. It brought to the mind of human tragedy of large masses of people struggling to escape with their lives, uprooted from their hearths and homes and reduced to utter misery and destitution. This has been happening again and again over large parts of the country. This year's floods are stated to the worst over a long period.

3. After this overwhelming experience the feeling is natural that, however important our other pre-occupations may be, the most urgent task before us now is to save the people from these horrors. I have also come back with the sense of assurance that this can be done.

II. Flood Situation

(a) 1954 Floods

4. An examination of gauges (Appendix I) and the rainfall

records for above 30 years for stations for which information is available does not establish the fact that the 1954 flood is altogether exceptional, barring the case of Kosi and a few other rivers. What is exceptional about 1954, however, is that the floods in all the northern rivers of the country seem to have occurred more or less at the same time this year creating an unprecedented situation in point of duration, extent and intensity. On some of the rivers very heavy floods were experienced more than once. Various meteorological factors during the last 10 days of July and again at the end of August combined to cause heavy rainfall over and near the entire stretch of the eastern Himalayas, resulting in an excessive spilling of the tributaries of the Ganga and the Brahmputra.

5. According to the reports so far received, the total area encompassed by floods exceeds 25,650 sq. miles. Nearly 94 lakh people have been affected. 226 lives have been lost. More than 7,200 cattle have perished. It has been reckoned that crops have suffered damage over an area of about 132 lakh acres, valued approximately at Rs. 38 crores. Several towns situated on the banks of rivers are threatened with severe erosion. No comprehensive estimate has yet been made of the total number of houses that have collapsed on account of floods. The number of houses damaged or destroyed as so far reported by Assam, Bihar and U.P. is 50,000. In West Bengal, many thousand houses have been damaged or destroyed. Destruction of property in Assam has been roughly valued at Rs. 1.39 crores. Estimated value of property lost in Bihar, West Bengal and U.P., is not readily available. Loss on account of damage to roads, railways and bridges in Assam is estimated at Rs. 85 lakhs. In West Bengal, damage to communications runs into crores of rupees. Reports from Bihar and U.P. are still awaited. The extent to which communications have been disrupted this time exceeds all past experience.

6. As known so far the position of the various States, chiefly involved in the floods this year may be seen from the following table:

Name of State	Area affected	Damage to crops	Damage to property	Damage to communication	Loss of human life	Loss of cattle	Remarks
1	2	3	4	5	6	7	8
Assam	12,000 sq. miles	Over Rs. 9 crores	Rs. 138.52 lakhs	Rs. 85 lakhs	17	3094	
Bihar	10,000 sq. miles	*Over 32 lakh acres	+About 40,000 houses damaged or destroyed	Figures not available	42	*608	*Complete report not available. +Final figures are likely to be much higher
West Bengal	Three floods 1st flood 54 sq. miles 2nd flood 900 sq. miles 3rd flood 1000 sq. miles	Rs. 7.5 crores	Many thousand houses have been damaged or destroyed	Damage runs into crores of rupees	142	1500	
U.P.	17 lakh acres (2660 sq. mils)	**Extensive damage to crops	Over 8000 houses damaged	Figures not available	25	2000	**Floods still continuing

(b) Earlier Floods

7. I asked the States of Assam, Bihar, West Bengal and U.P. to report the figures of the area affected as also the extent of damage to life and property during the last 5 years. The information received from them is given in Appendix II. It will be seen that in Assam, during the last 5 years, there have been four heavy floods — two covering extensive areas and the other two somewhat restricted in extent while in 1953 the floods were of a mild nature. In Bihar during the last 5 years, there have been two severe floods and two mild ones while 1951 was a normal year. In U.P. there have been three heavy floods and one mild ones during that last five years. 1951 was a normal year when there were no floods in U.P. In West Bengal there were three heavy floods out of which two were restricted in extent and one, i.e., of the current year was exceptional both in the severity and extent of flooding. In addition there were mild flood in 1951 and 1953.

8. Last year there were heavy floods in the Godavari in the South when a discharge of 2.8 million cusecs was recorded over Dhowlaiswaram weir. This flood over-topped and eroded flood banks and caused a good deal of havoc to the Rajhamundri town and the delta areas. The town was inundated and a number of houses collapsed. There was heavy loss of cattle and other moveable property amounting to several crores of rupees. Both telephone and telegraphic services were completely dislocated.

9. Floods were experienced in July 1948 and September 1950 in the Kashmir Valley. During both floods, a number of breaches occurred in the embankments on the left side causing heavy damage to the standing crops, roads, buildings and other property. The floods in 1953 were of medium intensity.

III. *Relief Measures Undertaken*

10. The following figures reflect the extent of action taken by various State Governments in connection with the floods this year:

(*Rs. in lakhs*)

State	Gratuitous relief	Agricultural loans	Test Relief	Rehabilitation & house-building grants & loans	Total
Assam	13.50	30.00	10.00	[illegible].00	83.50
Bihar	*175.00	++240.00	—	[illegible]	415.00
+West Bengal	5.67	233.80	4.13	2.52	46.12
U.P.	2.20	**25.00	2.70	—	29.90
	196.37	328.80	16.82	32.52	574.51

* This amount includes schemes for providing employment and other similar measures.

++ This includes agricultural and other types of loans.

\+ Figures given do not include rice doles, garments, cloth, blankets, milk powder, medicines, etc., distributed to the affected persons.

** Takavi loans.

11. In the previous years (1950–1953) the total cost of relief measures in these States as follows:

(*Rs. in lakhs*)

State	Gratuitous relief and Governor's relief fund	Agricultural Takavi loans	Test Relief	Rehabilitation & house-building loans and grants	Total
Assam	21.9	45.3	—	—	67.2
Bihar	527.0	1141.0	—	—	1668.0
West Bengal	**4.54	—	—	—	4.54
U.P.	7.16	91.0	—	105.56	
	560.60	1277.3	6.40	—	1844.30

** Figures for 1950, 1951 and 1953 have not been furnished by the State Government.

12. Central Assistance (in 1954): The following statement indicates the Central Assistance already/sanctioned/under consideration in connection with the current year's floods (position

as on September 1954).

State	Required			
	For re[illegible]airs to roads [illegible]mbankment[illegible]nd building[illegible]lakhs)	Gratuitous Relief and test relief (Rs. lakhs)	Takavi	Assistance given
1	[illegible]	3	4	5
Assam	85.06	Full expenditure incurred by State Government to stave off famine conditions caused by floods, and reimbursement of expenditure incurred on relief work last year		Under consideration
Bihar	Reimbursement of 75% of expenditure on relief schemes			50% of contribution for first two crores of expenditure and 75% contribution in excess of Rs. 2 crores
West Bengal	100.00	25.00		As grant, half the cost of (i) gratuitose relief and (ii) rebuilding of houses by poor people in affected areas subject to a ceiling of Rs. 2.5 lakhs as Central share for each item. At loan, half the cost of relief work subject to ceiling of Rs. 7.5 lakhs
U.P.		30.00*	21.30*	

* 50% as subsidy and 50% as loan.

IV. *Nature of Problem*

13. The rivers of India are broadly divisible into three types:

(1) Peninsular;
(2) Central Indian; and
(3) Himalayan.

14. Floods in Peninsular rivers like the Cauvery and the Krishna are caused by heavy rainfall in the Western Ghats. Such occasions, however, are not frequent. The floods in the Cauvery are controlled to a great extent by the Krishnarajasagar and Mettur reservoirs, floods embankments in the Krishna Delta afford reasonable protection to that area.

15. Floods occur more frequently in the Central Indian rivers like Tapi, Narmada, Godavari (major portion), Chambal, Mahanadi and Damodar. These are caused by heavy precipitation of rainfall in the Western Ghats, Madhya Pradesh and Chota Nagpur.

16. The Himalayan rivers stand out as a separate class, the occurrence of floods in them is almost an annual phenomenon. The factors responsible for the destructive floods in these rivers are: (a) heavy rainfall in the Himalayas, (b) steep slopes of the rivers before they debouch into the plains, and (c) absence of easy out-fall facilities. Most of the Himalayan rivers drain themselves either into the Ganga or the Brahmaputra; and when these two mighty rivers are themselves in high floods the effective discharge of waters of the swollen tributaries is not possible. Uncontrolled rivers tend to form numerous channels and extend their area of inundation. The flood problem, particularly in the North, has been aggravated by the fact that with the increasing pressure of population the areas liable to floods have been occupied for agricultural purposes.

17. The effect of earthquakes in increasing the volume of floods has not been fully established but there is evidence to show that the 1934 earthquake in Bihar has caused subsidence even up to 4 ft. in the middle portions of North Bihar. In Assam, it is stated that the earthquake of 1950, as a result of extensive hill slides in the catchments of the Brahmaputra and its north-eastern tributaries, the beds of these rivers have got silted up in varying degrees. It is also alleged that the road and railway embankments built across the drainage lines on both banks of the Brahmaputra hold up the flood

waters in many areas, causing local flooding and aggravating the flood damage to crops in low areas. It is, therefore, important that complete examination be made of the carrying capacity of the waterways in these embankments.

18. On some of the rivers the situation has been further aggravated by deforestation in the upper catchments causing soil erosion and increase in silt content of the rivers. Silt in the rivers does not generally cause trouble unless it is in very large quantities or is of coarse type. When the river carries an appreciable quantity of coarse silt, instability of its regime occurs, especially if the slope of the bed gets flatter. This results in a lateral movement of the river which can cause good deal of damage. Of the Himalayan rivers which cause floods, Kosi and Teesta are noted for this dangerous tendency. Except for the Kosi there are hardly any surveys showing the changes in the courses and the bed levels of the rivers.

19. Flood inundation this year has been extensive in the States of U.P., Bihar, West Bengal and Assam.

20. *Uttar Pradesh*: The most severely affected districts of Uttar Pradesh are in the eastern part. The rivers which cause damage in this area are the Gogra and the Rapti. The former submerges an area of 3,000 sq. miles and the latter about 1,200 sq. miles normally every year. Inundation also occurs, as in the current year, near the confluence of the Ganga and the Ram Ganga and also in the upper reaches of Bari Gandak (Narayani).

21. *Bihar*: Practically the whole of North Bihar is liable to submersion during floods. The inundated areas can be broadly divided into three zones Western (6,000 sq. miles), Central (Kosi portion) 2,380 sq. miles and Eastern (1,690 sq. miles). The rivers causing spill in the Western zone are nearly 50 of which 10 are of medium size and three big size, these last being Burhi Gandak, Bagmati and Kamla. The numerous streams are spaced 2 to 4 miles apart. This area exhibits considerable similarity to the Huai basin in China.

Gandak: Against the highest known discharge of 7,00,000 cusecs, this year's flood registered 6.5 lakhs cusecs. The main embankments remained intact. Some areas within the loops were however flooded.

Bagmati: The spill channels emanating from these rivers such as the Sugia, Sugia Pradesia, Hiraman, etc., caused considerable flooding in the Bagmati Basin. The spill of the river Bagmati on both banks in Nepal Tarai caused considerable flooding north of Darbhanga-Narkatiaganj railway line. The spill on the left bank combined with the Lakhandei spill caused considerable havoc in and around Sitamarhi sub-division. Sitamarhi town ring bund was over topped.

Burhi Gandak: The river was in high floods and there was considerable inundation in valley.

Kamla: This river was also in high floods and caused considerable damage in Madhubani and Benipatti areas. The level at Jayanagar is reported to have gone 2 ft. higher than last year's highest level.

Kosi: The central portion of Bihar is traversed by the Kosi and is the most devastated portion of North Bihar. The present Kosi scheme (1953) will enable considerable control of the river. Recent July flood of 6.5 lakh cusecs has not shown any features which necessitate a change in the scheme. Since the inspection of the area in the third week of August 1954, further unprecedented floods of over 8 lakhs cusecs intensity have occurred. While this high level water would have spread across a larger area, it is not likely to warrant any material alterations to the 1953 scheme.

22. *West Bengal*: Three successive high floods were experienced this year, first in mid June, second at the end of July and the third at the end of August. Of the many rivers causing destruction and havoc in North Bengal Teesta and the Torsa stand out prominently, of these the first is the more difficult to tackle as it has a tendency like the Kosi to change its course.

Jalpaiguri and Cooch Behar districts and parts of Darjeeling district were affected. The Assam Rail Link and the National Highway were breached. Cooch Behar was completely isolated for several days. Several towns have already suffered erosion and the threat continues.

23. *Assam*: Assam has a large number of rivers running from the hills to Brahmaputra. Extensive areas on both banks of the Brahmaputra were flooded. Heavy erosion has occurred at Palasbari and Dibrugarh. A number of villages north of Kamrup, Goalpara and North Lakhimpur have been affected. Areas around Saidya and Saikhwaghat were under heavy inundation.

The damage caused by the floods in Brahmaputra was aggravated by the fact that many of its major tributaries were in high spate at the same time.

24. *Jammu & Kashmir*: For a fortnight, during May 1954, the Wular level rose considerably due to Pohru floods and submerged some cultivated lands. This would necessitate reconsideration of the proposal for diversion of the Pohru torrent into the Wular Lake.

V. *Action Taken So Far*

25. Although floods have been causing serious damage to property and inflicting terrible hardships on the inhabitants of certain States, no systematic attempt has been made so far to devise adequate measures for flood protection in the areas so affected. Each time a heavy flood is experienced it has been the practice for the States to meet the situation by the adoption of such emergency measures as remissions of land revenue, grant of loans, gratuitous relief, etc., designed to mitigate hardship. Flood committees have also been appointed from time to time by the various States, but their recommendations have, for the most part, remained a dead letter. In Assam committees were appointed in 1929, 1934, 1947 and 1950 and they suggested the collection of hydrological and other data. Bihar appointed two committees in 1926. But few, if any of the recommendations were carried out. Very little was done in West Bengal to implement the recommendations of a flood committee which was appointed in 1922. It must be pointed out that all such committees were greatly handicapped in their investigations for want of basic information regarding the behaviour of rivers. Unfortunately the recommendations of successive committees for the collection of hydrological data were not followed up effectively.

26. After the attainment of Independence greater attention has been paid to flood control measures. The multi-purpose development of the Damodar, the Mahanadi and the Kosi, three of the most destructive rivers in the country will, after the completion of the projects now under way, provide substantial protection from floods in the areas they have been devastating hitherto. The Bhakra Dam on the Sutlej, the Matatila Dam on the Betwa, the Rihand Dam on the Rihand, a tributary of the Sone, the Gandhi Sagar Dam on the Chambal, are multi-purpose in conception and although flood control was not the dominant consideration, the areas through which the flow will be protected to a large extent from floods.

27. A scheme for the control of floods in the Kashmir Valley has recently been worked out with the assistance of the Central Water

and Power Commission. The main features of the scheme are:

1. Construction of a supplementary channel to divert 50 per cent of the peak floods from the Jhelum;
2. Improvement of the remaining outfall channel taking off from the Wular Lake; and
3. Strengthening of the Jhelum bunds in the entire reach.

28. To obtain data as a preliminary step to drawing up of schemes, Investigation Circles have been opened in Assam and Bihar at the instance of the Central Government. U.P. Government has set up a Special Investigation Division. Investigations are also in progress in connection with multipurpose schemes with flood control as one of their objectives in the Tapti and Narmada Valleys.

VI. *Lines of Remedial Action*

29. It is possible to have recourse to the following measures of protection and flood control:

1. Embankments were feasible to keep the flood out of areas which are otherwise subject to inundation.
2. Storage reservoirs, preferably on the tributaries.
3. Detention basins where the excess of flood water may be stored for a short time.
4. Diversion of the water of one river into the other.
5. Increasing the slope of the river by cutting down loops.
6. Dredging and channelling portions of the river where waterway has been reduced due to silting.

Besides these, some other measures like revetments and spurs will be necessary to safeguard any particular town exposed to the danger of being eroded. After collection of the requisite data, the choice of a appropriate method or combination of methods can be made. Hydraulic model tests will also be conducted for indications of proper solutions.

The preparation of a balanced scheme for a river basin is an extremely complex engineering, economic and social problem. All the known devices must be carefully considered and suitable combinations selected for each river basin.

Specific

30. As investigations proceed and data accumulate, the specific measures appropriate to each case will be formulated. What at the moment appears to be feasible for feeling with the flood problem in the different States is as stated below:

Uttar Pradesh

31. As the main problem is due to spilling and inundation, the State Engineers feel that a suitable remedy would be the construction of embankments on either side of the rivers so as to restrict the flooded area from an average of 10 miles width or so to about 1½ to 2 miles for normal flood discharges. Other suggestions are:

1. to improve the slope of the river by cutting out loops and unnecessary bends so as to increase its silt carrying capacity,
2. to divert a portion of high peak flood discharge of one river into another by means of diversion channels and regulators where possible,
3. to provide silt catching basins at the points where a high silt-carrying tributary meets the main river,
4. to dredge portions of the rivers where waterway has been considerably reduced due to silting.

To the above measures must be added the possibility of detention reservoirs.

Bihar

32. North Bihar is a big inland depression which, if left to itself, would built up in course of time by river action. Owing to the pressure of population, however, these areas have been extensively cultivated necessitating measures for flood protection. The Gandak plain has already been protected by embankments. A scheme for the Kosi area, consisting of embankments and diversion of part of flood waters is ready for construction immediately after the flood season.

33. For the areas between the Gandak and the Kosi a combination of embankments and storage reservoirs on the upper catchments may be necessary. Further consideration should also be

given to the possibility of diverting some water from Bagmati into Burhi Gandak. There are possibilities of using some natural depressions as emergency flood detention basins. The congestion of flood below Jhamta will relieved to a certain extent by the construction of medium reservoirs in the upper reaches.

West Bengal

34. Basic information regarding the behaviour of the Teesta and the Torsa which cause most of the destruction in this area in North Bengal has not yet been collected. Some of the data relating to these rivers will have to be collected in the upper catchment area, outside India. Short-term schemes for the protection of Jalpaiguri, Siliguri, Cooch-Behar, Alipurduar and Mathabhanga towns are an immediate necessity.

Assam

35. Immediate short-term measures are necessary to protect Dibrugarh and Palasbari which are in danger of being wiped out. Revetment work at Dibrugarh is in progress and the portion completed has withstood the recent heavy floods. Proposals are being worked out to ensure that the entire programme of revetment designed to give complete protection to the town will be completed in the shortest possible time. A similar revetment for the protection of Palasbari town will also be necessary. An estimate for this work has already been prepared. Certain areas in Brahmaputra valley can be protected against floods by the system of embankments. It would probably be necessary to construct storage reservoirs of small streams in their upper catchments.

Jammu & Kashmir

36. A scheme for 'Flood control and reclamation of the Kashmir Valley', has been worked out. At present a 10 ft. wide pilot channel along the centre line of the supplementary channel is being dug. It will soon be made 100 ft. wide. In addition to this, strengthening of the Jhelum bunds is also in progress. The target is to complete the entire scheme by the spring of 1957. Efforts are being made to complete the work earlier.

VII. *Investigations and Data*

37. Floods are causing damage not only in India but also in our neighbouring countries like Nepal, Sikkim and Bhutan. Large areas are being eroded and if proper soil conservation measures are not taken in time, large tracts will become un-inhabitable. Collection of rainfall and other hydraulic data of rivers will greatly help all concerned to devise measures to avoid erosion of land and destruction due to floods.

38. An indication of the minimum data required for the preparation of an overall plan is given in Appendix III. The collection of data will naturally take some time. Every effort will, however, be made to expedite this work.

VIII. *Outline of Programme*

39. The programme of flood control and protection can be divided into three phases:

Immediate: The first phase will extend over a period of two years. This period will be devoted to intensive investigation and collection of data. Comprehensive plans will also be drawn up and designs and estimates prepared for short-term measures of flood protection.

Some measures such as revetments, construction of spurs and even embankments may be applied immediately in selected sites.

Short-term: During the second phase which may be taken to start with the second year and extend to the 6th or the 7th year, flood control measures such as embankments and channel improvements will be undertaken. This type of protection will be applicable to a major portion of the areas now subject to floods.

Long-term: The third phase will relate to selecting long-term measures such as the construction of storage reservoirs on tributaries of certain rivers and additional embankments wherever necessary. This may take 3 to 5 years more.

40. A complete answer to the problem of flood may not be found in any single measure. Each case will have to be considered on its merits and a measure or a combination of measures adopted if a proper solution is to be found.

41. The question of constructing storages on major streams such as the Kosi, the Lohit, the Dihang and the Dibang, etc., can be

considered only in combination with other water uses. While investigations may be carried out, when staff becomes available, it is not possible to include the construction of storage reservoirs at this stage amongst the short-term measures now visualised for flood control.

42. Although embankments do not provide absolute immunity from the floods they will ensure a very large measure of protection which, given good maintenance, should prove to be of a lasting character. Provided the enthusiasm of the people can be aroused, as it is stated to have been in China, and their cooperation secured for this work of national importance it should be possible to complete the embankments in about 7 years if a start is made immediately. This programme of flood protection work will incidentally provide on a tremendous scale opportunities for employment of a simple character, scattered over large areas.

43. The State Governments are primarily responsible for the execution of project for the control of floods in their area. As many of the major rivers of India pass through more than one State, the control of floods is an inter-State rather than a State problem. Denudation of forests by reckless exploitation in States where the head waters lie may expose a State in the lower reaches to devastating floods and yet the State affected would be helpless in taking remedial action. Furthermore, the financial resources of States may not always be adequate for undertaking major flood control works. It is therefore obvious that unless the Centre takes the initiative in this matter and helps the State Governments to formulate and if necessary implement a systematic plan of flood control, no tangible progress is likely to be achieved in this direction. An Inter-State River Valleys Bill which aims at empowering the Central Government to take the initiative in matter pertaining to the regulation and development of inter-State rivers and river valleys will be introduced in the Parliament shortly.

IX. *Immediate Measures*

44. Collection of hydrological and other data should be given the highest priority and the efforts of the various departments of the Central and State Governments should be directed to this end. Data will have to be collected in Nepal, Sikkim and Bhutan for rivers rising in those countries and running through India. Besides the States

concerned, Central agencies such as Survey of India, Geological Survey, Meteorological and Forest Departments would have to participate in the effort.

45. The States as well as the Centre should make preliminary arrangements immediately for concentrated survey work and field investigation parties should commence work by the 1st October, 1954. Flood Control Organisations should be set up immediately for the recruitment of staff.

46. Equipment required for field parties such as transport vehicles, survey instruments, etc., should, in the first instance be diverted, from the existing departments and replaced later on.

X. *Organisation*

47. To ensure that the measures outlined above are carried out, it is proposed to create, with the consent of the States concerned, Flood Control Boards in the States which are liable to frequent floods. The Boards will be constituted in U.P., Bihar, West Bengal and Assam in the first instance. Andhra and other States which are liable to floods will also be requested to adopt the same course. It will be duty of these Boards to assess the flood problem in their areas and to: (a) collect data, (b) prepare a comprehensive flood control scheme for the State, (c) indicate priorities, and (d) ensure the implementation of approved schemes. These Boards will be assisted, wherever necessary, by technical committees for the collection of data and the preparation of schemes.

48. A Central Flood Control Board will also be constituted on which the Union Ministry of Irrigation and Power and the State Boards will be represented. The Central Board will consider the schemes submitted by State Boards and draw up a national flood control programme, having regard to the availability of finance and technical personnel. The Central Board will also be assisted by a strong technical committee consisting of experts in flood engineering, soil conservation and agriculture. Experts from ECAFE and other foreign countries will also be invited to assist this committee wherever necessary. The Central Technical Committee will work in close cooperation with the Central Water and Power Commission.

49. Having regard to the magnitude of the work that will devolve on the Central Water and Power Commission it will be necessary to strengthen that organisation by appointing an additional Member

with ancillary staff to be exclusively in charge of flood control.

XI. *Personnel*

50. A large number of supervisors will be required for survey work. It would be necessary to press into service all qualified men, whether retired or fresh from college. We may have to direct the final year students of overseer classes to undertake survey work treating, if necessary, the interruption of a year as a year of service as they enter Government service later on. It may also be necessary to get the engineering students of all denominations to work with the investigation parties during their summer vacation. These arrangements which are of an emergent character will not wholly meet the needs of the situation. The requirements of technical personnel should be carefully planned and arrangements made in good time for training wherever necessary.

XII. *Cost*

51. It is difficult to estimate with any degree of accuracy the cost of the measures that are being envisaged to ensure flood protection in all the States in India. Only a very rough estimate is possible at this stage. For U.P., North Bihar, West Bengal and Assam, an approximate estimate based on incomplete data comes to about Rs. 75 crores, Rs. 100 crores for 'immediate' and 'short-term' measures and Rs. 75 crores for 'long-term' measures involving storage on the tributaries of rivers in North Bihar and Assam. The short-term programme in these States can be completed over a period of about 6 to 7 years. The picture will become clearer and the estimates more firm as investigations progress and designs are drawn up. Similar measures required in relation to the problem of floods in other States will need a relatively small amount. The cost of the works can be reduced to a substantial extent by enlisting the co-operation of people in various ways. Contribution in the shape of voluntary labour is an important form in which people can help while graded protection levies would be perfectly legitimate where protection works are undertaken at the cost of the State.

52. The problem, however, does not cease with the building of flood protection works like embankments for an embankment that is not kept in shape is no embankment at all. These structures are liable

to deteriorate unless the people protected by them are ever vigilant with regard to their maintenance. Not only is it therefore essential to kindle enthusiasm for the initial construction but to organise them for subsequent maintenance so that they may pass on these structures as a sacred trust to future generations.

APPENDIX I

Comparison of 1954 Floods with Maximum Recorded Floods

Name of the river	1954 Flood		Max. Flood between 1934-53		Previous maximum flood	
	Max. level	Date	Max. level	Date	Max. level	Date
1	2	3	4	5	6	7
Bihar:						
1. Kosi at S.T. 13 (Baraksheira)	419.96 8,00,000 c.s.	24-8-54	405.26	1948	414.86 (Computed 7,05,000 c.s.)	1927
	413.06 6,60,000 c.s.	27-7-54			405.26 (observed 4,78,000 c.s.)	1948
2. Gandak at Triveni	367.70	30-7-54	364.90	1950	367.75	18-8-1902
3. Lal Bakya at Gobari.	106.00		106.20	1935	107.60	2-9-1916
4. Tour at Ekadri	242.30	26-7-54	244.00	1947	246.24	1892
5. Burhi Gandak at Secunderpur	174.64		176.85	1946	178.85	1916
6. Baya at Bhagwanpur	164.42	3-8-54	167.74	1953	167.74	1953
7. Bhagmati at Dhang	232.90		231.30	1946	234.80	1902
8. Kamla at Rajnagar	195.75		197.75	1947	197.75	1947
9. Ganges at Digha	165.01	17-8-54	172.41	1947	172.41	1923

APPENDIX I (Contd.)

Comparison of 1954 Floods with Maximum Recorded Floods

Name of the river	1954 Flood		Previous Max. Flood	
	Max. level	Date	Max. level	Date
1	2	3	4	5
U.P.:				
1. Gogra at Manjhi Inchcape Bridge	182.75	24-8-54	185.02	1936
West Bengal:				
1. Torsa at Cooch Behar	191.50	28-7-54	189.85	1952
2. Kaljani at Alipur Duars	202.00	26-7-54	204.00	1952
3. Tista at Jalpaiguri	269.60	24-8-54	270.51	1950
4. Sutanga	212.00	29-7-54	214.43	1952
5. Jaladhaka		28-7-54		
6. Mahananda	382.00	28-7-54	380.00	1950
Assam:				
1. Brahmaputra at			343.88	1946
Dibrugarh	343.00		343.30	1931
2. Tejpur	219.00		221.40	1906
3. Gauhati	164.86		169.26	1906
4. Dhuri	97.62		97.29	1931
Kashmir:				
1. Jhelum at Khannabal			5240.40	1950
2. Sangam			5229.70	1950
3. Awantipura			5219.40	1950
4. Badshahibagh			5212.20	1950
5. Munshibagh			5209.80	1950
6. Banyari			5180.80	1948
7. Sopore			5182.80	1948
8. Baramula			5178.80	1948

APPENDIX II

Statement Showing Damage to Crops and Houses due to Floods in the States of Uttar Pradesh, West Bengal, Bihar and Assam for the Quinquennium Ending 1954

Year	Area under floods (lac of acres)	Damage to crops (crores) Rs.	House damaged (in thousands)	Damage to houses (in crores) Rs.	Cattle lost	Human lives lost	Total (in crores) Rs.
1	2	3	4	5	6	7	8
Uttar Pradesh:							
1950	26.00	12	25	1.25	2200	128	13.25
1951	No floods						
1952	No appreciable floods						
1953	22.51	10	80	4.0*	341	23	14.00
1954	17.00	7	8	0.4	2000	25	7.4
Total 5 years	65.51	29	113	5.65	4541	176	34.65
Average	13.00	5.8	22.6	1.13	980	36	6.93

* Assessed at Rs. 500 as suggested by the Revenue Secretary, U.P. on Telephone.

1	2	3	4	5	6	7	8
West Bengal:							
1950	.64	0.10	.55	.04	3000	80	0.14
1951	.003	0.03	—	—	—	—	0.03
1952	.64	0.10	.55	.04	severe	8	0.14
1953	.064	0.05	—	.01	—	—	0.06**
1954	6.40	7.50	N.A.	N.A.	1500	142	7.50
Total	7.747	7.78	1.23	.09	4500	230	7.87
Average	1.55	1.56	0.25	.02	900	46	1.58

** 7 acres of Cooch Behar town washed away.

1	2	3	4	5	6	7	8
Bihar:							
1950	3.35	1.0 com-	—	—	—	—	1.0
1951	0.07	— pu	—	—	—	—	—
1952*	0.99	.3 ted	—	— compu-	—	—	0.3
1953	over73.00	29.0	84	6 ted	—	—	35.0
1954	32.00	15.0	40	5	608	42	20.0+
Total	109.41	45.3	124	11	608	42	56.3
Average	21.88	9.06	24.8	2.2	122	8	11.26

* Area under crops destroyed in 73 lac acres and this has been adopted against 64 lac acres total flooded.

\+ Figures incomplete.

1	2	3	4	5	6	7	8
Assam:							
1950	5.76	2.5	N.A.	N.A.	5000	564	2.5
1951	64.00	2.1	N.A.	2.2	7000	4	4.3
1952	2.07	2.3	N.A.	1.9	5441	7	4.2
1953	not given	0.2	N.A.	.3	837	4	0.5
1954	76.80	9.0	N.A.	.34	3094	17	9.34
Total	148.63	16.10	N.A.	4.74	21372	596	20.84
Average	29.73	3.22	N.A.	0.95	4274	119	4.17

N.A.: Not Available.

1	2	3	4	5	6	7	8
Total of States:							
1950	35.75	15.60	N.A.	1.29	10200	772	16.89
1951	64.01	2.13	N.A.	2.20	7000	4	4.33
1952	3.70	2.70	N.A.	1.94	5441	15	4.64*
1953	96.15	39.25	N.A.	10.31	1178	27	49.56
1954	132.20	38.50	N.A.	11.74	7202	226	50.24+
Total	321.80	98.18	N.A.	27.48	31021	1045	135.66
Average	64.44	19.63	N.A.	5.50	6202	209	25.13

* Severe in West Bengal.

\+ Figures incomplete.

Note: This statement is based on the latest material supplied by the respective Governments, except that in some places costs have been computed where not supplied by the States. The figures for Bihar for 1954 may increase considerably.

APPENDIX III

A. Surveys

Ground and Aerial

1. Correct course of the river from emergence from Himalayas to confluence with Ganga or any other river must be correctly known. The locations at which tributaries of the river join it and the angle must also be known.
2. A longitudinal section showing the average bed level, maximum and low water levels must be obtained.
3. Cross sections at intervals of one mile extending up to either five miles on either side or till the high ground, which is above MWL (a Maximum Water Level), whichever is less.
4. Surveys of chaurs or low depressions adjacent to the river course.
5. Mosaic aerial maps of the river system, scale 4 inches to 1 mile.

B. Silt Data

1. The sizes and percentage of silt particles at different periods of flow in the river at (i) exit from gorge, (ii) end of steep slope, and (iii) in the last reach of the river.
2. Size and composition of bed material and banks on either side at intervals of a mile.
3. Bed load determination-particles size and quantity.

C. River Flow

1. Observation of rainfall data in the hill and plain catchment areas of river-study of the data collected previously.
2. Actual gauge and discharge observations of the river at 2 or 3 places.
3. Determination of maximum flood levels by marks or enquiries.
4. Incidence and intensity of storms.

D. Storage Sites

1. Preliminary reconnaissance survey.
2. Detailed survey of a few of the sites.
3. Geological survey at the probable sites.
4. Minimum Drilling.
5. Materials of construction-soils, stone and sand.
6. Transport facilities.
7. Storage requirements and possible capacities.
8. Capacity survey at a later date after the site is fixed.

E. Hydraulic Model Tests

1. Study of the flow in a single river.
2. Interaction of flows in different rivers.

F. Effect of Floods in the Main River on the Drainage of Tributaries

1. Observation of flood levels in Ganga or Brahmaputra and its back water effect on the drainage of tributary rivers.

2. Simultaneous observation of water levels in Ganga or Brahmaputra and tributary rivers.

G. Special Characteristics of the River Data Leading to

1. Heavy silting.
2. Meandering.
3. Violent movement.
4. Heavy erosion.
5. Effect of shortening or dredging.

H. Miscellaneous

1. Survey of villages affected.
2. Survey of existing waterways in road and rail embankments.
3. Details of inundated areas and flood damages.

8

RAILWAY ACCIDENT INVESTIGATION REPORT ON DERAILMENT OF 234 DOWN MIXED TRAIN BETWEEN GOLAGHAT AND FURKATING STATIONS ON MARIANI-JORHAT TOWN–FURKATING M.G. SECTION OF TINSUKIA DIVISION OF NORTHEAST FRONTIER RAILWAY AT ABOUT 20.56 HOURS ON 14-7-1976

July 19–21, 1976[1]

One Man Commission Shri A.V. Jacob, Additional Commissioner of Railway Safety, North Eastern Circle Gorakhpur.

Officers Present Shri B.R. Pahwar; Shri P.K. Banerjee; Shri A.K. Ghosh; Shri S.R. Sarkar; Shri B. Basu

Appointment

The Commission was constituted under Rule 4 of the Statutory Investigation into Railway Accidents Rules 1973 (notified by the Ministry of Tourism and Civil Aviation Vide No. RS 13-T(B)/71 of 19th April, 1973.

Terms of Reference

To inquire into the Derailment of 234 Down Mixed Train Between Golaghat and Furkating Stations on Mariani-Jorhat Town — Furkating M.G. Section of Tinsukia Division of Northeast Frontier Railway at about 20.56 hours on 14-7-1976.

---

1. Ministry of Tourism and Civil Aviations, Commission of Railway Safety, Government of India, New Delhi, 1985, i + 20 p.

Conclusions

Cause

On full consideration of the factual, material and circumstantial evidence, I have come to the conclusion that the accident was caused due to combined effect of defect in wagon No. NE C 29740 and the defects in the track at the site of the accident.

Responsibility

Responsibility for the accident is shared between Station Master, Barua Bhamungaon, Shri. A.C. Routh who allotted the wagon No. NE C 29740 for loading after the expiry of due date of re-packing and Mate, Shri Manindra Dey of Gang No. 1 and Permanent Way Inspector, Shri U.P. Choudhary. In considering the extent of their culpability, my remarks in the chapter 'Discussion' may please be kept in view.

Service Particulars

Sri A.C. Routh, aged about 54 years was appointed as Signaller on 1-4-1943 and promoted as Assistant Station Master on 19-4-1951 and Station Master on 24-9-1966. He has had about 5 punishments, mostly for offences connected with commercial working.

Sri U.P. Choudhary aged about 41½ years was appointed as Apprentice Permanent Way Inspector on 17-3-1962 and promoted as Permanent Way Inspector, Grade III on 5-8-1970. He has had no punishments during his service.

Sri Manindra Dey, aged about 57¾ years was appointed as gangman on 19-1-1945, promoted as Keyman on 16-3-1966 and as Mate from 26-5-71 from which date, he has been in charge of this section. He has had no previous punishments during his service.

Relief Measures

Looking to the circumstances of the accident, the relief arrangements were in time and adequate. The N.F. Railway will no doubt convey their appreciation to the Doctors of the Civil Hospital at Golaghat for the care given to the injured passengers.

Recommendations

35.1 In regard to the general condition of the track on N.F. Railway, successive Additional Commissioners of Railway Safety had to comment adversely on the same. In a similar accident which happened in the same section in 1972 (Department of 238 Dn. Mixed Train on Furkating-Jorhat-Mariani section between Rowariah and Bhalukmara on 4-12-72) the then A.C.R.S., Shri Arya Bhushan had commented on the fact that the condition of track was not satisfactory. He ascribed this mainly to the fact that track renewal works (both through and casual) were much behind acceptable minimum. In his report on the derailment of 176 Down Mixed Train between Dhemaji and Gogamukh stations of Alipurduar Jn. Division also the then ACRS, Shri J.Y. Marathe while concluding that the cause of accident could not be established beyond doubt has stated that the derailment was most probably due to poor condition of track and high maximum speed of 50 KMPH for a mixed train permitted on that track. The ACRSs have also in a number of annual inspections pointed out the short-fall in relayings on N.F. Railway and the deteriorated condition of the track, I would again urge the Railway Board to give specific attention to rehabilitation of track on N.F. Railway.

35.2 In the extant case, however, the percentage of unserviceable sleepers at the site of the accident and in other stretches of the section where checked was *below 20 per cent*. But the rails, second hand, 60 1b. are *very old* and have lost *11 per cent in weight*. Though the number of rails found with cracks which require removal in a 2 km stretch on checking with ultra-sonic detector was not large, still the fact that the rails are now more *than 60 years* old (having been rolled in *1913*) points to the need for an annual check with ultra sonic apparatus and replacement of rails which have developed cracks. The Chemist and Metallurgist in his report has pointed out that the composition of these rails does not conform of extant specifications and as per R.D.S.O.'s recommendation required to be changed. The administration may examine the matter further.

35.3 The maintenance practices followed in this section as has come to light at the inquiry points to the need for enforcement of schedules and greater attention to other details. As elicited by questioning neither the Permanent Way Inspector nor the Assistant Engineer had carried out a foot-plate inspection of the section for quite sometime. The P.W.I. stated that he had carried out a last vehicle inspection on 14-6-76 but an examination of his diary gives reason to doubt whether the inspection was in fact carried out as it appeared that he travelled in the train only and the track readings recorded were subsequent entries. As cross level deficiencies cannot be picked up from a push or motor trolley, trolley inspections alone are not sufficient and engine and last vehicle inspection as per Schedule by P.W.I and AEN must be ensured.

35.4 I understood from Additional Chief Engineer (Track), N.F. Railway that periodical engine inspection by P.W.Is. and AENs have been prescribed and that charts of these are seen by Headquarter Officers and shortfalls taken up periodically. If so more vigorous administrative action is called for to enforce schedules unless this is an isolated case.

35.5 In this connection, it is relevant to point out that the jurisdiction of Assistant Engineer is much more than the norms prescribed in the efficiency Bureau's Study of Workload of Assistant Engineers. According to information furnished by N.F. Railway the AEN/Mariani has an ITKM of 562.83 (with 4 PWIs and 3 IOWs, under him) against recommendation of E.B. Study for 400 ITKM for purely M.G. Section (Page 43, Para 5.03(I) Efficient Bureau Study No. 11/67). Similarly, Permanent Way Inspector, Furkating has route K.M. 107.87 against recommended 80 to 90 route K.M. on branch lines (Page 13, Para 2.04(c) ibid). The norms in E.B. Study were recommended by Railway Board's own efficiency Bureau and accepted by the Railway Board. In this case the work-load of Assistant Engineer is too high. Over-extended sections and heavy workload create a vicious circle of inability to meet inspections schedule laid down and apathy towards the schedule due to such failure which in turn further accentuates the shortfalls finally leading to demoralisation of the staff. I would urge the Railway Board to review the jurisdiction of Assistant Engineers and Permanent Way Inspectors on the basis of yardstick and where additional posts are found necessary, create the same.

36.1 Apart from the question of scheduled inspections of track by Officers and Inspectors, another important aspect of track maintenance which appears to have been neglected is the checking of the equipment of the gang. In view of the existence of wide variations in cross levels at the site of the accident, I checked the cross level at another site at K.M. 3/3 to 3/5. Here again, cross levels were not satisfactory. On check of the particular gang's spirit level, it was found that the bubble was maladjusted. Neither any one in the gang nor the P.W.I. knew how to use a maladjusted spirit level, i.e., by taking the mean of the two position of the bubble. The instructions to the gang was to work with one uniform position of the bubble which if correctly adhered to would have given a uniform Super elevation on straight. But the fact that the cross levels actually recorded were varying and reversing showed that even this was not being followed.

36.2 There appeared to be no periodical checking of the gang equipment at least on this section as laid down in Para 627(b)(ii) of I.R.W.W. Manual. The need for checking and rectifying where necessary the gauge and level in use with the gangs cannot be over emphasised. The date of such checking should be invariably pointed on the gauge, and level Board as a token of the check having been carried out. Action may be taken by N.F. Railway administration in this respect early.

37. In regard to maintenance of wagons, the question of ensuring that wagons plying on branch lines receive periodical 'fit to run' inspection requires to be looked into. In the specific case of Furkating-Jorhat-Mariani section, it is understood that the practice is for loads coming from Lumding for destination upto Barua Bamungaon to be cut off at Furkating and despatched onwards by 233 Up Mixed Train. Wagons for stations further up are worked to Mariani on main line and worked by 234 Dn. mixed to destination. Thus while the latter set of wagons receive a further fit to run examination at Mariani after the examination at Lumding the former do not get any such examination as Furkating has no Train Examining staff for the purpose. In both cases, wagons once sent to a branch line stations, can continue to ply between stations on the branch line and stations upto Lumding via Furkating for any length of time without any TXR examination. The distance between Lumding to Furkating is 139 km. In order to ensure that such wagons are examined by qualified Train Examiners at reasonable intervals, it appears necessary to post TXRs staff at Furkating or lay down that all wagons going into the branch line section will be routed through Mariani irrespective of the station on the branch line to which they are booked even though this may involve a longer haul. This recommendation will apply to all branch line loops on which at one junction there is no TXR establishment.

38. At way side stations, wagons are allowed to be loaded by Station Masters/Goods Clerks after a superficial examination of

their fitness to run and then attached to trains. Their road worthiness is not checked by competent TXR staff till they pass through a station where such staff are posted. There is, therefore, need for proper training of Station Masters and Goods Clerks as well as Guards in inspection of wagons to see that they are fit to run. It is understood that while practical demonstration is given during initial training, this does not form part of the curriculum for refresher. The extent of the training even in the initial stage is not known. It is considered that the initial training of Assistant Station Masters/Goods Clerks/Guards should include intensive training in examination of wagons and that provision for brushing up their knowledge of this should be included in their refresher curricula also.

39.1 Para 21(c) of Chapter II of the Operating Manual of N.F. Railway originally provided that in respect of traffic to and from stations on sections where there are no goods trains but only mixed trains, only wagons marked 'M' as fit to be attached to mixed trains are to be used. Otherwise the contents are to be transhipped into wagons marked with 'M' at junction stations. It is understood, however, that this system has since been abandoned as it interferred heavily with operation and as it was considered that since speed of mixed trains has been reduced to 40 KMPH, this restriction was no longer necessary.

39.2 According to information furnished by N.F. Railway, there have been 16 derailments of mixed trains on that Railway from 1971-72 to 1975-76 out of which 14 have been in mid-section. Out of this, 7 have been due to combined track or wagon defects or one of them, 2 due to over-speeding and 3 undetermined. It will thus be seen that number of derailments of mixed trains is quite high and that at least 50 per cent of them are due to combined or individual track or wagon defect. As all such accidents are potential danger to passengers travelling by these trains, it appears necessary to revert to a system by which only wagons which are maintained to a higher standard than the average are attached to mixed trains. On the Broad Gauge, there is a system of marking wagons fit to run by passenger trains. In the circumstances, it appears desirable to revert to the system of marking wagons with special symbol 'M', only such wagons being attached to mixed trains.

40. It is one of the recurring recommendations of ACRSs after every mixed train accident that four wheelers on a mixed train be attached in the rear of the coaches to mitigate the consequences of

any derailment of the former on passengers travelling in the latter. Board while issuing instructions in the matter vide their letter No. 72/Safety (A&R)/1/2 dated 16-12-72 have stated that in certain cases, there would be no alternative to marshalling the wagons next to the engine. I have been shown letter addressed by N.F. Railway to Railway Board in which the Railway Board has been requested to exempt this section among some others from operation of the rule that goods stock be attached in rear only. It is true that apart from the fact that marshalling of wagons in the rear would increase the time required for attaching and detaching wagons at way side stations by train engine, on this section there is a reversal at Jorhat Town and, therefore, even if the wagons are marshalled in the rear at the starting junction, they will come next to engine at Jorhat Town unless further shunting is done at that station to remarshall the train. However, the continued incidence of derailment on this section (there has been six since May, 1972 including this one) warrants a review of the position to assess the exact extra time required for the purpose and to insist on marshalling wagons in the rear if the time required is not excessive.

41. Moreover, it is seen that average daily inward and outward wagons moved by the mixed train from Furkating in the last one month are about 10 to 12. If so, it is a matter for considerations whether a separate goods train each way on alternate days with an inferior steam engine cannot be justified. Also the occupancy of this train on date of accident was only 25 against a capacity of over 250. The thin occupation of this train may be due to its slow speed or parallel bus services. It may also, therefore, be worthwhile to examine whether this mixed train cannot be abolished altogether and converted into a goods rain pure and simple.

41.1 According to para 21 of Chapter II of the Operating Manual of N.F. Railway, Station Masters are not to load wagon with expired return date or due re-packing. However, whereas the return date is marked prominently on the body of the wagon, the due re-packing date has to be calculated from the date of last re-packing stenciled in small figures on the sole bar of the wagon. It seems too much to expect Station Master or Goods Clerks to check the due date from this before permitting loading of a wagon. I would recommended that due re-packing date be also prominently displayed below the return date on the body of the wagon.

42.2 Incidentally it is a common sight on both N.E. and N.F. Railways to see wagons with expired return date moving in loaded conditions against the direction of the owning Railway with or without extensions of return dates stencilled on them. Apparently no serious attempt is being made by Railway administration to enforce the rule regarding not loading time expired wagons except in the direction of owning Railway. The freedom with which traffic staff are allowed to break this rule naturally breeds contempt for allied rule of not loading over due re-packing wagons. There is, therefore, need to enforce both rules vigorously on the Railways.

43. The engine of 234 Dn. YP 2339 was not provided with a speedometer. As brought out at the inquiry, it was turned out from Dibrugarh Workshop after POH on 29-5-76 without this fitting. Though excess speed has not been found as a cause of the accident in this case, it is unsatisfactory that despite repeated instructions from Railway Board, passenger train engines still continue to run without speedometers.

44.1 Though the accident occurred at 21.00 hours on 14-7-76, sanction of Civil authorities to start restoration operation was given only at 15.00 hours on the 15th, i.e., after 18 hours. This time appears excessive.

44.2 According to the Railway, S.D.O. and S.D.P.O., Golaghat were informed of the accident by written memo at 00.20 hours as their phones were out of order and none could wake them up. They confirmed receipt of information at 5.50 hours, DC/Jorhat could be informed only at 05.55 hours as Trunk phone remained out of order during night. S.D.O and S.D.P.O., Golaghat is reached the site of accident at 8.00 hours on 15-7-76 and CC and SP, Jorhat at 10.30 hours.

44.3 In the extant case, there was no suspicion of sabotage at all but as per extant orders the sanction of the Civil authorities had to be awaited. The Railway Board may consider how best the need for giving full opportunity to state Government officials to inspect the site of accident can be reconciled with the need for early restoration of through communications and take suitable action.

Railway Board's Comments on Various Paras of the Report

Para 42.2: Instructions on the subject been reiterated to all concerned by the railway administration.

Para 43: The loco of the ill-fated train which was turned out from Dibrugarh workshop after POH on 25-9-76, could not be fitted with a speedometer as facilities for fitment of the speedometer on NBC roller bearing axle boxes were not available in the shops. These facilities have, however, since been developed and instructions issued to ensure fitment of speedometers during POH of the locomotives.

Para 44: In the context of CRS's observations in para 44 of the report, the matter was referred to the zonal Railway to indicate their experience regarding delay on the part of civil and police authorities in granting permission to commence restoration operations after an accident. The Central, Northern, South Central, South Eastern, Western Railways have advised that in the recent past there had been no case on their railways where civil/police authorities took excessive time in granting permission to commence restoration operations. Even on N.F. Railway, where the subject accident took place, there has been no other accident (not ascribed to sabotage) where any abnormal delay occurred in getting permission from the concerned authorities. On the Southern Railway during the period 1974 to August 1979, there was only one case where the police took 12 hours to give permission to start restoration work. The delay in that case was attributable to a dispute between the local police and Railway police. On the Eastern and North Eastern Railway, however, there have been a few cases where excessive delays were reported to have taken place in getting permission for restoration operations. Barring this, no other case has come to the notice of the Board where abnormal delay has taken place in granting permission to start restoration after an accident. It may be mentioned here that instructions already exist on the State Governments vide Ministry of Home Affairs letter No. 19/7/70-GAP/1, dated 14-12-70 (copy enclosed), stipulating the need for prompt attendance of the police authorities concerned at the site of the accident and permit clearance of restoration of traffic.

It is considered that delays in granting the permission by the police usually occur in the cases of sabotage when police authorities may decline to sign the factual note as to the conditions obtaining at the site after the accident. In this connection, it may be mentioned that the Ministry of Home Affairs had emphasised on State Governments vide their letter No. 19/6/73-GAP/1 dated 18-7-73 (copy enclosed) that to avoid delays in restoration of communication after derailment/accident suspected to have been caused by sabotage, the concerned police authorities visiting the site of the accident should prepare and sign a joint factual note as to the conditions obtaining at the site. These instructions were reiterated to the State Governments by the Ministry of Railways vide letter No. 72-Sec. (SPI)/152/12, dated 7-3-75. This issue was recently taken up with the Home Ministry by Chairman, Railway Board vide his D.O. letter No. 82/Security (Crime)/152/1, dated 17 July, 1982, (copy enclosed). The Ministry of Home Affairs have been requested to have their extent instructions reiterated to all State Governments, indicating that these instructions should be incorporated in the police manuals.

Para 35.1: Some arrears of track renewals have accumulated over the Indian Railways during the past 10 years due to inadequate availability of funds for this purpose. The Ministry of Railways is seized of the issue and action has already been taken to make more funds available for track renewals commencing from the financial year 1979-80 with a view to wipe out the arears. It must, however, be emphasised that on no section is the track unsafe for the movement of rolling stock at the authorised speeds. However as the density of traffic on this section is only 0.25 GTKM and the maximum sectional speed has already been reduced to 25 Kmph no track renewal is justified on condition basis. Accordingly, no programmes for track renewal on this branch line has been formulated.

Para 35.2: As mentioned above, the traffic on this section is very light. Further, there was only one case of rail fracture on this section during the past two years, which would indicate that the situation is not at all alarming. Action is, however, in progress to procure more ultrasonic rail flaw detectors and when these become available, it would be possible to test the rails on this branch line more frequently. The Railway will, however, be asked to expedite action, as necessary, in the light of the RDSO's observations/analysis of the rail-pieces of this section, which is proposed to be sent by the Railway to the RDSO for examination.

Para 35.3: The Railway administration would ensure that the prescribed schedule of engine and last vehicle inspections is carried out by the engineering officials regularly.

Para 35.4: The Railway administration has noted the ACRS's observations for compliance, and would take suitable action in the matter.

Para 35.5: The workloads of PWIs and Asstt. Engineers have been assessed by the Railways administration. Whereas the jurisdiction of PWIs has been readjusted, the workload, of AENs are under scrutiny and redistribution of jurisdiction as necessary, would be effected. This Railway would be asked to expedite action in this respect.

Para 36.1: Necessary action in the matter has been initiated by the Railway administration, who has been asked to procure sensitive levels and supply the same to the permanent way gangs.

Para 36.2: Necessary action has been taken by the Railway in compliance to this recommendation.

Para 37: The routing of all wagons playing on the branch line via Mariani, is not necessary. Instructions have, however, been reiterated by the Railway that wagons, which are date expired, should not be loaded.

Para 38: It may be pointed out that the wagons which are made available or are sent for loading at way-side stations are those whose road-worthiness is already checked by a competent TXR. The road-worthiness of such vehicles is again checked when they pass through a station where TXR facilities are available. It is not possible for a Station Master/Goods Clerk/Guard to examine the wagons as minutely and intensively as a TXR can do. Such staff cannot be expected to see as to whether fitment of components of the wagons is complete in all respect and is within the prescribed limits and that a particular component or a part is properly welded or rivetted. It may be mentioned here that apprentice Mechanics are given full 5 years intensive training, both theoretical and practical, before they are put to work as TXRs. If the Station Masters/Goods Clerks/Guards were also required to examine the road-worthiness of a vehicle at a particular station, such staff will have to be taught full mechanical engineering relating to the maintenance and upkeep of wagons. This is neither feasible nor desirable because such a proposal, apart from diffusing responsibility, would be at the cost of the efficiency of the respective departments. This would add to problem rather than solve it.

Under the circumstances, this recommendations is not acceptable.

Para 39: The speed of mixed trains on all the sections of this Railway has been reduced to 25 Kmph. Instructions have also been issued by the Railway administration for intensive examination of the goods stock attached to mixed train at the TXR headquarter stations, and the station where no TXR is posted, the goods wagons would be examined at the next TXR examining station. This would meet the requirements embodied in the ACRS's recommendations.

Para 40: The extra time required for shunting by reversing of the train engine, in the event of goods wagons being attached in the rear of the mixed train, has been worked out by the Railway. The total additional time required for the purpose is approximately 3 hours which is excessive and would also create further problems of changing the crew enroute.

It is seen that CRS has noted the position explained by the Railway.

Para 41: As explained by the Railway administration, the existing materialisation of traffic on this section does not justify the running of a goods train either daily or on alternate days or bi-weekly. Since a large number of passengers from Jorhat Town, Bhalukmara, Barua Bamungaon and Golaghat use this mixed train, the recommendation to abolish the mixed trains on this section is not acceptable. It is seen that CRS is satisfied with the remarks given by the Railway.

Para 42.1: The repacking date is already there on the sole bar and it is not at all difficult to read this. It is not considered necessary to point the repacking date on the body panel.

9

INDIRECT TAXATION ENQUIRY COMMITTEE, 1976 – REPORT[1]

Chairman Shri L.K. Jha

Members Shri G.B. Newalkar; Shri J. Sen Gupta; Shri M.V. Arunachalam; Shri Raja J. Chelliah; Shri S.S. Marathe (replaced by Dr. Man Mohan Singh in September, 1976)

M. Secy. Shri K. Narasimhan

Appointment

In pursuance of the Finance Minister's Budget Speech of 1976, announcing the decision to appoint a committee to review the existing structure of indirect tax system. The Indirect Taxation Enquiry Committee was set up under the Government of India, Ministry of Finance, Department of Revenue Resolution F.No. 331/3/76-TRU dated July 19, 1976.

Terms of Reference

(i) To review the existing structure of Indirect Taxes – Central, State and Local, in all its aspects,

(ii) To examine the role of indirect taxation in promoting economic use of scarce resources,

(iii) To examine the structure and levels of excise duties, the impact of excise duties on prices and costs, the cumulative effect of such duties, their incidence on various expenditure groups, the scope for widening the tax base and increasing the elasticity of the system,

(iv) To examine the feasibility of adopting some form of Value

---

1. Ministry of Finance, Department of Revenue, New Delhi, [in two parts (Part I, 1977, 195 p.; Part II, 1978, 794 p.)]

Added Tax in the field of indirect taxation where appropriate and, if found feasible, to suggest the appropriate stage to which it should be extended having regard to Indian conditions, i.e., whether the stage of coverage should be manufacturers, wholesalers or retailers,

(v) To examine whether and how far it would be advisable to assist any particular industry or particular sectors of an industry by grant of concessions in indirect taxes; in doing so, the Committee will doubtless take into account all the normal canons of taxation, and the balance of administrative convenience. In those cases where these devices are found to be advisable, to suggest norms for the same.

(vi) To examine the structure and levels of import duties from the point of view of import trade control, protection to indigenous industry and pricing of indigenous products and suggest changes, if necessary.

(vii) To advise the Government on the steps to be taken to implement the recommendations made, including changes in the administrative and organisational set-up.

(viii) To suggest changes, if any required, in the constitution and in the related taxation statutes, for the implementation of the changes suggested in the tax structure and having regard to the revenue needs of both the Centre and the States,

(ix) to consider the interaction and the proper balance between indirect and direct taxes in our tax structure while examining the role of indirect taxation in mobilising resources.

(x) To make any other recommendations germane to the enquiry.

Contents

Taxes in India; The Role of Indirect Taxes; Principles of Reform of Excise and Customs; Approach to Rationalisation; The Revenue Angle; Stimulus to Production and Investment; Encouragement to Small Producers; Reforms of Sales Taxation; Other State and Municipal Taxes – Measures of Reforms; Procedural Reforms; Administrative Framework; Value-added Tax – Basic Features; Long-Term Reform of the Indirect Tax Structure; Summary of Conclusions and Recommendations; Appendices from 1 to 22.

Recommendations

The prime purpose of a tax system is to mobilise real resources needed for promoting economic and social progress. But the very process and manner of resource mobilization, the incidence of taxation, and the encouragement or discouragement that it gives to diverse economic activities, are not without their own socio-economic consequences. From the social angle what is most needed is that taxation should have an adequate measure of progression. From the economic view point, the tax system should encourage the kind of economic activity to sustain which resources are being mobilised, while at the same time, should least reduce the efficiency of resource use.

For the tax system to subserve these objectives it must have stability. It should not be thinkered with frequently either in the interest of revenue or to deal with day-to-day problems or to resolve the difficulties of particular producers. The need for higher revenues should be met in a manner which does not upset the structural balance of the system once it has been rationalised. Thus, we believe, should be possible if the system is rationalised and changes effected along the lines of our recommendations.

In conclusion, we would like to summarise the highlights of our findings and recommendations so as to bring the major directions of change in the tax system that we envisage. The system of indirect taxation that we have today is the result of a more or less uncoordinated growth of major individual indirect taxes levied independently by the Centre and State Governments and Local authorities. The structure of each of the major individual indirect taxes is itself not entirely rational or internally consistent, and their interaction often serves to compound their harmful effects. The objectives of tax reform should, therefore, be to eliminate the overlapping of different taxes and to rationalise the internal structure of each of the taxes in such a way that they are rid of their major deficiencies and would become the building blocks for a harmonious indirect tax system in the country. The most serious deficiencies in the system of indirect taxation can be traced to: (a) the widespread taxation of raw materials and other inputs under import, excise and sales taxation, mainly for raising revenue and not always with adequate regard to the economic consequences flowing from such taxation; (b) the overlapping coverage of excise and sales taxation over a wide range of products; and (c) the inequitable distribution of tax burden among States *inter se* through the attempts of particular States to export part of their taxes to the residents of other States.

In the field of excise taxation, our major proposals relate to: (a) the rationalisation of the duty structure on final products such that progression could be more easily achieved and our economic priorities fulfilled; (b) rationalisation of the rates of duties on raw materials such that materials that are close substitutes will be treated similarly unless there are special economic reasons to the contrary and high rates of taxes on particular materials imposed for special reasons in the past will be curtailed in the interest of lowering the cost of production in the economy as a whole; and (c) taking major steps within a time-bound programme of action towards the solution of the problem of cascading, first by extending the application of existing procedures for the relief of input taxation and finally moving over to a system of Value Added Taxation at the manufacturers' stage.

Import duties on products fall mainly on raw materials, intermediates and machinery. This has the effect of bringing about a general increase in the cost-price structure which, apart from being undesirable in itself, tends to make our industries less competitive in the international market. The very high level of import duties on some products generates a vicious circle which leads other industries to seek higher protection in order to survive. A reversal of this trend, particularly when our foreign exchange position is comfortable, is necessary. The long-term objective of the reform of import taxation should be to lower the rates of taxation on different inputs and machinery to levels that would be necessary to give adequate protection and have an element of discouragement of imports. Such adjusted levies would serve purely economic purposes and to them would be added a counter-vailing duty equivalent to the excise on similar commodities/products. We recognize that this reform could only be gradually carried out. Once import duties are rationalised along the lines suggested above, they could be harmonised with the operation of the excise tax system because then the countervailing duty on imported products would be given the same treatment as excise duties on domestic products.

In the field of sales taxation, our proposals are based on the principles: (a) that sales taxation by a State should essentially be imposed on its residents without impinging on costs of production in the economy and without significantly affecting the residents of other States; (b) that the principle of a unified market within the country should be preserved; (c) that if the tax is to play a distinctive role it should cover also value added at the post-manufacturing stages; and (d) that there should be as far as possible uniformity in procedures and even in the broad structure of taxation in different States. Accordingly, we have recommended that the State Governments should gradually move over to a single-point tax at the last stage. Secondly, sale of inputs to registered manufacturers should be free of taxation so that, as under excise, so also under sales taxation, inputs would be complete free from levies. Thirdly, the inter-State sales tax, now subject to a ceiling rate of 4 per cent, should be gradually brought down to one per cent.

The principle of a unified market implies that there should be no import or export duties when goods move within the country from State to State or from place to place. We have, therefore, recommended that octroi, which are in the nature of import levies and often act as transit levies, should be totally abolished.

If our major recommendations are implemented, the resulting system would approximate to an integrated and extended indirect tax system ranging from the import and manufacturing stages to the stage of the large retailers, with full relief for input taxation and therefore completely free from problems of cascading and distortions in the allocation of resources. At the same time, excise and sales taxes would have clear and distinctive roles within their rightful spheres and would enable us to maintain relatively unchanged the division of tax powers as contemplated in the Constitution.

Indirect Taxes as a Source of Revenue

In the effort to mobilise resources for development, indirect taxes levied by the Central and State Governments have been playing an increasingly important role; in 1976-77, they accounted for 79.3 per cent of total tax revenues. The share of indirect taxes in India was appreciably higher than the average of such taxes in many developing countries as well as industrialised countries.

Among the indirect taxes, the share of excise duties and sales taxes has been rising steadily while the share of customs duties, which has been subject to wide variations, has lately shown a downward trend.

A study of the automatic change in the tax yields in response to charges in national income in respect of individual indirect taxes for a recent period, shows that while sales taxes and customs duties had a fairly high degree of income elasticity, excise duties had an elasticity much below the desired level. The main reasons for the higher degree of elasticity in respect of import duties and sales taxes have been their universal coverage and predominance of *ad valorem* duties. As against this, excises, until recently, have been selective and have been by and large specific in nature.

Central Taxation – 1. *Central Excise Duties*

A major step in the rationalisation of excise duties was initiated in 1984 when their coverage was extended to sugar, matches and steel ingots. Since then, there have been selective additions beginning with products in the nature of mass consumption goods. As revenue needs increased the emphasis shifted to inputs. Year after year, the excise tax base was widened till almost the entire range of manufactured products was covered under excises in the year 1975.

For the purpose of control and assessment, several procedures and systems have been evolved leading to self-assessment and more reliance or documentary control. The administration of tax concessions to small scale manufacturers has also been sought to be simplified by introducing special procedures.

Of the consumer products subject to excise, the major portion of revenue is derived from a select range of mass consumption goods. However, during recent years excise revenues from wage goods as a percentage of total excise revenues have shown a declining trend.

Apart from the extension of excise tax base, a notable feature of the excise tax structure is the move towards *ad valorem* duties in the place of specific duties. Nevertheless, a substantial portion of excise tax revenue is still derived from items subject to specific duties the more important of which are petroleum products, unmanufactured tobacco and ferrous and non-ferrous metals.

One of the considerations which has been kept in view, while fixing the rates on final products, has been the progression in tax burdens. Similarly, objectives such as correcting imbalances between demand and supply, promotion of exports and protection to small scale industries and several other less important social and economic considerations have influenced the excise rate structure. There has been an extensive use of exemptions bringing into effect differential rates. As a consequence, the rate structure consists of a multitude of rates on consumer products, raw materials, intermediates and other inputs which differ not only between commodity groups but even within the same commodity group.

The taxation of inputs has been looked upon as an important source of revenue even after excises have acquired a universal character. Procedures to mitigate the distortions caused by multi-stage excise taxation are applied on a limited scale.

Central Taxation – 2. Customs Duties

Import duties, though primarily used for revenue purposes, have also been made use of to afford protection to domestic industries and to conserve foreign exchange.

After several attempts at rationalisation, the structure of basic import duties has now acquired stability. The scale of import duties has been related to the degree of processing undergone by different kinds of imported products. Accordingly, lower rates have been prescribed for basic raw materials and capital goods. A middle rate has been fixed for goods which have undergone some processing from the basic raw material stage and a high rate has been prescribed for fully processed goods. Some products, e.g., foodgrains, skimmed milk powder, etc., have been exempted from import levies on social considerations and some others on considerations of assisting exports. In contrast, on considerations of protection, higher import duties have been prescribed for some other articles of import. In the course of the evolution of the tariff, release from bindings under General Agreement on Trade and Tariff (GATT) for several items has been secured on considerations of protection to indigenous industry and revenue.

Apart from the basic import duties which have been fixed on a three-tier basis, there are auxiliary duties applied on a similar basis and countervailing duties which are calculated on the basis of c.i.f. price plus the basic duty and auxiliary duty. Thus, even though the basic duty structure has apparently been rationalised, application of auxiliary and contervailing duties ultimately results in a large variety of rates.

The yield from import duties when broken up shows that the major contribution is from the import of inputs — raw materials and intermediate products.

Export duties have begun to perform more of a regulatory than a revenue earning function.

There has been a limited adoption of the Customer Cooperation Council Nomenclature for import duty purposes. The new tariff merges a very large number of nomenclature headings in the CCCN and, in the process, has apparently led to an increase in the effective rates of duty on a number of products.

Indirect Taxes at State and Municipal Levels

Sales taxation is the most important source of revenue to the States accounting for about 57 per cent of their total tax revenues. Its share has been steadily increasing. Correspondingly, the importance of land revenue and State excise has been declining.

Following the recommendations of the TEC, a major change was brought about in the sphere of inter-State sales tax with the enactment of the CST Act whereby exporting States were conferred powers to impose a tax on inter-State exports at the rate prescribed in the Act. The development of the sales tax systems subsequent to the TEC Report, did not adhere to the pattern recommended. It has rather been conditioned by several considerations such as raising revenue encouraging investment and providing simpler administration. There are three types of sales taxes levied — the single point, the double point and the multi-point. In practice, there are mixtures of these types in individual States. There are variations in the systems of sales taxation found in different States, but a common trend towards the imposition of a single-point tax can be discerned.

The rate of multi-point sales tax is generally 4 per cent. In the States following the single point system, the general rate varies from 4 per cent to 7 per cent. Luxuries are generally subjected to a single point levy and taxed at higher rates up to 15 per cent.

As regards the treatment of raw materials and intermediate products under sales tax, the practice followed by individual States varies. While some grant full exemption, others grant only partial concessions. These are often linked to the fulfilment of certain conditions.

As sales taxation in the country is based both on origin and destination principles, it often happens that the sales tax levied by one State falls on the residents of other States.

One of the measures of Central regulation of sales taxation is the enactment of the CST Act. The provisions of this Act have been used to regulate the rate of sales tax on goods of special importance in inter-State trade and to fix a ceiling on the rate of CST; with the efflux of time the CST rate has increased to four per cent from the original rate of one per cent.

Another important development is the levy of Additional Excise duty in lieu of sales tax on tobacco, sugar and textiles. As the State Governments complained that their share of revenue from Additional Excise duties had not kept pace with the increase from time to time in the yield of Basic Excise duties, the matter was considered in 1970 by the National Development Council which decided that the rates of Additional Excise duties should be revised upwards within a period of two to three years so as to yield 10.8 per cent of the value of clearances and that in future the ratio between Basic and Additional Excise duties should be roughly 2:1.

Sales tax on motor spirit is levied under a separate enactment in many states, while others have merged it with the general sales tax. The yield from this source has increased fairly rapidly in the last 15 years.

After sales taxation, State excise on liquor is an important source of revenue for the States. In addition, excise duties on medicinal and toilet preparations containing alcohol and narcotics are levied through a Central Act. The rates of duty under this Act on such preparations are considerably higher than those applicable to medicines leviable under the Central Excise Act. Other taxes, which include, *inter alia*, tax on motor vehicles and tax on passengers and goods taken together contribute about 18 per cent of the State tax revenues.

For many States, electricity duty does not have considerable revenue significance. The base and rate of electricity duties vary from

State to State.

In many States, octroi is the foremost source of revenue to local bodies. In some states, revenue has been raised for local bodies without resorting to octroi. The system of collection and the rate for octroi vary considerably as between States as well as between local bodies within a State.

Interaction of Central and State Taxes

The overlapping co-existence of excises and the sales tax, each compounding the effects of the other through interaction has given rise to uncontrolled and unintended incidence on different commodities. Where the commodities involved have an imported content, the compounding effects are further aggravated.

The extensive taxation of inputs as well as final products and that too by different authorities has led to the following effects:

(i) The total burden on the consumer is usually much higher than the rates of tax imposed on final products. The levy of taxes on taxes and higher profit mark-ups and financial burden due to the need for a larger amount of working capital resulting from multi-stage excise and sales taxation of inputs contribute to an all-round escalation of costs and profits. Extensive taxation of inputs has caused divergence between the nominal rates on final products and the cumulative rates on them.

(ii) A heavy tax at the input stage also tends to be regressive. It encourages manufacturers to produce more of expensive varieties out of the same input.

(iii) Taxation of inputs also tends to encourage vertical integration, the manufacturer producing more and more of the inputs needed by him rather than buying these from ancillary industries.

(iv) Taxation of inputs affects exports adversely inasmuch as the former becomes a part of the costs of production. The effectiveness of the drawback system is eroded, as it becomes virtually impossible to calculate exactly the total quantum indirect levies on a product which is to be exported. Further, sales taxes and octroi duties are not taken into account in the drawback calculations, while the States generally extend only limited concessions in respect of inputs under their sales tax systems.

The Incidence of Indirect Taxes (1973-74)

A study of the distribution of the burden of indirect taxation among different expenditure groups has revealed the following features:

(i) The share of the tax burden on the rural sector in 1973-74 is seen to have fallen as compared to 1963-64, while the share in population of the rural sector declined slightly.

(ii) In terms of percentage of expenditure, the tax burden appears to have been distributed in progressive manner. The progression is also seen to prevail among rural and urban households taken separately. As far as indirect taxes alone are concerned, despite widespread taxation of inputs, the tax burden turns out to be uniformly progressive.

Indirect Taxes Fall even on the Poorest Sections of Society

Central taxes account of the largest share of incidence in both the rural and the urban sectors. As between Central and State indirect taxes, the former are more progressive. In the rural sector, the incidence of taxes on intermediate goods is higher than that of taxes on consumption goods for the lowest two per capita expenditure groups; for all the groups above them, the incidence of tax on consumption goods is higher. In the urban sector, the incidence of taxes on intermediate goods is slightly lower for the same two lowest per capita expenditure groups.

In respect of excises as well as import duties, intermediate goods claim the largest share of the incidents both in the rural and urban sectors.

In the case of State taxes, consumption goods account for a very high share of incidence as compared to the other two groups of commodities in both the rural and urban sectors.

Among food products, the taxes on sugar, foodgrains and *atta* affect all expenditure groups but their impact is regressive with respect to total expenditure. A reduction in the weight of taxes on mass consumption goods such a sugar, foodgrains and kerosene that tend to be regressive or proportional would serve to increase the degree of progression of the indirect tax system. The taxation of certain intermediate products such as iron and steel, diesel oil and tyres and tubes has a pervasive effect. However, incidence of these taxes turns out to be progressive.

The Role of Indirect Taxes

Since one of the prime objectives of taxation is to restrain increases in consumption with a view to divert real resources for purposes of development, taxation has necessarily to fall on the bulk of the population.

Taxation, while raising resources for the Government, should also subserve important socio-economic objectives.

A system, where articles of comfort and luxury are taxed at substantially higher rates than basic necessities of life, will be in accord with the objective of progression.

In India, indirect taxation will have to be non-neutral for bringing about reallocation of resources according to Plan priorities and for achieving progression.

Indirect taxation should be non-discriminatory in so far as the objective is to raise revenue; but where intervention is called for, indirect taxation may be selectively used for causing diversion of resources through changes in relative prices.

If the tax system were made more income elastic than in the past, there would be less need for raising the rates of tax on individual commodities from time to time.

Some features of the tax structure like heavy taxation of raw materials or differential taxation of raw materials and other inputs imposed mainly to raise revenue reduce the efficiency of the system.

Principles of Reform — Excise and Customs

The rationalisation of indirect taxation in the country hinges on the reform of the excise tax system into which other components could be dovetailed.

In the sphere of Central indirect taxation, though import duties and excises are to be treated similarly from the point of view of raising revenue, they have to be given their distinctive roles and tailored to produce the desired economic effects.

On various considerations, single integrated indirect tax system in the country extending from import and manufacturing stage down to the retail stage might have to be ruled out in favour of two or more taxes to be levied by more than one authority. If so, the endeavour should be to ensure that they are rid of their major deficiencies and become the building blocks for a harmonious indirect tax system.

Low elasticity of excises has been due to inadequate coverage and widespread reliance on specific duties in the past. The crux of the reform of excise taxation is the fashioning of an extended system with an adequate device for eliminating the harmful effects of input taxation. Further, *ad valorem* duties are preferable to specific duties to avoid frequent revisions of rates for meeting revenue needs which tend to create distortions and irrationalities.

The basic structure of the system should not bring about unintended re-allocation of resources or influence producers' choice in relation to the use of inputs, location of industries, etc., in a manner that leads to loss of efficiency and welfare.

Where there is no special reason for interference, like products should be taxed in a non-discriminatory fashion. While consumer goods largely consumed by upper income groups should be taxed at higher rates to ensure progression and to restrict the flow of investment into the production of non-essential goods, it would be desirable to apply the same high rates to the entire range of products in this class unless there are goods social or economic reasons for introducing differentials.

A plethora of rates makes tax administration as well as tax compliance a complicated matter. Various consumer products should in course of time, be fitted into four or five (cumulative) rate categories.

It may be necessary to have some in-between rates in the initial stages of rationalisation of nominal rates. Certain category of products such as petroleum products, tobacco, matches and textiles, whose taxation has its own logic, may have to be kept out of the above rate structure.

There would be considerable advantage in introducing as early as possible a scheme of comprehensive classification so that in effect tariff item No. 68 should be done away with and each new product from the very beginning be brought under the appropriate rate category. It would be necessary to examine whether some of the items that are now taxable only at two per cent should not be taken out of that list and fitted into the appropriate rate categories.

The yardstick of price before tax would be the best one to employ in determining whether particular varieties of a product should be considered as being primarily consumed by the rich or the poor.

As a general rule, a single rate should be applied to a class of similar products unless there is a clear cut distinction, arising on account of a differentiation based on substantially different prices.

The heavy reliance on the taxation of inputs has led to several undesirable effects. In an extended system of taxation of final products, it would not be possible to unconditionally free from taxation goods that are used as inputs or components. The ideal solution would be to make a distinction, for tax purposes, on the basis of the nature of use and not on the basis of category of goods. Whatever is used for further production by manufacturers, who are themselves subject to tax, should be given suitable tax relief, while the same product, if it goes direct to the consumer, will pay tax at the appropriate rate.

Studies undertaken show that basic raw materials as a class bear a substantially higher average rate of duty than semi-processed and final products. One of the steps towards rationalisation of the excise duty structure would thus be to bring about a reduction in the average rate of taxation on raw materials. Any significant reduction in the average rate of tax on raw materials would, however, have to be accompanied by a compensatory upward revision in the rates on final products to safeguard revenue.

It would neither be feasible nor desirable to reduce the rates of tax on raw materials to such a low level as to obviate the need for a system of tax credit. In the long run, a proper relationship between the rates of tax on final products and on raw materials will have to be brought about.

The following general guidelines for the taxation of inputs are recommended:

(i) A generalised system of tax credit should be introduced in course of time.

(ii) Various raw materials and other inputs should also be subject to a limited number of rates of duty in place of the present wide variations in rates.

(iii) Raw materials which are substitutes for each other, should, as a rule be taxed at similar rates unless the use of a particular raw material needs to be economised on wider considerations justifying a higher levy. In the latter case, it would be desirable to levy a separate differential duty which should not be eligible for tax offset at later stages.

(iv) Inputs which are capable of being used as final products should be subject to such rates of duty as may be appropriate for them as finished consumer products, while those goods which are primarily used as inputs and do not have much use for replacement purpose should be subjected to the same rate of duty as applicable to the finished products in whose manufacture they are mostly used. In both cases, the aim should be to provide tax credit in respect of duty paid on such inputs to producers who use them for further manufacture, even if it needs some adjustment in the rates of tax on final products.

(v) Taxation of packaging materials also calls for rationalisation. In general, the excise duty burden on different packaging materials should be broadly the same except for the discrimination in favour of packaging made of waste material. Further, wherever the duty on packaging materials adds considerably to the cost of manufactured commodities, which are essential in nature, suitable relief in respect of duty paid on packaging materials should be considered.

A value added tax system at the manufacturer's stage would be the best means of achieving the twin objectives of having an extended tax system and avoiding the distortions that flow from input taxation. Pending its introduction, the fullest use should be made of the existing provisions and procedures to give relief from the cascading effects of input taxation.

There should be a substantial extension of the application of rule 56-A. The tax credit allowed under this rule should cover, wherever economic considerations so warrant, packaging materials and consumable stores also.

The provisions of rule 56-A should be preferred to other procedures for extending relief of input taxes. However, the differential excise duty that may be specially imposed on some raw materials for promoting their economic use should not be eligible for tax relief.

The steps towards rationalisation of the excise rate structure should be take in the following order:

(i) Rationalisation of the duty structure in relation to basic raw materials, keeping in mind the constraint that the resultant reductions in the average rate of tax on raw materials should not appreciably exceed 5 percentage points for the time being.

(ii) Rationalisation of the rate structure of final products (excluding certain groups such as petroleum and tobacco products, but including consumer goods now falling under tariff item No. 68) in terms of nominal rates of duty ranging from 2 to 35 per cent.

(iii) Extension of the application of rule 56-A to the manufacturers of all products (whether final or intermediate or capital goods) in respect of which the difference between the nominal rate and cumulative rate is significant indicating the presence of appreciable cascading.

(iv) Corresponding adjustments in the nominal rates of duty on the same final products so that they will fall under one or other of the cumulative rate categories we have suggested.

(v) More or less simultaneous adjustments in the rates of duty on packaging materials, components and goods that are used both as inputs and final goods for replacement purpose.

While under Indian conditions it may not be justified to free capital goods of taxation as in European countries, there are good reasons for keeping the rate low. By and large, the cumulative rate on most machinery items now range from 2.6 to 5 per cent. This being so, it would be preferable to leave the nominal rate of duty on capital goods at two per cent barring certain exceptions.

The measures recommended should impart sufficient elasticity as well as a measure of stability to the system. If, at any time, it is desired to divert a still higher percentage of national income to the exchequer, then a small and uniform percentage increase in the rates of tax on all products should be preferred to selective increases so that the basic structure of taxation and the relative rates on different products are not disturbed.

Long-term investment priorities can be built into the long term structure of the excise tax system. Moreover, there are a number of other objectives which need to be considered separately and the means of achieving them, in so far as it is desirable to do so through indirect taxation, would have to be grafted on to the basic long-term structure. In general, adjustments in levels of excise taxation should not be used to achieve minor or trivial objectives. To prevent abnormal profits being made in a situation of scarcity of a product, there could be a temporary increase in the excise duty in the form of an additional levy, with readiness to lower it as the supply position improves. It must not, however, be so high as to discourage fresh investment which would be necessary to relive the shortage. It would be preferable to keep the additional levy distinct from the Basic excise duty, and its period of validity should automatically expire when the next Budget is presented — unless a decision is taken at that time to continue it for a longer period. Similarly, if for an unforeseen contingency substantial additional revenues have to be raised, there may be advantage in making a small surcharge applicable across the broad to all the items which are subject to excise duties for a fixed temporary period.

Apart from being a revenue measure, import duties have also two important economic functions to fulfil, namely, to protect domestic industries as decided upon by Government and, wherever necessary, to discourage the expenditure of scarce foreign exchange.

In the absence of quantitative import controls, protection to domestic industries has to be afforded by the protective components of import duties. A coordination of import control policies with the import tariff would be necessary where import control is in existence and is the major means of giving protection and conserving foreign exchange.

Where imports of a number of goods are severely restricted and substantial excess demand is generated at prices equal to the landed costs of imports, heavy import duties could be justified to prevent the import licensees or others from making large unearned incomes. It would be preferable, in such cases, wherever possible, to canalise imports through a State agency or to arrange that they go directly to the actual users with appropriate arrangements to ensure that the benefits of the low price is passed on to the ultimate consumers. This would help keeping the protective element at the appropriate level so that potential domestic producers would get the right signals.

A rationalised structure of import duties should broadly consists of the following elements:

(a) A levy adequate to give the degree of protection deemed necessary for particular products,
(b) A revenue element, which may be called the countervailing duty, being equal to the excise duty leviable on the same or similar domestic products,
(c) A discriminatory duty on products necessary to skim off the

excess profits. This can be looked upon as a surcharge for discouraging imports.

Of these, between (a) and (c), whichever is higher should apply. For the purpose of arriving at the base for the countervailing duty, it would be proper to include only the landed cost of imports (excluding duties) and the national protective element, if that should be lower than the discriminatory duty.

The import duty structure, as it obtains today, does not satisfy a consistent set of principles. The economic effects of high duties have been severely ignored in the interests of revenue. As a result, several high-cost, uneconomic industries have come to be established. The rates of duty on most products today appear much higher than what would be justified on the basis of the principles enumerated above. Duties on intermediates and machinery will particularly have to be brought down to lower levels. In view of the substantial revenues involved, this could be attempted in phases.

It is not possible to adumbrate a general principle or policy as to whether import duty in respect of capital goods should be fixed at a level sufficient to give protection to domestic industry and their import should be liberalised or whether it would be necessary to continue a fairly strict import control policy in order to continue the protection to the domestic industry producing machinery. For capital goods industries which are well established, it would be preferable to liberalise imports, the protective tariff being retained at a level sufficient to give protection to domestic producers. For newly set up industries meeting only a part of the country's requirements, a much greater reliance on import control will have to be continued.

The present rate of duty at 75 per cent on intermediates and semi-processed materials is too high to be justified on any rational economic considerations. Where indigenous capacity of intermediates and semi-processed goods already exists, or is likely to be set up in the near future, the rate of duty on them should be much more than what is just adequate for protection, provided the level of imports is sufficient to meet the full requirements of industries using such intermediates and semi-processed goods.

The level of duties on individual products or categories should be determined on an industry by industry study, which might appropriately be entrusted to an organisation like the Bureau of Industrial Costs and Prices. Such an organisation could also indicate the level of imports necessary for proper utilisation of capacity of user industries.

The scaling down of duties on imported products will have to be both selective and phased. The following areas may deserve priority action—

(a) where a reduction in duty will help lowering the price of basic necessities such as food, clothing, shelter, education, health and transport;
(b) where a reduction in duties while lowering the revenue realisation per unit of import, would in fact augment revenues because the volume of imports would go up;
(c) where the cheapening of certain imported products would have a long term favourable impact on the development process, including the promotion of employment; and
(d) where the duty on a particular input is unduly high, compared with the levies on competing inputs.

As import controls continue to exist, there should be proper coordination of tariff policy with import control policy while effecting changes in duties on any product. The following general approach in certain category of cases is recommended:

(a) On items in which we are self-sufficient and it is considered desirable to meet the additional demand (with the growth in economy) by way of imports rather than increasing indigenous production, import duty levels should be such as to equate the landed costs of imports to domestic prices.
(b) In the case of inputs, a substantial proportion of the demand for which, is met out of local production and only a relatively small gap between domestic production and demand is met by imports licensed to actual users, the level of duty should be such as to keep domestic and import prices at par.
(c) Where a small proportion of demand of a product is met out of local domestic production and the rest of the demand is met out of imports that are much cheaper, the proper way of protecting domestic industry would be either to give a subsidy to the domestic producer or to arrange for a pooling of prices.

Import duties on inputs have become a major contributor to cascading and general escalation of costs, besides often producing distortions in relative prices.

Keeping in view the revenue implications, in the immediate future input tax relief may be extended even for import duties (under a procedure similar to rule 56-A) in relation to a limited number of products in whose cases cascading and other distortions seems to be particularly severe and harmful.

No countervailing duty should be levied on imported goods not being produced at home and not competing with any indigenous products. However, it would be legitimate to subject them to a revenue duty at the appropriate level, after a careful consideration of the duties likely to be applied to them if produced at home.

The role of export duties in the future would be essentially an economic one of driving a wedge between high overseas prices and lower domestic prices so that export demand does not unduly raise internal prices. It should be ensured that frequent and sudden changes in export duties on short-term considerations do not damage the long term prospects of our exports.

Approach to Rationalisation

The task of rationalising the indirect tax system has to be viewed neither as a revenue raising exercise nor as an occasion for lowering the overall tax burden.

If account is taken of the levy on the inputs, the average cumulative rate of excise on consumer products works out to something like 20 per cent (excluding tobacco and petroleum products as well as goods falling under tariff item No. 68); but, the nominal and consequently the cumulative rates show a wide amplitude. However, a study of the prevailing rate structure does not indicate that the levies on different products have in fact been determined on clearly defined criteria, like progression, economic considerations for discouraging consumption of an article, making a draft on scarce resources, and prevention of investment in low priority areas.

A multitude of rates is not desirable either on considerations of progression or on economic and administrative ones.

In fitting different consumer products into the appropriate categories, the approach could be to examine whether there are reasons to tax a given product at a higher or lower rate than 20 per cent (cumulative). Where the levy on inputs does not cause a divergence of more than three per cent between the nominal rate and cumulative levy of excise, the final rate could well be fixed, ignoring the levy on inputs. Where, however, the divergence is greater and relief under rule 56-A or other procedures is not available, the rates of duty on final products could be fixed at appropriately lower levels to narrow the gap. When a rate higher than 40 per cent (cumulative) is to be imposed on any product, its implications should be carefully considered.

If relief to the lower income groups is considered to be desirable, powers under the CST Act can be used to lower the tax on inter-State sales of foodgrains.

While the rates on levy sugar may well be kept low, a wide disparity in the rates of tax on levy and free sale sugar can lead to some undesirable consequences.

Consumers' choice between like products should not be unnecessarily interfered with by differential levies on refined oil and vanaspati. Consideration should be given to applying the same *ad valorem* rate to both products.

Having *ad valorem* duties increasing with the price is one of the simplest ways of achieving progression, in the excise levy on textiles. With the compulsion on textile mills to use a certain proportion of synthetic fibres and yarns instead of cotton only and in the light of the reference in the Industrial Policy Statement to the use of polyester fibre as a raw material for *khadi*, it would be safe to presume that the initial policy of discouraging the use of synthetic fibres and yarn stands reversed. Various studies show that lower income groups do make use of synthetic and blended fabrics, provided the price is low enough.

The real test to apply in distinguishing between the cloth consumed by the rich and the poor should be the price factor. On this basis, the cheaper cloth should be taxed at a lower rate. If progression is desired, those in higher price brackets can be taxed at higher *ad valorem* rates. This should be done on a slab system. Such a gradation will encourage mills to produce lower priced fabrics and at the same time eliminate the dangers of abuse.

The mere fact of the cloth being categorised as coarse or fine is not a good basis for discriminating levies, either on social or economic considerations.

A switch over to *ad valorem* duties on cotton yarn would have the added advantage of reducing assessment disputes, laboratory tests and other complications which arise because a difference of even one count can make a material change in the tax liability. If it is necessary to levy discriminating duties on fabrics on account of difference in raw material content, it would be appropriate to introduce the necessary differentials at the yarn or fibre stage.

About the extent of the discrimination at the fibre/yarn stage and the considerations on which it should be based, trends of Government policy as well as an assessment of the situation suggest that the very wide differential between cotton and yarn of man-made fibre has to be steadily reduced. In bringing about a reduction in the cumulative levy on fabrics made of man-made fibres and yarn, the trend should be towards shifting the levy from the raw material stage towards the more processed articles. Overall, the attempt should be to shift as much of the burden to the fabric stage and to fix the tax at the yarn stage at such a level that its incidence on the decentralised sector is just adequate to obviate the need for excise control.

To overcome the cumbersome process of ascertaining denier/count/composition and to ensure progression and equitable incidence of duty, the levy on fibre and yarn should be on an *ad valorem* basis.

Taking into account the wide disparities of climatic conditions in the country, woollens should not be ranked much below cotton in importance. Considering that hand-knitting woollen yarn has a potential of becoming a major source of employment and for meeting domestic demand and for export purposes, the existing levy thereon seems to be much too high on any criterion.

The duty incidence on woollen textile should be shifted forward and to start with the customs duty on raw wool should be substantially lowered. The duty on the final product should be graded in a manner which will weigh more heavily on the more expensive fabrics than on cheaper ones. High levies on polyester and acrylic fibres create distortions and undesirable repercussions.

The present odd rate, on printing and writing paper, which is used by the student class, should be maintained at the existing low level and rounded off to five per cent *ad valorem*.

Wide tax differences can adversely affect the production of varieties of paper taxed at relatively higher rates, whose production may be otherwise desirable. It would be more rational for all printing and writing paper, other than those subject to an informal price and distribution control to be taxed at a uniform rate.

A reconsideration of the need for continuing the duty differential between packing and printing paper, which often leads to classification disputes, is called for.

There is need for making changes in the existing excise duty concessions to smaller paper mills. It would be more scientific and rational to link the concession with the value of production tax based on capacity considerations. Unless it is Government's intention to discourage production of certain varieties of paper by smaller paper mills, there seems to be no strong reason for the denial to them of the benefit of concessional duty in respect of those varieties of paper and all varieties of paper boards.

In regard to certain industrial varieties of paper, there is a case for lowering the present rate of customs duty of 100 per cent, as they are used as inputs and not as consumer products.

The list of medicines in the nature of life saving drugs, which are taxed at specially low rate needs more frequent review and suitable expansion.

While a higher rate of duty on medicines, which can be properly regarded as patent and proprietary, could cause a beneficial shift towards the production of medicines sold under a generic name, the existing difference in rates should be narrowed down.

A panel of qualified experts should to set-up to suggest (i) a list of drugs covered by the Medicinal and Toilet Preparations Act, which cannot possibly be used for non-medicinal purposes, in that they could be excluded from the scope of high levies and (ii) a list of drugs-needed for treatment in critical ailments of which despite and risk of diversion, may merit taxation at lower rates.

Import duties on bulk drugs as well as intermediates have also to play a protective role. In considering any adjustments in order to reduce the cumulative levies which are judged to be too high, would have to be ensured that domestic production of like products, if it exists, is not hurt. Where there is no domestic production, the import duty could well be lowered to a level, which is deemed adequate for affording protection to new investment.

The special study on the taxation of road transport industry shows that:

(a) indirect taxation of road transport has a perceptible impact even on the lowest expenditure groups.

(b) The pervasive and multi-stage taxation on manufacture and sales of trucks and buses results in a very high cumulative levy.

(c) The system of taxation results in the locking up of extra working capital.

(d) Trucks and buses meant for transport are taxed higher than personalised transport like cars and scooters.

(e) Taxes that affect the cost of operation increase operating costs by about 50 per cent for trucks and 45 per cent per passenger bus per passenger km.

(f) There is considerable divergence between States in the tax rates on goods and passengers.

A strong case seems to exist both on social and economic considerations for a reduction in the total burden of the various levies affecting road transport.

Since the Centre and the States tax the road transport industry, a concerted plan of action is needed. Discussions between representatives of the Centre and the States would be worthwhile. The following suggestions are made:

(a) A measure of uniformity in rates of taxation of this industry by the State Governments with no further increase in the rates should be made for, say, 10 years.

(b) To start with, the Centre could bring down the capital cost of vehicles by giving relief from input taxation. The loss in revenue will be more than made up by the increased contribution arising on account of the augmentation of urban bus fleets and expansion of operations by small operators.

There is need for rationalisation and a measure of uniformity in respect of the plethora of taxes and fees levied by State Governments and local bodies.

The question whether the time has come when with the improved foreign exchange position, price of petroleum products should be lowered, merits consideration.

If in Government's view the time has not yet come for a general revision of the price structure of petroleum products, a fresh look may be given at least to the prices and taxes applying to individual products for giving appropriate relief.

If the prices of different steel sections are themselves determined with due regard to having such elements of discrimination as are socially and economically justifiable, there is no particular reason why the tax structure should also seek to introduce differentials. A uniform *ad valorem* rate could well be introduced to determine the revenue element and thereafter the Joint Plant Committee could have the freedom to adjust prices of individual sections. In any case, the rate should be *ad valorem* rather than specific so that there is an automatic and proportionate change in the tax whenever prices change.

A lower incidence is recommended in respect of alloy and special steels as they are generally for industrial purposes.

Too high a level of customs duty for alloy and special steel and stainless steel not only encourages high cost producers but reduces possibilities of additional employment at subsequent stages.

There is a good case for reducing levies on copper, zinc and lead as these have a wide variety of applications in the production of electrical goods and accessories and capital goods. The conversion of the import duty on copper into a specific one because its international price is subject to violent fluctuations is recommended. Import of metallic concentrates should be made duty free so that spelters in the country do not have their costs raised. The exemption for copper concentrates can be continued and similar exemption provided for zinc concentrates. Alternatively, the whole question of pricing and differential taxation could be looked at *de novo*.

Commercial grade aluminium has multifarious uses but the present duty on non-levy aluminium which is high affects industries significantly. Though the present juncture is not opportune for reducing the duty due to the scarcity of this metal, there is a good case in the long run for considerable lowering of the existing duty and extension of duty free clearances in deserving cases.

There should be a shift in taxation in respect of plastics from the raw material stage to the final product stages as well as a net reduction in the average incidence on final products. This would enable greater progression being achieved with reference to the finished products consumed by the well to do and those that largely cater to the lower income groups.

It would be desirable instead of having different rates for different plastic resins to have a uniform rate of customs duty for all of them.

A reduction in the burden of tax on raw materials as is likely to result from the rationalisation exercise could be partly made up by increases in rates at the final products stage and partly be compensated by increase in output.

On balance, the taxation of inputs of agriculture has to be determined on a wide variety of considerations including the possibilities of raising the requisite revenue from alternative sources.

Although machinery as a class has till recently been free from excise levies at the final stage, the fairly heavy taxes on is main raw materials, namely, metals, has meant that capital goods generally have been contributing to revenues on a not insignificant scale.

Having regard to all considerations, a levy of the order of 5 per cent (including the taxation of inputs) on capital goods could in the interests of revenue be retained. A separate tariff classification should be created and machinery items should be taken out of tariff item No. 68. Government may wish to re-examine whether there are adequate economic reasons for retaining higher levies on some of the industrial items of machinery, particularly those needed for improving irrigation.

The view that machinery items which are not indigenously produced at present, should be allowed to be imported without any duty, cannot be accepted.

The present rate of duty of about 28.5 per cent on cement is very high, as it raises the cost of all capital projects. The rates of duty on cement should be gradually reduced as more supplies become available.

In any restructuring, rates on many final products, even those which are consumed by lower income groups, may have to move up.

The Revenue Angle

One of the reasons, which today makes the structure, seem in need of a major change is that while most of the existing levies had adequate justification when they were imposed, it was but rarely that there was any subsequent re-examination of these to see whether the circumstances which had warranted them, had changed and a reduction would be desirable.

Due to the greatly widened scope for self-assessment procedures, most of the considerations that stood in the way of bringing more products under excise and led to the heavy reliance on taxation at high rates of a few product families and basic inputs, have lost much of their validity.

Developments in the economy necessitate changes in the indirect tax structure as a whole having regard to the social and economic impact of the existing levies.

A restructuring of consumer product rates including those new falling under tariff item No.68 and taxing them at rates of 10, 20, 30 or 40 per cent (cumulative), with exceptions — where justified on special considerations — would throw up revenue possibilities of a sufficiently large order; the yield being Rs. 20 crores per percentage point increase, even in respect of items now falling under tariff item No. 68 other than capital goods. Whilst a generalised and substantial revision of the rate in respect of items covered by tariff item No. 68 has large potentialities, the appropriate course would be to fix suitable for identifiable groups of products covered by this tariff item.

It should be examined whether the exemption granted to certain products, because the rates applicable to them under the appropriate tariff had been earlier considered to be too high, should be withdrawn and if this could not be taxed at the rate applicable to items covered by tariff item No. 68.

Where as a result of the reduction of duties on inputs, there is a consequent reduction in the cumulative tax burden on certain products using them, the revenue loss can be recouped by making appropriate increases in the nominal rates of duty.

It may not be possible or even desirable to make all the changes that are considered advisable in one single Budget. The pace of change may well be spread over three years or so. The complete phased programme for bringing about the needed changes might be accepted by Government even at the first stage.

If a reduction in excise duties stimulates production or reduction in import duties leads to higher imports and — in the case of inputs — also to increase in domestic production, the loss of revenue may well be amply compensated, because though the rate of duty would have gone down, the volume of goods to which it applies will have gone up.

Insofar as reductions in duties have to be phased, priority should be given to a reduction in customs duties over a reduction in excises because in terms of resource mobilisation, imports not only contribute to the Exchequer by the amount of duties they bear but they also help to cushion the impact of Budgetary deficits by bringing about a contraction in the money supply to the extent that the foreign exchange reserves as well as external credits are drawn upon.

A resource mobilisation effort which is spread in an equitable way across the board is preferable to selective increases which inevitably lead to distortions. Instead of a flat percentage point increase which may tend to be regressive, the better method would be to have a surcharge at a fixed per cent of the existing rates of duty on consumer products. This method of mobilising additional revenues will obviate the need for raising the rates applicable to inputs, which should only be undertaken if it is intended to discourage the use of particular inputs because of their short-term or long-term scarcity.

Stimulus to Production and Investment

Although, psychologically, a sacrifice of revenue gets more readily accepted than an outflow from the Exchequer, which subsidies entail the fact that the latter, by their very nature, attract constant attention tends to ensure that they are neither excessive nor continued even though circumstances might have changed.

Excise duty reductions are more likely to be effective, where the prevailing level of excise duty is significant and the price elasticity of demand for the product is relatively high.

When an investment has already been made with Government approval, and subsequently it is felt that the industry should be accorded a lower priority, it would be preferable to take steps to prevent new investment rather than to render the investment already made wholly or partly infructuous.

It should be ensured whilst extending any concession to a sector of industry facing difficulties that the benefit accrues only to deserving units and not those suffering from the results of mismanagement.

In considering reliefs in the indirect tax system for encouraging production, a comprehensive view has to be taken of the total relief available under the fiscal system.

The existing scheme for granting excise relief for higher production has resulted in benefits, which are far from uniform as between industries to which it applies and even between units in the same industry.

If preliminary indications are any guide, the major impact of the scheme would seem to be a redistribution of the same level of production among different manufacturers in which the more efficient have been the net gainers. The scheme should be discontinued after the period of three years is over.

In its initial years, a new capital-intensive unit may be confronted with a situation in which if it has to sell its products at the prevailing market price it would suffer losses due to its higher capital costs and the time lag in reaching the optimum production level. Concessions in direct taxation may not adequately take care of this situation

In respect of capital intensive industries which are considered essential and which any how have to be expanded, concessions under the direct taxes do not provide an adequate answer, some concessions in regard to levies in the initial years of production both to new units and to cases of substantial expansion of old units would be justified. The concession could well be in the form of a 10 percentage point reduction in the full rate of tax on the product. It should become applicable from the date of and commencement of commercial production and remain valid for a limited number of years not exceeding five. The total amount of the concession should be expressed as a percentage of the investment in fixed capital. This would enable a composite view to be taken including other concessions like the investment allowance under the direct taxes, so that the total quantum is reasonable and adequate, but not excessive. A review should be made to enable making of changes that are warranted, but with adequate notice.

In respect of the sugar industry, which is already subject to a dual pricing system, any incentive to compensate for the higher cost of production during certain seasonal periods, should, to the extent possible, be in the form of modification of the existing pricing system rather than be at the expense of the Exchequer.

Differential excise taxation for encouraging the production of low-priced consumer durables, especially for those which are now out of the reach of the poor and lower middle class people, is a welcome step. A case by case examination is, however, necessary, the prime consideration being the provision of relief in cases where the price reduction could be sizeable and the product would become cheaper. The criterion to be applied should be the price or value rather than physical specifications.

In deciding upon the nature and magnitude of concessions to the particular sectors or types of production, a distinction should be made between cases where the desired objective is to stimulate a particular type of economic activity and those where it is merely to protect and ensure the survival of the existing units.

In future, any exemptions granted should have a time limit appropriate to particular cases but not exceeding five years.

Encouragement to Small Producers

Most of the Committees/Commissions which examined the case for fiscal preference, in the form of excise duty concessions, for the small scale sector *vis-a-vis* organised units had accepted the preference in principle.

Though it would be advantageous to lay greater emphasis on measures other than taxation to encourage the growth of the small scale sector, purely from the revenue angle, a measure of protection to them through differential excises is as legitimate as protection through import tariff is for an industry as a whole.

The industries having potential for growth and new avenues of employment would certainly deserve fiscal concessions, but they should be supplemented by other measures to improve quality, design and marketing facilities, so as to avoid over-dependence on fiscal benefits.

The existing scheme of concessions, particularly in respect of the criteria which should be applied for the grant of concessions and the extent to which concessions should be given, needs to be rationalised.

The value of production of a unit would be the most rational basis for granting concessions to smaller producers.

There should be a total exemption from excise up to a certain value of production; any excess over it should be taxed at a concessional rate subject to an upper limit, beyond which the excess should be liable to normal rates. Where the production reaches a sufficiently high level in a given year, the producers should be subject to the normal rate of taxation from the following financial year.

First clearances up to Rs. 2.5 lakhs (an assessee is required to maintain accounts under Section 44AA of the Income-tax Act if his turnover exceeds this figure) could be exempted fully for all units eligible for concessional treatment in an industry. Concessions based upon investment criterion are not favoured. Clearances falling in the slab Rs. 2.5 lakhs – Rs. 10 lakhs may be charged at a concessional rate of duty which may be lower by 3 percentage points as compared to the effective rate of duty payable by the organised units.

With the introduction of the concessions based on the value of production, it would be imperative to withdraw the existing concessions based on various criteria. A case by case review could also be made to ascertain whether there is any tendency to abuse the exemption or whether such concession causes serious distortions in the pattern of production between different sectors of the industry for appropriate follow-up action.

A review of the working of the scheme of simplified procedure of assessment for small producers at present applicable to 46 industries shows that there has not been as much response to the scheme as was anticipated.

If appropriate modifications are made in the scheme, there is no reason why it should not find greater acceptance by the small scale sector.

(a) The approach could be to give concessions to small producers on the value slab basis as indicated earlier.

(b) There should be a concerted attempt to educate the small manufacturers about the attractive features of the scheme. For this purpose, notifications and other provisions should be simplified and a version of it couched in understandable non-technical language should be made available.

(c) It should be considered whether the three-year block period for which the duty liability is fixed could not be shortened. If the period is reduced, Government should also consider whether there is any need for the duty liability fixed for the shortened period to be revised, even if the value of production exceeds the base value by 50 per cent.

(d) To help financially weak small producers, it may be provided that the duty could be paid within 7 days of the commencement of the month as against the present requirement of payment a week before the commencement of the month.

There is little justification to limit the benefits meant for smaller producers to a selected number of industries. It should be extended, if necessary, phases, to all commodities with few exceptions (e.g., tobacco, petroleum products, matches and goods falling under tariff item No. 68).

Reform of Sales Taxation

A decision on the final choice regarding the future role of the sales tax system, as to whether it could be made a Central subject to bring about an integrated and rationalised system of indirect taxation on domestic production and consumption extending from the manufacturing to the retail stage or whether it would be enough if the existing systems themselves are reformed so as to free them from most of their weaknesses, has necessarily to be political.

The excise system, despite the considerable widening of the base in recent years, is still not, and cannot also become, universal in coverage. The sales tax, on the other hand, is much more in the nature of a general tax, covering all commodities except those where the intention is to spare the consumer. *Prima facie,* there is a strong case for preserving sales taxes in addition to excise duties on the ground that both play distinct roles.

The levy of sales tax on inputs, without appropriate procedures for relief through drawback or refund, deflects from the distinctive role of sales tax as a levy on consumers within the State and turns it, like excise, into a tax on production. It also gives rise to and compounds the problems of cascading, distortions in relative factor prices and vertical integration. The sales tax system should, therefore, be suitably amended to ensure that the taxation of inputs does not impinge in the way that it does today on the prices of final products, regardless of whether the production and/or consumption of the product is within the State or outside.

It has been a mistake to raise the rate of tax on inter-State sales to its present level of 4 per cent as it goes against its basic rational, namely, that while some revenue should accrue to the exporting State, the tax should not result in a significant burden on the importing State. Further, it has led to ways of avoiding the tax altogether. The trend, therefore, needs to be reversed.

On a balance of all considerations, a single point sales tax at the last stage is favoured as it would eliminate cascading effects and make it easy for State Governments and State Legislatures to consider and determine the kind of burden that should be imposed on consumers to different products. The complete switch-over could be staggered over a period of years by having a double point system in the interregnum in respect of commodities where the risk of evasion is great.

The limit of turnover of or above Rs. 2,50,000 prescribed by the Income-tax Act for compulsory maintenance of accounts could be taken as a line of demarcation for purposes of compulsory registration of dealers for sales tax purposes with provision for compulsory registration without limits for manufacturers and importers. The law should also provide for voluntary registration of dealers whose turnover is less than Rs. 2.5 lakhs.

Different rates of sales tax result in divergence in prices from State to State, even in respect of items for which maximum prices are fixed by the Government or manufacturers. A case, therefore, exists for introducing uniformity in sales tax rates in the case of such selected goods.

The Regional Council for sales tax should be made to play a more active role in investigating and discussing matters relating to sales tax.

If the States do not switch over to a uniform pattern of taxation, it would obviously be difficult to bring about equality of rates. There are, however, some products of widespread consumption, produced by a relatively small number of producers, where the desired uniformity as well as savings in cost of collection and elimination of harassment can be achieved by imposition of Additional Excise duty in lieu of sales tax.

The rate of Additional Excise duty in lieu of sales tax should move proportionately with the change in the basic duty. There should be an attitude of partnership between the Centre and the States. Wherever there is agreement about applying a uniform rate of sales tax to any product, it should be the endeavour to have a similar uniformity in rates in respect of the most important its inputs which do not have any other significant alternative use.

Keeping in view the extra territorial impact caused by CST, it should in stages be brought back to the original level of one per cent.

While there may be a good case for lowering the rate of sales tax on some of the basic necessities of life, such as foodgrains and pulses, limitations imposed by Parliament on the levy of local sales tax in regard to internal consumption should be the minimum.

If on national considerations it is regarded desirable to lower the imposition on any product, it would be quite legitimate, in the context of the Centre lowering the excise duty, to take recourse to the declared goods procedure in respect of them.

The definition of "backward areas" for the purpose of sales tax concessions should be uniform and no concessions should be given to industries located outside the backward areas as nationally defined.

Steps should be taken to implement the recommendations contained in the 61st Report of the Law Commission in regard to taxation of works contracts, hire-purchase transactions, as well as the enactment of a provision for facilitating and enforcing the recovery of any amount illegally realised as tax by a private person, whether as sales tax or any other tax.

It would also be advantageous both to State Governments and to business and industry, if uniformity in sales tax legislation and procedures is achieved in all States either through Central legislation or by the drafting of a model law by a Central agency like the Law Commission which each State could adopt. If need be, the provisions of Article 252 could be availed of for this purpose. Alternatively, a small group of representatives from different States could be set up, who could jointly evolve the draft of such a law after agreement.

As regards the apprehended loss of revenue pursuant to some of our suggestions, a reduction in the rate of CST need not result in a proportionate loss of CST revenue, as the subterfuge of consignment transfers presently adopted to avoid CST will not be a paying one. Further, the capacity of the importing State to have a higher sales tax on products originating outside the State would increase.

Octroi and Other Taxes

Almost every Committee that examined octroi in the past found it to be undesirable and harmful.

It is harmful and obnoxious as it interferes with the movement of trade and commerce and acts as a major source of delay and harassment. Its economic demerits are that it is a regressive duty, violates the principle of free flow of trade across local boundaries, and encourages the concentration of industries in metropolitan areas.

A decision to abolish octroi should not be linked with the finding of alternate sources or avenue. It could be abolished in stages.

Resources for the upkeep of municipal areas consequent on the abolition of octroi should be found by taxation by local authorities or by the State Government; the burden of compensation should not be passed on to the Centre. Alternatives, like levy of a surcharge on excise duty on HSD, removal of check-post followed by self-assessment by transport operators, levy of an entry tax are not suitable because of various undesirable consequences.

If commodity taxation is to be its substitute, the levy should be made by the State rather than by municipal bodies. A flat turnover tax with its rate being limited to less than one per cent would be a viable alternative.

Each State Government could constitute a Standing Committee which could determine the basis on which the receipts from the additional taxation would get allocated to different local bodies.

There are several arguments to support the taxation of services. However, the matter has to be proceeded with cautiously, taking into account the revenue potential and other practical problems.

If it is intended to tax services, it should be through a Central legislation the proceeds from the service tax should go to the States.

For alternative sources of revenue, the question of increasing the ceiling of Rs. 250 fixed by Article 276 of the Constitution for levy of Profession Tax could be considered after proper incidence studies.

It would be advantageous to have studies about indirect taxes conducted by competent bodies, comprehensive enough to take into account all the resource possibilities. It would be better if the same body or agency undertook such a study for all the States.

There is a good case for the abolition of electricity duty in view of the importance of electricity in the economic development of the country and also because it is a necessary input in almost all industries.

If electricity duty is to be retained, its structure should be simplified to achieve at least near uniformity of treatment.

State revenues from electricity can be increased if attention is paid to recoveries of dues, reduction of losses in transmission and rationalisation of the tariff.

In fixing the rates of electricity duty, no considerations demanding differential treatment of different categories of consumers need be taken note of.

The levy could be at a flat rate of one paisa per unit. If this is not considered progressive, it could be a flat *ad valorem* rate.

The Central Government may seriously consider, in consultation with the Finance Commission, whether it would not be a good thing to provide that the income-tax paid by any undertaking which is wholly State-owned should, in its totality, be give to the State Government which owns it.

Procedural Reforms

Among the desirable features which a sound tax system should possess, operational efficiency in the matter of assessments, collection and enforcement of the various taxes is of great importance.

What needs special emphasis is that, unlike in the case of direct taxes, delays and uncertainties about the amount of excise duty payable can cause serious hardship and entail financial losses. Further, it creates opportunities for corrupt practices.

A time has come when statutory time limits should be fixed in the excise and customs laws in respect of the following:

(a) Approval of classification and valuation
(b) Sanction of refunds, rebates and drawbacks of excise and customs duties
(c) Finalisation of provisional assessments and assessment documents
(d) Decisions in short assessment demands. For each of the above, different time limits could be stipulated.

Where a manufacturer does not generally sell to or through a related person, the submission and approval of the price lists prior to the removal of the goods may be altogether dispensed with. In other cases, a definite time for approval of both the classification and price lists should be fixed. The approval should not take more than three months. Where this is exceeded, the classification and value claimed by the assessee should be deemed to be final. Any revision in the lists should only be prospective in operation. Similar provisions should be made in regard to finalisation of assessments made on a provisional basis.

A time limit of three months for the grant of refunds/rebates/drawbacks would be liberal enough. Interest should be payable in cases of delayed refunds.

In regard to valuation, transactions between holding and subsidiary companies and companies under the same management can clearly be treated as transaction between related persons.

Prima facie, transactions between relatives who are either liberal ascendants or descendants could be regarded as transactions between related persons, but not with other relatives, in the widest sense. There is much less reason for treating all agents and distributors as related persons. The standards followed in direct taxation should apply to indirect taxation also.

In regard to other relatives and a distributor of sub-distributor of the assessee, the onus should be on the Excise Department to establish the kind of interest whether direct or indirect which would affect the price charged by the assessee.

Difference between ex-factory price and the re-sale price of the dealer/distributor, may include transport, packaging, marketing and other costs. These elements should not be treated as part of the assessment value. The same approach should apply in regard to the transactions with a related person.

Where the manufacturer establishes his average transport cost, he could be allowed to claim a deduction from the all India price while determining the assessable value.

The cost of packaging without which the product cannot be sold even to a customer at the factory gate should be a part of the assessable value. But the cost on account of outer packaging required for transport or packaging to meet the special needs of any class of customers should not form part of the assessable value.

The need for arriving at an early finality in matters regarding valuation is imperative and the question of amending the law should be examined urgently. In regard to pending disputes in High Courts, the Government should consider availing of the procedure prescribed by Article 139A of the Constitution, so as to get an early and final verdict.

The time is now opportune for a total restructuring of the existing Central excise tariff schedule, so as to evolve a tariff based upon a scientific system of classification, comprehensive in scope and more precise and unambiguous.

Adoption of BTN even for excise tariff procedures would have a number of advantages.

Whilst it would be desirable to extend the application of BTN for excise purposes, it would be preferable to use the Indian commercial or trade identity for describing a range of products, whenever appropriate.

No refined in respect of past clearances due to a revision in classification should be permissible to the manufacturer. The law could be amended to make the position clear. Unless forgery, fraud or collusion is involved, a change in the classification should have only prospective effect.

The provisions relating to the taking of bonds should be streamlined and either a single bond should be devised to cover all operations or in the alternative a drastic reduction should be made in their number.

In cases where goods are generally not sold at the factory gate or the sales are very few, the extension of warehousing facility with appropriate safeguards may be given favourable consideration.

In excise matters also, production norms should be gradually evolved, particularly to cover industries which have a large number of producers.

The balance of advantage lies in not imposing any pre-Budget restrictions on clearances.

A self-contained and comprehensive Act replacing the existing Central Excise Act, with adequate provisions to deter evasion, would make excise procedure and administration smooth, efficient and objective-oriented. The views of the trade and industry should also be taken while drafting the new Bill.

Bills of entry may be taken up for processing without waiting for the manifest and should normally be accepted if it shows evidence of classification.

The period of 3 years for warehousing imported goods may block goods on the imports of which foreign exchange has been expended and may be cut short by a year or even two.

In the interests of operational efficiency, and to ensure comparability between the Customs schedule and the Import Trade Control schedule, it is imperative that the Customs schedule is also wholly CCCN-based without any contractions or adaptations. This will also help in the matter of comparing international trade statistics. Further, the Customs administration would derive an immediate and continuing benefit from the explanatory notes and classification opinions of the Nomenclature Committee.

It would be worth considering whether the manner of computation of drawback amount could be liberalised by suitable changes in the Customs Act, so as to obviate the precise determination of the exact quantum of duty burden on the components/ingredients of the products exported.

As sales taxes falling on inputs enter into the cost of production of export products, the coverage of drawback might be made more comprehensive so as to authorise refund of an amount equivalent to the element of sales tax and terminal taxes.

The present minimum qualifying amount of drawback may be raised to Rs. 25 in respect of exports by post parcels and Rs. 100 for other exports.

For reducing the scope of litigation, Government should carefully consider whether, when the verdict goes against them, they should or should not accept it. If they find it unsatisfactory, they should further consider whether the better answer would not be to seek to amend the law so as to place the matter beyond doubt rather than to attempt to get a higher judicial authority to reverse the legal view already taken.

For classifying a particular medicinal preparation as restricted or unrestricted, the latter course would be to provide in the law itself appropriate criteria.

If the end product in its final form does not contain alcohol, no duty should be levied under the Medicinal and Toilet Preparations Act. To set at rest doubts in this regard, it would be desirable to writer the correct position in the law itself.

Adoption of the metric system as against the present practice of determining duty in some cases at a specific rate per litre of the strength of London-proof spirit is preferred.

Administrative Framework

Whilst reforming the tax system, it is necessary simultaneously to ensure that the administration of the laws, while being objective, sympathetic and human in its approach, does also enable taking of expeditious decisions.

One of the objectives of a reformed administration should be to explain each law, notification or procedure in the language of the layman. A public relations approach has to be built into the tax machinery so that people of small means, particularly the small producers, are fully aware of their rights and obligation. Publications, like working schedules, tariff guides and digest of important rulings, should be regularly updated and published.

In the context of the growing complexity of Customs and Excise administrations and with the switch-over to more account based controls under excise, there is an immediate need to reorient the training of the officers to meet the professional needs of administration.

Keeping in view the phenomenal increase in the responsibilities of the Central Board of Excise and Customs, the restraint stipulated by the Central Boards of Revenue Act, 1963, limiting the number of members, should be removed.

The Collectorates should be reorganised so that each Collectorate ordinarily should not have more than four to six divisions.

To make the internal audit system efficacious, the audit function should be performed by an independent organisation within the control of the Central Board of Excise and Customs. Prompt follow-up action should be taken on audit objections, so as to avoid repetitive mistakes.

It is well recognised that an adequate information system is a prerequisite for the effective administration of broad based or comprehensive taxes, such as extended excises and general sales taxes.

Steps should be taken to (a) enlarge the coverage of data collection, (b) strengthen the data collection wing; and (c) strengthen the Research wing, so as to be equip it for carrying out more comprehensive studies on a continuing basis. The process will be considerably facilitated through computerisation. The same improvement in the information system should also be effected in relation to the State indirect taxes.

Early steps should be taken to eliminate the deficiencies and inadequacies in respect of test facilities.

An independent body to hear appeals would inspire public confidence, which the decisions of executive officers, no matter how impartial they try to be, do not. Whilst delays in settling issues pertaining to indirect taxation must be avoided, there is no reason to assume that the replacement of an executive agency by a quasi-judicial one must necessarily mean the adoption of dilatory procedures.

A two-tier appellate machinery with a Tribunal independent of the Board for bearing appeals both on facts and law from the first court of appeal should be established. All relevant procedural provisions in the Income Tax Act, can, with suitable adaptations, be incorporated into the Central Excise and Customs Acts, with the variation namely, that the procedure in vogue under the Income-Tax Act whereby an assessee/department has to move the Tribunal for drawing up a statement of the case to the High Court be dispensed with.

The members and the Chairman of the Tribunal should have appropriate status and to inspire the necessary confidence, the membership should have an equal sprinkling of professional experts and judicial officers besides departmental officers. For the present, the Tribunal should have six members. The question of further strengthening the Tribunal could be taken up on an appropriate future occasion.

Uniformity and any early final ruling on classification are of utmost importance for the healthy growth of trade and industry and for normal interplay of commercial competition. As the desired objective cannot be achieved through the normal appellate machinery, the balance of advantage, would be in a single body being vested with the necessary authority to dispose of disputes relating to classification, such decisions being made binding on all concerned including the Appellate Tribunal. An All India Classification Tribunal should therefore be set up with the members having appropriate status and qualification.

Every State should have also a uniform pattern of appellate procedures.

Value Added Tax—Basic Features

VAT, in its comprehensive form, may be simply defined as a tax to be paid by all sellers of goods and services, other than those specifically exempted, on the basis of value added by their respective firms. By contrast, a cascading type turnover tax, which may also be comprehensive, falls on the total value at each stage.

The difference between a retail sales tax and VAT is that while the former is collected at one stage, VAT is collected in instalments at successive stages of production and distribution.

The main characteristics of VAT are:

(i) It is a multi-stage tax rather than a single stage one like the retail sales tax, and, in its ideal for, is to be levied on all stages of production and distribution.
(ii) It is, in principle, comprehensive unlike selective excises.
(iii) It is collected in bits at each stage of production and distribution which, when added, equal a tax on the retail sale of the final product at the same rate as the VAT.
(iv) Finally, it falls on each input entering into final products once and once only.

The essential feature of VAT is not neutrality but rather the fact that it avoids cumulative taxation of inputs.

The chief merits of VAT are:

(i) it ensures that an input is taxed only once and hence not only is cascading avoided, but the incidence on any final product can be controlled.
(ii) It combines the advantages of being a general tax, without the

disadvantages of extended input taxation.

(iii) It is free of other economic demerits of cascade type turnover or sales taxes.

(iv) It does not promote vertical integration so long as there are no exemptions to important sectors in the middle of the chain of production.

(v) It does not discriminate against products embodying a larger part of value added at the earlier stages of production.

(vi) It does not change the relative prices of inputs and give wrong signals to producers regarding factor combinations.

(vii) It does not raise costs through input taxation and since under it exports could be fully relieved of internal indirect taxation, it helps a country to maintain the relative competitiveness of its industries in the world market.

(viii) It could be made non-neutral with regard to consumers' choice between final products.

(ix) In developing countries, a mild bias could be built into the system against capital intensive methods.

(x) Economy in the use of scarce inputs could be promoted through an additional non-refundable duty.

As against its merits, there are several features which demand a strong and efficient administrative structure as well as additional efforts on the part of tax-payers. These features are:

(i) More elaborate book keeping is required of the tax-payers, probably involving additional expenditure.

(ii) Where small traders are insufficiently educated, it will be too much to expect them to maintain adequate records of purchases of inputs to match against output.

(iii) There would be a large increase in the number of tax administrators, in countries where sales taxation does not exist, because of the need to bring in a multitude of retail outlets.

(iv) It is possible for a number of tax-payers to collude and evade taxes, like those who sell services directly to consumers.

Introduction of several rates complicates the administration of VAT considerably. In a developing country where large inequalities of income exist, a set of differential excise duties which would not come under the system of tax credit might be called for.

For various points of view, the tax credit method is easier to apply, which can be enforced even with specific duties at some stages. The need to submit vouchers of tax paid also acts as a check on artificial increases in claimed deductions.

The introduction of VAT in almost all countries was preceded by detailed public debate in chambers of commerce, industry, associations and other firms; in Parliament and educational institutions, etc.

Due to the detailed training imparted to revenue officials and the education of assesses by Government and trade chambers, etc., the introduction of VAT in several countries did neither create many problems nor did it cause much distortions.

Long Term Reform of the Indirect Tax Structure

The excise tax system at the Central Government level forms the bulwark of the entire tax structure of indirect taxes in the country and unless it is placed on a sound footing, it would not be possible to bring about a full rationalisation of that structure.

From the economic point of view and for easily achieving a determinate degree of progression, it is best to have a tax system which covers value added at all stages of processing and trade but which, however, does not create problems of cascading and distortions in relative factor prices.

VAT enables a country to have extended commodity tax system and yet avoid the familiar problems created by other general taxes like the cascade-type sales taxes and excises. It is also relatively easy under the VAT system to free exports almost completely of internal commodity taxation.

There could be two major agreements against the introduction of a comprehensive VAT in India — one is political and the other is administrative. The political argument is the obvious one that the loss of power to levy sales taxes would seriously erode the fiscal autonomy of the State Governments and weaken the federal principle that each subordinate level of Government should have the discretion to raise more or less revenue as the people of the State concerned desire. The administrative argument is that the endorsement of VAT in relation to wholesalers and retailers is likely to create serious problems due to the need for dealing with a large number of tax-payers and the difficulties likely to be faced by a majority of the traders to cope up with the accounting requirements.

It would not be prudent to think in terms of extending VAT to the retail and even wholesale stages in the near future. However, if the benefits of reform of the other parts of the tax system are not to be nullified, taxation at the wholesale and retail stages must be freed of the defects associated with the usual forms of sales taxation.

Given our federal system and the administrative problems of enforcing VAT at the post-manufacturing stages, the right course of action is not to pursue the theoretically best solution, namely, one integrated system based on the VAT principle but to adopt the second best solution of VAT applied to the manufacturing stage (to begin with) combined with a reformed system of sales taxation.

While formally VAT would be applied at the manufacturing stage in lieu of the present excise system, it would be extended to cover imports; and the essential principle of VAT, namely, freeing of inputs from taxation, would get embodied in the sales tax systems. This long term objective should be achieved through a time-bound programme.

Under the MANVAT, there will be no indirect tax component in the price of exports. The MANVAT would not mete out any discriminatory treatment as other systems do, on account of the differences in the stages at which value is added. Relative price distortions would also be eliminated, because in effect inputs are freed from taxation. Administration should not also present insurmountable difficulties.

If the existing restrictions and checks are retained, a general application of rule 56A to all or most of the inputs would involve several problems of administration and compliance. Whilst in the interim, there should be a wider application of rule 56A, the long term solution lies in a switching over to a system of MANVAT.

MANVAT could be operated on the basis of four or five rates that would be applied to the vast majority of consumer products, as a result of the rationalisation of the duty structure on the basic raw materials and inputs.

Under Indian conditions it would be preferable to keep a certain number of industries outside the scope of MANVAT and continue on them the present system of excises. These are industries in respect of whose final products not much cascading is involved as well as those whose products have to be taxed at special or at high rates for economic or sumptuary reasons. These will include petroleum products, tobacco and tobacco products, sugar, coffee, tea and matches.

The introduction of MANVAT in the first instance could be confined to three or four industries which produce final products like automobiles and diesel engines where there is evidence of considerable cumulation of levies. Such a pilot project would enable tax administration to identify problem areas, test cut procedures and study the reactions of tax-payers. Studies have revealed that a VAT confined to the manufacturing level would not be beyond the capacity of tax authorities in India. In the interests of safeguarding revenue, it is necessary to establish the workability of the new system before its widespread application is contemplated.

An erosion of the benefits enjoyed at present, may come about because under VAT, a total exemption from tax is not an unmixed blessing. Non-payment of tax at one stage would automatically brought the chain of tax credit which would be denied to the consumers of the exempted producer. A practical solution would be to ingrant tax credit on a notional basis to manufacturers in respect of inputs bought by them from smaller producers working under a special scheme to be introduce for that purpose.

In our country, it should not be difficult to devise special schemes for the smaller producers whose turnover is below certain value limit.

To prevent abuses and evasion, apart from elaborate audit of accounts by trained personnel, periodic physical checking of inventories of goods on hand would be necessary under MANVAT.

If recommendation for the adoption of MANVAT is accepted by the Government, it would be necessary to send a small team to study the operation of VAT in some countries including a few developing countries.

Simultaneously with the introduction of MANVAT or even preparatory to it, the existing system of sales taxation would have to be reformed as indicated in Chapter 13. As regards import duties, the revenue element in course of time should be made equivalent to MANVAT on the same or similar domestic products, which would thus become a true countervailing duty; and when revenue needs permit, relief under MANVAT should be made admissible in respect of such countervailing duties.

METEOROLOGICAL DEPARTMENT REVIEW COMMITTEE, 1976 – REPORT[1]

Chairman Dr. R. Ramanna

Members Prof. D. Lal; Prof. R. Narasimha; Dr. M. S. Pawar; Shri P. Kumaraswamy; Prof. P.R. Pisharoty; Prof. B.V. Srikantan; Dr. K.G. Vohra; Shri J.D. Philomen Dos

M. Secy. Shri N.K. Mukarji

Appointment

The Committee to review the organizational structure and functions of the India Meteorological Department was Constituted by the Government of India under order No. ME-11011/1/75-M dated 25th July 1976 on the advice of the National Committee on Science and Technology. The terms of reference set out in the Government order are to make recommendations on.

Terms of Reference

(i) the most effective means of bringing about close and continuing interaction between India Meteorological Department and the users of meteorological information;

(ii) facilities needed to be established for the expeditious collection and dissemination of the meteorological information needed by these users by means of an optimal application of latest scientific and technological advances in the area;

(iii) the broad dimensions of the nature and scale of R&D effort which the India Meteorological Department should undertake together with the Institute of Tropical Meteorology and in collaboration with other institutions such as the National Institute of Oceanog-

1. Bombay, Meteorological Department, 1977, 96 p.

raphy, Indian Space Research Organisation, etc., as also experts drawn from India's Scientific Community as a whole;

(iv) the status of the India Meteorological Department in relation to other scientific agencies of the Government;

(v) the internal organisational structure of the Department;

(vi) the internal management structure of the Department with particular reference to practices relating to personnel, procurement of stores and equipment, construction and civil works, financial sanctions, etc., and

(vii) any other aspect of the character and operations of the India Meteorological Department which might improve the Departments efficiency and effectiveness.

Contents

Introduction; Recommendations on the Administrative Structure for Scientific and Technical Programmes of the India Meteorological Department; Recommendations on the Policy for Recruitment, Promotions, Transfers and Pay Scales; Recommendations on the Policy for Purchase and Stores and Delegation of Financial and Administrative Powers; Recommendations on the Reorganisation of Instrument Production by the India Meteorological Department; Recommendations Related to Agricultural Meteorology; Recommendations on Hydrometeorology and Flood Forecasting Programmes; Forecasting and Climatology; Autonomous Institutes; Recommendations on Training Programmes; Appendices; Summary of Recommendations

Recommendations

The India Meteorological Department is more than 100 years old and as such it is one of the oldest scientific organisations in the country. It has had many distinguished scientists who have made outstanding contributions to the development of Meteorology and Seismology in the sub-continent. In fact, it can be said that the study of tropical meteorology was first started in India. In the years before Independence, in spite of many difficulties, several Indian Scientists were able to make outstanding contributions to meteorology. It would be good be refer to Dr. K.R. Ramathan, who is happily still with us, for his important contributions to the science of the upper atmosphere. The IMD seems to have suffered from the worst aspects of the remnants of colonial bureaucracy and but for a few individual exceptions, has become to a certain extent an institution for routine production of data. The research effort has been limited and of a routine nature. The recognition of scientists has been on the criteria of seniority of service and number of papers published rather than quality. These developments are in no way due to the scientists, but have resulted from the type of organisational structure in IMD has found itself with the very fact that the department is treated as a subordinate office of the Ministry has been greatly responsible for this state of affairs. The classification as a subordinate office in government parlance is determined only by the total expenditure of the concerned Department and irrespective of the nature of the decisions, the secretariat has an overriding role, which is not very conductive for the promotion of science. As a result, the scientists are deprived of whatever initiative or feeling of responsibility they may have and keeping good relations with the secretariat becomes a dominant role in all decision-making. The Review Committee, while fully aware of the difficulties and problems of the IMD as it exists, has concentrated itself on making a series of positive recommendations, to make it once again an important arm of Indian science. The recommendations have been made from the point of view of finding a suitable structure for a Government Scientific Department in general and meteorology in particular. They are being made with a view to identify and improve the quality of the work of the department as quickly as possible, but phased in a manner so as to make their implementation feasible.

General

It is our view that the pace of scientific activity gets retarded because of two reasons. One is the administrative structure which is intended to support it and the other is lack of input of competent people into the system. In both these aspects, the IMD has suffered very badly, first because of its subordinate position in Government and secondly because of the lack of proper training programmes both at the scientific and technical levels. In recent years, not many competent people have joined the department at the lower ranks mainly because of unsatisfactory methods of recruitment. Some reorganisation has been attempted in the past through the formation of autonomous bodies, etc. Though these steps were in the right direction, they have not led to satisfactory results. We believe, this is due to lack of sufficient imagination in the implementation of these decisions, and lack of proper direction and follow up.

The Committee has gone into some details as to the type of structure the IMD should have and how dominance of the Ministry and the central office can be reduced so that the scientists can take quick decisions and implement useful projects as quickly as possible without being answerable to many people whose knowledge of the subject is in adequate. It is true that one cannot introduce a completely new system into an organisation which has worked under severe handicaps for several years and where the attitude of mind of the scientists has been severely conditioned by the old system.

The basic spirit of these recommendations has been to increase interaction between the scientists in the various sections of the IMD and with the autonomous bodies, *at all levels*, rather than expect collaboration by decisions taken only in high level committee which are never truly effective in science. However, high level committees are required to formulate policy to choose scientists who will lead groups and to ensure that things are going in the might direction, wherever financial implications are involved, people at the top will have to be fully involved for getting the necessary sanctions and for ensuring that the support is fully sustained. In the spirit of the above comments, the formation of the following committees has been recommended in the report.

1. Council for Meteorology and Earth Science (CMES)
2. Meteorological Executive Committee (MEC)
3. Regional Committee for Meteorology (RCM)
4. Meteorological Programme Advisory Committee (MPAC)

The detailed justifications and terms of reference of these committees are given in the report. It is hoped that finally a system is evolved where decisions can be taken quickly and not by means of long notings on files and other out dated procedures. If the above recommendations on the administrative. Structure can be made to work, it does not seem important as to which Ministry the IMD is administrated by. There is great advantage in being with a user ministry. It could stay where it is, since the Ministry of Tourism and Civil Aviation is also an important user of the data. The Committee is averse to centralising all scientific activities of the country co-ordinated by a single ministry, as this can lead to isolation from users.

Seminars/Visiting Professors

For getting good ideas in science, people between the ages of 20 and 40 are the most active and they should be encouraged to hold free discussion amongst themselves irrespective of the units or the autonomous bodies they belong to. Relevant data must be made available to all concerned without the need for official sanctions. Regular seminars, discussion groups, etc., on subjects of meteorology and other branches of science play an important role in all scientific activities and it is by "constructive criticism" on such occasions that scientific progress is achieved. These should be encouraged. Visiting Professors from India and abroad over a period of time will help in keeping the scientists up to date. A tradition has to be built up for using seminars, etc., to act as catalyst for proper planning and quality research work. It also brings about maturity and discipline among junior workers which is necessary for team work – an essential aspect of modern scientific development. This tradition seems to be lacking in the IMD.

Central Office

The Committee has discussed at great length the improvements in administrative policy that have to be introduced to increase efficiency. These refer to policies regarding training, stores, promotions, transfers and organisation of research and service activities, etc. The Committee has also discussed the functions of the central office and is of the view that its very reason for existence is to promote scientific activity rather than restrain it because of some irrelevant centralised regulations which may have been issued for a very different reason. The relevance of such regulations should be decided upon by the Director General in Consultation with the Council (CMES), the formation of which has been suggested earlier.

Instruments

It is clear that meteorology in India will not reach the same status as meteorology abroad unless there is a sustained programme for the production of quality instruments and induction of a high degree of automation. The instruments required for meteorological work can be produced in India. Since we are planning for programmes in meteorology for India till towards the year 2000, there should be no hesitation in introducing automation for data collection in a large way wherever it is feasible and considered necessary. Automation would provide high quality data and its quick dissemination, which is vital to the users, e.g., civil aviation, defence, agriculture, irrigation, etc. The Committee suggests large scale automation in a phased manner because it is not possible to depend on a large number of semi-skilled people together required scientific data. At the moment, the Tahsildar's office has an important say, in measuring and reporting the amount of rainfall and many a times the validity of these data can be doubted. The IMD at present produces many routine instruments. The production of such routine type of instruments should be passed on the Indian industry which is now ready to take it over. The development of instruments requiring a high degree of sophistication and automation should be the main programme at various instrumentation centres of the Department.

The Committee has special comments on intensive training because this is probably the weakest side of the IMD and its present efforts are most inadequate. It is suggested that prior to final selection all entrants should be made to go through at least a year's training programme, which involves not only meteorology as defined normally but the basis of meteorology which includes relevant portions of Physics, Mathematics, Chemistry and Biology. The teachers should include the staff of the IMD for teaching is an essential part of any scientific organisation. This is one of the most effective ways of keeping the scientists abreast of the new developments in the subject. In case where there is lack of expertise, scientists from other organisations can also be requested to take part in the teaching programme.

The Committee considered the question of starting meteorology courses in universities and took note of the courses offered by the Andhra University which have been running now for many years. It was of the view that meteorology being a highly applied and interdisciplinary subject, a 2-year post-graduate course by itself will not solve the problem of providing the type of persons with the appropriate base. What is required is a training programme of the IMD where the scientists of the Department benefit by being teachers in the programme. The co-operation of the institutes of higher learning like the Indian Institute of Science, or some IIT where a multidisciplinary atmosphere is available for research in basic meteorology is also necessary. The IMD should make efforts to interest some Institutes of higher learning to take up such studies on their behalf. It would not recommend starting M.Sc. courses in meteorology in universities without an interdisciplinary research programme.

The technicians must also be trained so that they are aware of the basic principles of the instruments which they are using, understand the requirements for their maintenance and repairs and also have a feeling for the use of data which they are collecting. The more promising of the technicians who show capacity for innovation should be specially encouraged. This seems to be singularity lacking in many of the observation centres. Efforts should be made so that automated instruments are well serviced from their concerned centralised units by capable technicians.

The importance of training cannot ever be overstressed and it should be planned that every officer at whatever level he be, has a chance to improve his knowledge by refresher courses throughout his entire career.

In all these activities, the IMD should not underestimate the need for clean and well maintained buildings, staff punctuality, proper dress for its lower staff and quick disposal of files. Class IV (now Group D) staff, not engaged in technical work should anyway be reduced to a minimum. All these go towards the creation of an atmosphere of discipline.

Promotion Policy

The promotion policy of the IMD should be such that scientists due for promotion are interviewed by people who know the subject and also by those who work closely with the scientific workers concerned. The recruitment and promotion system as it exists now, where only very high level officers and the secretariat decide on most of the promotions is an unsatisfactory one for recruitment of scientists and it should be replaced by a system of the type in use in the Council of Scientific and Industrial Research (CSIR), Tata Institute of Fundamental Research (TIFR) and Bhabha Atomic Research Centre (BARC).

Much of the dissatisfaction that exists in scientific organisations is due to the fact that promotion is identified with availability of posts at all levels and an official position is coupled with salary. Both of these are not essential in a scientific organization. The Committee has suggested that while the total number of posts in the IMD can increase at a predetermined rate, the number of posts at various levels should be very flexible and promotion determined on quality of work rather than on availability of a post. For such promotions, assessment will have to be done in a way very different from the present system.

Autonomous Bodies

The Government has on previous occasions taken some decisions to separate some of the activities of IMD and make them the function of autonomous bodies. While in principle this is a good idea, in practice, however autonomy has not helped the younger and middle scientists to have access to data for discussion with their colleagues in other branches of science. We believe that there must be close collaboration between the Indian Institute of Tropical Meteorology and India Meteorological Department. These institutes should work in close collaboration as units working under the council (CMES). The autonomy must reflect itself in the ability of constituent groups of complete research projects quickly and not promote isolation of scientists as it does now. In fact, there should be facilities for the change of personnel from one unit to the other, for suitable periods of time, so that the expertise of one branch of science is available to the other. The work done in any of the units should be recognised for the purpose of promotion, etc., we define autonomy as one which allows for quick movement of personnel, quick procurement of stores, fast recruitment, efficient availability of data and in general, quick implementation of decisions without being hampered by existing rules.

Stores

The availability of materials, i.e., stocking of stores is a very vital item for a department which has laboratories spread all over India. Important work may be held up for comparatively small items of purchase because of procedures, centralisation of stores and purchase operations. Suggestions such as delegation of powers all along the time, the distribution of stocks, etc., have been made for improving availability

Users Communication

The IMD has an important role to play for various users such as agriculture, civil aviation, defence, shipping, irrigation, etc. The Committee has made suggestions as to how data can be quickly collected and disseminated to the users organisations by modern communication methods. The type of data to be communicated is also important, if meteorology is to play a part in the economic life of the nation. The communication of data in India requires special study as the existing methods are not adequate. It is essential that we do not depend entirely on international bodies and foreign countries for defining what type of data are required by our users. For example in civil aviation, the data required for our conditions of flight may be different from that required in other areas of the world. These differences must be identified by those interaction between the users and the IMD. On the irrigation front, the IMD can contribute enormously in the prediction of floods, cyclones, etc., by the study of snow depths in Himalayas and such other phenomena. All this requires closer collaboration at working levels and the concerned units must attempt to build up confidence in our data and its analysis. A National Meteorological Data Centre should be set-up so that all meteorological data of interest are available for dissemination to relevant users. Foreign expertise should be used only to supplement Indian efforts.

The activities of Nautical Almanac Unit of IMD one of a different nature as compared to those of other units of IMD and require collaboration with Indian Institute of Astrophysics, Nainital Observatory, Osmania University, National Physical Laboratory, the Tata Institute of Fundamental Research and other institutes working on various aspects of Astronomy. The field of operation of this unit should be expanded and a research wing added to initiate theoretical research on celestial mechanics and observational aspects of positional astronomy. More detailed recommendations on the expansion of this unit are included in the Appendix S.A.

The Committee has made an attempt to identify future areas of research but this is done more in the nature of suggestions than to provide a plan for the future. It is clear that scientists of the IMD themselves must define their detailed programmes.

Training Programmes

The Training Directorate of IMD: The present training Directorate is responsible for the training of staff to be recruited in various cadres in the Department. The Directorate functions under the DDT (Forecasting) and is responsible for conducting a Meteorological Training School with the following courses:

(1) Four months' course for observers.
(2) Six months' course for Meteorological Assistants.
(3) Six months' course for Meteorological Officers (in consultation of item 2)
(4) Four months' course for Meteorological Officers (abridged course of item 3).

Advanced courses of 2-week duration on selected topics are also conducted from time to time, to aquaint the staff with recent developments. Occasionally training courses for the benefit of the Defence Services are also arranged as per their requirements.

During 1975-76, 281 candidates underwent training, including 15 trainees of the advanced course for the benefit of the Defence Services are also arranged, as per their requirements. Training in operation maintenance and servicing of radio-meteorological observational equipment, like Radio sound/Radiowind equipment, Radiotheodolites, Radars, etc., is imparted by the Training Centre at New Delhi which was established in 1962. This Centre conducts two courses viz. (i) Radio-meteorological operators' course (3 months) and (ii) Radio-meteorological officers/Engineers' Course (6 months).

A training centre to be located at Poona exclusively for agricultural meteorology has recently been sanctioned. This centre provides training in this specialised field to departmental personnel as well as to those sponsored by State Governments, agricultural institutions and universities.

The Sanctional Staff strength of the Training Directorate is 40, with one Director and three Meteorologists Grade I (Appendix X-A). The Syllabus for the regular courses is in conformity with the standards laid down by the World Meteorological Organization.

Views of the Committee

Appendix X-B gives the present staff strength of the India Meteorological Department. It is seen that during the next five years, more than 100 Meteorologists Grade II and more than 220 Assistant Meteorologists will be required by IMD.

The Committee views training as the single most important factor in the success of a complex set up like IMD and feels that the training programme for the staff recruited in different cadres should be quite intensive, including training in the relevant portion of basic sciences as well.

In planning for the future, it is useful to make a distinction between training and education. The purpose of training should be to impart special knowledge and skills to fresh recruits so that they can contribute to the operational services offered by the Department (this includes maintenance of equipment and instrumentation, proper recording and transmission of observations, provision of forecasts and other services by methods developed and accepted by the Department). Efforts to advance the state-of-the-art in meteorology and in the quality of the services offered need a creative and innovative approach that can only be provided by suitable educational programme with a broader base and deeper appreciation of the problems. Modern professional practice emphasizes quantitative aspects of meteorology and these demand a considerable background in the basic sciences of engineering in addition to meteorology. One possible curriculum for such a programme is listed in Appendix X-C. It is not intended that every recruit to IMD take all the courses listed, but most of them should be available so that selections are possible to suit the needs of students and of IMD.

The staff for teaching should be drawn from different Divisions of the Department based at Poona and Delhi. This would provide an opportunity for the staff to refresh their knowledge of fundamentals and keep abrest of new developments.

The IMD should make efforts to interest some of the national institutes of higher learning to take up research programmes of interdisciplinary nature. This would provide opportunities for the staff of IMD to go to these Institutes for training in advanced topics in atmospheric sciences and also to take up short-term and long-term research programmes at these places.

Training is also necessary for the technical staff at all levels, so that the members of such staff understand the instruments they are using or repairing and know the importance of the data they are collected.

The Training Directorate should review the courses offered and the syllabus, and have a wider spectrum of specializations in the teaching a staff by asking the departmental staff to deliver lectures for the candidates. The Directorate should have permanent staff mainly for organising the courses, including the selection of candidates setting the syllabus, scheduling the lectures, preparing lecture notes, conducting examinations, organising field training, etc., with the sanctioned strength of 40 the Training Directorate should be able to organise a broad spectrum of training activities.

All the meteorological officers entering the Department should undergo at least one year's training, including education in basic sciences and meteorological sciences. During the training and at the end of training period examination should be conducted and only the successful candidates should be absorbed as officers (Met. Grade II). This condition should be stipulated at the time of recruitment.

All the technical staff including observers should undergo a training course of six months. In this category, however, the marks scored in the examination should be kept impersonal records, for future promotions of the candidates.

A syllabus suitable for this country should be written up, instead of following the WMO classification and syllabus for training, particularly in view of greater involvement of basic sciences and interdisciplinary areas in the training programmes proposed. We recommend that the proposal for constructing the building and hostel for the training school at Pashan Land, Poona should be expedited.

Frequent short-term courses (3 to 4 weeks), and seminars and workshops should be organised by the Training Directorate to cater for the advanced training and specialisation.

The level of education of the students in any class should be high enough for the level of teaching, e.g., minimum qualification of II Class M.Sc. could be the criterion for the Meteorological officers course.

A joint programme in meteorological education should be organised by the IMD, IITMs and an institution of higher learning like the Indian Institute of Science, Bangalore. A suitable committee consisting of representations of each of the three organizations could take the responsibility for the entire programme.

The candidates who undergo the programme should be jointly selected by the above Committee, and paid a suitable attractive stipend during the programme.

At the end of the period of the course, those who pass should be eligible for positions of Met. Grade II in the IMD as recommended in 10.14, but it is expected that there will be at least a few who would decide (and find it possible) to continue on a programme of research or development at either of the other two institutions. Part of the training period must be spent at a multi-disciplinary academic institution; a part may similarly be spent in one of the IMD regional centres acquiring experience with the operational system at IMD.

As a corollary of such a programme, it is essential that opportunity be available to Scientist in IMD to move to universities or other research institutions for a fixed period for purposes of pursuing research. Periods spent in such work should not be treated as breaks in service, as they generally contribute to the growth of technical ability in the organisation.

A centre for atmospheric sciences should be established in an academic institution so as to provide facilities for all those who wish to do research in this field. Such a centre should be opened in an institution of outstanding calibre where multidisciplinary groups with high degree of specialisation are already functioning.

11

WORKING GROUP TO STUDY THE PROBLEMS OF BANK CREDIT IN THE NORTH-EASTERN REGION, 1976 – REPORT[1]

Convenor Kumari Nalini K. Ambegaokar

Members Shri P.S. Santhanakrishnan; Shri J.N. Pathak; Shri T.R. Shah; Shri A. Sathyamoorthy; Shri M.M.Lal; Shri S.K. Agnihotri; Shri C.K. Ramachandra; Shri N. Mukherjee (Vide Shri S.L. Khosla); Shri B.L. Gaur; Shri I. Sashimeran Aier; Shri B.B. Deb Roy

Secretary Shri P.I. John

Appointment

At the meeting of the Regional Consultative Committee for the North-Eastern Region held at Gauhati on July 5, 1976, it was decided that the Reserve Bank of India should appoint a small Working Group to examine, *inter alia*, the factors impeding the flow of bank credit in the region and make recommendations for the necessary changes in the procedures and practices of banks so as to bring about rapid and all round banking development in the region. Accordingly, the Reserve Bank set upon August 20, 1976, a small Working Group to study the specific aspects of banking problems in the region.

Terms of Reference

(i) To identify the factors impeding the flow of bank credit in the North Eastern Region;

(ii) To recommend in the context of the socio-economic features of the region, suitable arrangements for expeditious disbursal of

---

1. *Reserve Bank of India Bulletin*, February 1977, p. 174-200

credit by commercial banks, both directly as well as through intermediaries such as Farmers' Service Societies, Gaon Level Panchayat Societies, Anchal Samitis, Village Council, etc., and

(iii) To suggest improvements and modifications in the operational methods and procedures of the banks in the region for the rapid deployment of bank finance in the desired direction.

Later, by a Communication dated October 28, 1976, one more terms of reference was added by Reserve Bank which was as follows:

(iv) To indicate the location of Regional Rural Banks in the North-Eastern region and to examine the role to be played by them in the region.

The Working Group was asked to prepare an overall report highlighting the special problems of the North-Eastern region and indicate, in the report, separately, their specific recommendations in regard to each State/Union Territory in that region.

Contents

Introduction; Background to the problems; Factors impeding the flow of bank credit in the North-Eastern Region; Use of intermediaries for the expeditious disbursal of bank credit in the North-Eastern Region; Role of Regional Rural Banks in the North-Eastern region and their locations; Suggestions for improvements/modifications in the operational methods and procedures of banks in the North-Eastern region; Summary of recommendations.

Recommendations

The three important aspects relating to the expeditious disbursal of bank credit in the North-Eastern region, namely, the use of intermediaries, the role of Regional Rural Banks and the suggestions for improvements/modifications in the operational methods and procedures of banks have been discussed in detail and recommendations made in Chapters IV-V and VI respectively. The major recommendations are summarised in this chapter.

Use of Intermediaries

In view of the differing conditions in different States/Union Territories in the region and in deference to the views of the respective state Governments, the Groups suggests that the commercial banks may use different agencies/intermediaries and/or lend directly so as to reach the remote places and to disburse credit in the region. This is given in detail below:

(a) Thus, in Assam, the Working Group recommends that:

(i) Commercial banks may lend through the GPSs as well as engage in direct lending at least till the former can take up credit functions fully through appropriately trained managerial staff;

(ii) Operation of RRBs through co-operative societies should be taken up as it is now an accepted national policy, although, at present, the Assam Government has some apprehensions regarding the likely overlapping of functions of the RRB and the Apex Bank.

(iii) The State Government should take expeditious action on liquidation/dissolution and/or merger of old societies with new societies on the lines of Reserve Bank's guidelines, and

(iv) The State Government should expedite the re-allocation of societies among the different banks including the RRB.

(b) In Manipur, we recommend that:

(i) Banks should adopt existing co-operatives on a selective basis for credit disbursal and also undertake direct lending where societies are not so adopted;

(ii) Government should expedite restructuring of the primary credit societies into FSS or LAMPS, and

(iii) When RRB is set up, it should supplement efforts of banks in disbursing credit.

(c) In Tripura, while noting that the process of allocation of societies among the banks and State Co-operative Banks has already been initiated, we recommend that:–

(i) The State Government may expeditiously complete the task of reorganisation of societies and setting up of ISS and LAMPS; and

(ii) In the meanwhile, banks and the RRB may continue to lend directly.

In the Hill States of Arunachal Pradesh, Meghalaya, Mizoram and Nagaland, the Working Group make the following recommendations:

(a) In Arunachal Pradesh

(i) banks should lend directly on the basis of requisite surety/guarantee provided by Anchal samities, and
(ii) government should expedite the organisation of LAMPS, in order to enable banks and RRB (when set up) to rapidly expand their activities.

(b) In Meghalaya

(i) banks should use the primary co-operative credit societies, which are being reorganised, as intermediaries and also continue to lend directly, and
(ii) the Lead bank in collaboration with the State Government may initiate steps to demarcate areas among commercial banks, the RRB (when set-up) and the Apex bank, for channelising credit through co-operative societies.

(c) In Mizoram

(i) banks may finance the existing multipurpose societies;
(ii) the Government may expedite organising LAMPS which can then act as intermediaries for increasing the flow of credit by commercial banks and the RRB (when set-up), and
(iii) in the meanwhile, banks can lend directly on the basis of certificates from village councils.

(d) In Nagaland

(i) commercial banks may lend directly with the help of village councils, till the Government completes the task of activising co-operative societies in the form of LAMPS which can then act as intermediaries for disbursing credit by commercial banks and the RRB (when set-up), and

(ii) banks may follow the example of the Lead Bank which has already relaxed the security requirement.

Another type of intermediary which can be used by banks in the North-Eastern region, particularly for medium and long term purposes is the Government sponsored and/or partly/wholly Government/owned/managed corporate agency, and if necessary, with equity participation by commercial banks, through whom banks can give credit for development of the region. In this connection, the Group recommends that:

for medium and long-term development activities such as land shaping, terracing, horticulture and plantation development, the State Governments may organise agencies like Land Development Corporations, Irrigation Corporations, Horticulture and Plantation Corporations, etc., to undertake these activities under professional management and banks should extend the necessary finance to them for that purpose.

Setting Up of RRBs

As regards the role of the RRBs in the North-Eastern Region and their location:

(i) the Working Group, after considering the various aspects has come to the conclusion that banking expansion in the region may also be brought about through a local based and rural-oriented institution like a RRB.

(ii) in view of the geographical lay-out of the different states in the region, difficulties of communications and the aspirations of the Government and people in each state to have an involvement in an institution like a RRB, the Working Group feel that there would be a case for each State having one RRB in its territory; however;

(iii) considering the guidelines of setting up of RRBs laid down by the Government, the Group feels that there is a clear case for modification of these guidelines in the North-Eastern region and recommend that the Government of India and Reserve Bank may consider taking steps towards that end.

Changes in operational methods and banking procedures:

The Working Group feels that there is an urgent need for introducing changes in banking procedures and operational methods in the North-Eastern region. The improvements and/or modifications that need to be made relate to the following aspects.

Thus, for rapid banking expansion in the region, we recommend that:

(i) the new branch licensing formula introduced in 1977, viz., for 2 banked centres, 4 unbanked centres should be applied to measure the performance of individual banks operating in the region and not on an all-India basis as at present and the shortfall in the coverage of the unbanked rural centres may be made good by a time-bound programme of say, a year or so;

(ii) banks experiment with 'limited day operation' or 'village' type branches at suitable places in the region, and there should be a single permanent machinery to both formulate and monitor branch expansion programmes.

As regards organisational pattern and operational methods, we recommend that:

(i) banks review their policy of delegation of powers to branch managers and having regard to the difficulties in communications, should increase, wherever necessary, the number of 'controlling offices' in the region;

(ii) the different banks operating in the region should bring about some uniformity in the discretionary powers of their branch managers in the same centres, in respect of loans to weaker sections, and

(iii) banks should build up their own, extension service cadre for this region, with provision of suitable transport facilities to them.

As regards lending practices of banks, we recommend that:

(i) loan application forms should be simple and uniform as prescribed by Reserve Bank for agricultural loans and as devised for RRBs for non-agricultural purposes by "Working Group on simplified accounting and other procedures for RRBs."

(ii) such forms should be in local language and be made available in sufficient numbers whenever required;

(iii) as in the case of short-term loans to agriculturists (where anticipated crop is at present accepted as security and no further mortgage is required), in the case of term loans to agriculturists also, banks should accept a mere charge on land as security as suggested by the Talwar Committee and to expedite this, State Governments should have a time-bound programme for framing the rules and regulations of the Relevant Act;

(iv) till (iii) is implemented banks should lend on a 'Group Guarantee basis amounts up to Rs. 3,000 for crop' loans or working capital and Rs. 7,000 for term loans;

(v) in the case of term loans to agriculturists where they do not have mortgageable rights on land but where they are in continuous possession of such land, a certificate of possession signed by a village/Anchal Chief and countersigned by a Revenue Officer should suffice for sanctioning term loans for developmental purposes; and

(vi) in cases mentioned in (v) above, the State Governments should take timely action to ensure that such borrowers would remain in continuous possession of land during the currency of the loan and that they should exert moral pressure on borrowers to recover overdues, if any.

As regards other terms and conditions of bank lending, we recommend that:

banks, as a special case for this region, should adopt a flexible attitude and relax the terms and conditions of lending for priority sectors, e.g., they can lower rates of interest on bank loans in cases where the viability of the scheme/project can be improved upon by such relaxation.

Many schemes for concessional bank finance do not apply in cases where credit is disbursed through RRBs and agencies like co-operatives, e.g., credit under Differential Interest Rates (DIR) scheme or cover for credit under the Credit Guarantee Corporation of India Ltd. (CGCI). We, therefore, recommend that:

(i) Government of India should consider making suitable changes in the DIR scheme so as to benefit borrowing through RRBs, co-operatives and allied agencies in the North-Eastern region, and
(ii) CGCI cover may be extended to bank lending through RRBs, co-operatives and similar agencies in this region and the proportion of the risk borne by the CGCI be also raised in respect of advances in the region.

As regards other types of loans, we recommend that:

(i) for loans against trucks and other vehicles in the region, banks should give specific instructions to their branches in the region not to insist on several types of securities, and
(ii) banks should adopt a flexible attitude in regard to the farmer being insisted upon taking a package of cash-cum-kind bank loans, taking into account the several factors, affecting the farmer's activity and conditions of farming in the region.

It was noticed that the repayment dates of agricultural loans were fixed by banks, for different crops, at the same dates which were either much after or ahead of the harvesting period, e.g., date fixed was March 1977 for both the 1976 kharif and the 1976-77 rabi crops, we recommend that:

for agricultural loans, banks should fix dates for repayment around or near the harvesting time and issue suitable instruction in the matter of their branches in the region.

As regards manpower planning and training, we recommend that:

(i) Head Offices of banks operating in the North-Eastern region should evolve a special policy in regard to recruitment, selection and training of staff, for this region, and
(ii) the Lead Banks may set up a joint training centre in this region for all banks, with the help of an institution like the National Institute of Bank Management (NIBM).

As regards publicity and guidance to borrowers, we recommend that:

(i) banks should take up the various schemes of publicity of banking business and lending in local languages in the region, through, among others, radio and/or audio visual demonstrations, and

(ii) for educating rural borrowers in the use of credit, etc., and as a help to borrowers as well as to co-operatives and banks, the work of the Spearhead Teams started by the NIBM in Assam may be extended to other states in the region, with necessary finances being arranged by the State Governments and Banks.

In order to bring about coordination between the banks and the governmental agencies, we recommend that:

(i) banks at high levels — Chairmen/Managing Directors — meet top Government officials periodically to resolve problems facing them, and

(ii) even at field levels, where co-operatives operate, the responsibility of implementing the agreed credit plan may be squarely and jointly put on the bank's field officer and the concerned Assistant Registrar of Co-operative Societies.

COMMITTEE APPOINTED TO INVESTIGATE THE CONDUCT AND ACTIVITIES OF SHRI SUBRAMANIAN SWAMY, MEMBER OF THE RAJYA SABHA, 1976 – REPORT[1]

Chairman Shri Godey Murahari, Dy. Chairman of the Rajya Sabha

Members Shri Kamlapati Tripathi; Shri A.R. Antulay; Shri N.K. Bhatt; Shri D.K. Daphtary; Shri Bhupesh Gupta; Shri Suresh Narain Mulla; Shri Bhanu Pratap Singh; Shri D.P. Singh; Shri Mehta

Appointment

The Committee was appointed to investigate the conduct and activities of Shri Subramanian Swamy, Member, Rajya Sabha, in pursuance of the Motion adopted by the Rajya Sabha at its sitting held on the 2nd September, 1976, having been authorised by the Committee to present this report on their behalf, present this report to the House.

Terms of Reference

1. (a) To investigate the conduct and activities of Shri Subramanian Swamy, Member of the Rajya Sabha, during the past one year or more both within and outside the country, including anti-Indian propaganda calculated to bring the Parliament and the country's democratic institutions into disrepute and generally behaving in a manner unworthy of a Member of this House;

(b) To report to this House by the first week of the next session whether the conduct and activities of the Member were inconsis-

---

1. New Delhi, Rajya Sabha, Secretariat, 1976, p. 43

tent with, and seriously fall below, the standards which this House is entitled to expect of its Members; and

(c) To make such recommendation as the Committee may deem fit.

Recommendations

Shri Subramanian Swamy failed to appear as directed by the Committee at its third sitting held on October 29, 1976. The Secretary-General of the Rajya Sabha brought to the notice of the Committee a letter dated October 25, 1976 written by Shrimati Roxna Subramanian Swamy, styling herself as "Attorney for Shri Subramanian Swamy", with reference to the Secretariat's letter dated October 23, 1976. The Committee decided that this letter deserved no notice by it as Shrimati Roxna Swamy had no *locus standi* to address such a communication in the matter for the consideration of the Committee. The Committee took a serious view of the failure of Shri Subramanian Swamy to comply with its directions, but the Committee decided to give him yet another, and final opportunity to appear in person before it at its next meeting to be held on November 2, 1976. The Committee further directed that Shri Swamy should be specifically told that if he failed to appear in person before it on November 2, 1976, it would proceed with the consideration of the matter on that day and come to its conclusions. A letter was sent to Shri Swamy accordingly on the same day.

Shri Swamy again failed to appear before the Committee at its fourth sitting held on November 2, 1976. The Chairman referred to the clear and definite terms of the Rajya Sabha Secretariat's letter of October 29, 1976, to Shri Swamy, and suggested that in the circumstances the Committee may proceed with its examination on the matter on the basis of the material before it. The Committee, while agreeing with the Chairman's suggestion, expressed its displeasure at Shri Swamy's attitude in persistently defying its directions to appear before it.

Shri Om Mehta gave the Committee, in accordance with the desire expressed by some members, an analysis of the particulars contained in his statement of September 20, 1976. In doing so, he said that he had since been informed that the Indian Embassy in Washington (U.S.A.) had addressed a letter to Shri Subramanian Swamy on March 31, 1976, at his then known address in Washington conveying to him Government's orders regarding the impounding of his passport and that a photostat copy of his letter together with a report of certain observations made by Shri Swamy in this connection had appeared in the April 23, 1976, issue of a newspaper *India Abroad* published from New York. This report would establish that Shri Swamy was aware of the orders impounding his passport. The letter dated April 8, 1976, which an official of the Indian Consulate-General took for delivery to Shri Swamy at New York on April 10, 1976, was an exact copy of this letter. Shri Om Mehta also brought to the notice of the Committee an extract from a letter dated October 20, 1976 (Appendix III), addressed to him by Shri Swamy regarding his attendance at the sittings of the Rajya Sabha during the 93rd and 97th Sessions of the House which proved the points in respect of drawal of TA/DA without attending the meetings of the House.

At its fifth sitting held on 9th November, 1976, the Committee considered the draft report, and, after detailed deliberations on each of the issues involved, decided to appoint a sub-committee consisting of Shri Bhupesh Gupta, Shri C.K. Daphtary, Shri D.P. Singh and Shri A.R. Antulay, Members of the Committee, to redraft the report.

The sub-committee met on November 10, 1976 and after a detailed discussion decided to make a verbal report to the Committee at its next meeting. At the sixth sitting of the Committee held on November 11, 1976 the sub-committee reported accordingly. The Chairman informed the Committee that Shri Bhanu Pratap Singh by a letter dated 9th November, 1976, addressed to the Chairman, Rajya Sabha, had resigned his membership of the Committee with effect from 10th November, 1976. He also placed before the Committee a letter dated 5th November, 1976 received from Shri Swamy addressed to the Chairman, Rajya Sabha [Appendix II (iv)].

At its seventh meeting held on November 12, 1976 the Committee considered and adopted the report.

The Committee examined all the material including the documents placed before it. The Committee was of the view that in coming to its conclusions, it was not so much concerned with abstract technical and legal niceties, but its concern was the conduct of Shri Subramanian Swamy, whether he had acted in a dishonourable manner unworthy of a Member of the Rajya Sabha and his conduct was derogatory to the dignity of the House and inconsistent with the standard which Parliament is entitled to expect from its Members. A number of objectionable activities of Shri Subramanian Swamy were brought to the notice of the Committee and the Committee decided to confine its attention primarily on the following:

(1) Attention of the Committee had been drawn to the four "signatures" of Shri Subramanian Swamy during the 93rd Session of the Rajya Sabha on the daily attendance register of the House. Shri Subramanian Swamy in his letter dated October 20, 1976 addressed to Shri Om Mehta and his subsequent letter dated November 5, 1976 addressed to the Chairman, Rajya Sabha, claimed these signatures as his. On expert examination of these signatures, however, it was found that these signatures were not his. On the basis of Shri Subramanian Swamy's statement itself these signatures could not be his, because he had categorically asserted that it was the decision of his Party to boycott that session and therefore he did not attend it. Obviously therefore he could not have signed on the register to mark his presence. The question now arises as to the purpose for which these signatures were appended. The purposes could be two: (i) He may not forfeit his seat in the House under the provisions of Article 101(4) of the Constitution due ot continued absence from the sittings of the House, and therefore it was necessary for him through the agency of some one else, to have his signatures marked in the attendance registers, (ii) To support his claim for, and obtain, daily allowance. Here it could be argued that if his mere presence in Delhi would have entitled him to daily allowance, then why should he have had to resort to have his signatures on the register. The fact, however, remains that these signatures are there. It was in all probability done to lend credence to his assertions that he was in Delhi during the said period. Whatever the purpose for which the said registers were signed, the Committee is satisfied that the conduct of Shri Subramanian Swamy in claiming these four forged signatures as his, is reprehensible and far below the standards expected of a Member of Parliament.

(2) On the basis of the evidence placed before it and from the letters of Shri Subramanian Swamy received in the Secretariat, the Committee was of the view that Shri Subramanian Swamy knew about the impounding of his passport by the Government of India when he was still abroad. Instead of surrender-

ing the impounded passport to the authorities concerned as he was required to do, Shri Subramanian Swamy continued to travel on the strength of that passport knowing fully well that it was not a valid document for the purpose of any further travel. The conduct of Shri Swamy in this regard, in the Committee's view, was inconsistent with the standards expected of him as a member of Parliament.

(3) The Committee considered the reported activities of Shri Subramanian Swamy in the United Kingdom, U.S.A. and Canada where it appears he gave interviews on the radio and television. In his letter to the Rajya Sabha Secretariat, dated October 9, 1976, Shri Subramanian Swamy says, "I am a public man and I do not have a copy of all my interviews especially those given on radio and TV". In this letter as well as in his subsequent ones, Shri Subramanian Swamy does not deny he gave interviews and wrote articles in other journals during his visits abroad. In the letter referred to above, he writes, "otherwise I would request the Committee to help me obtain copies of my interviews/stories/artilcles in *Times* (London), *Guardian, Economist, New York Times, Washington Post, Los Angeles Times, Denver Post, India (Aborad) New York and TV interviews* on BBC, Public Broadcasting System (USA) and Canada AM." It would thus appear that Shri Subramanian Swamy had easy access to such mass media including radio and television. In this connection, the Committee cannot but take note of the fact that many of such journals in these countries as well as the TV and the radio were engaged in virulent anti-India propaganda after proclamation of emergency in the country. That Shri Subramanian Swamy was feeding their propaganda would be seen from what appeared, for example, in *Toronto Star*, Wed., February 11, 1976 under four column heading "Mrs. Gandhi could be killed, Indian MP in exile says" along with a photograph of Shri Subramanian Swamy. This report states:

> "There is a fear in India that Communists will assassinate Prime Minister Indira Gandhi, blame the democratic opposition and take over government, an Indian Parliamentarian in-hiding says.
>
> Harvard-educated economics Professor Subramanian

Swamy, 36, said."

The report further states:

"They (pro-Moscow Communists) could find a new Prime Minister among their own party, or a sympathizer in Mrs. Gandhi's Congress Party."

In his letter dated 9th October, 1976, to the Rajya Sabha Secretariat, Shri Subramanian Swamy does not repudiate this news item but only says that "I find the *Toronto Star* Interview on the basis of the extracts quoted quite garbled." He does not claim that he had sent any contradiction to what he calls "garbled" report to the editor of *Toronto Star*. If this report in the *Toronto Star* was substantially wrong, Shri Subramanian Swamy could easily have said so in his letters received in the Rajya Sabha Secretariat and placed before the Committee. There is, therefore, no reason for the Committee to believe that the report in the *Toronto Star* is untrue. The propaganda unleashed through these media by him is also in keeping with the line taken by the newspaper *Motherland* which propagated the philosophy of the Party to which he belongs, when recently a Central Cabinet Minister was killed.

Reports and other public utterances of Shri Subramanian Swamy in U.K., U.S.A. and Canada are in tune with the anti-India propaganda carried on by certain mass media including radio and television in these countries. It is altogether inexcusable that Shri Subramanian Swamy should have carried on such activities in league with well-known anti-India elements in these countries who made available to Shri Swamy the columns of some journals in the U.S.A. and Canada for running down and defaming the democratic institutions in our country.

Full reports of Shri Swamy's activities in the U.K., U.S.A. and Canada are of course not known to the Committee, but whatever report is available would show that Shri Swamy was virtually acting as a tool of anti-India elements during his visits abroad. It may be reasonable presumed that these elements had a part to play not only in inspiring his anti-India campaign in foreign lands but actually organising it. This is the first ever case of a Member of Parliament carrying on so blatantly his activities in collusion with anti-India elements abroad to malign our democratic institutions and to provide fuel to the fire of anti-India propaganda by the external enemies of our country. It may be noted that in the communications received from Shri Swamy in the Rajya Sabha Secretariat and otherwise, there is not a word of regret for his patently unpatriotic and anti-national activities during his above mentioned foreign tours. On the contrary, there is an attempt to justify his conduct. In the opinion of the Committee, Shri Subramanian Swamy's activities in the U.K., U.S.A. and Canada which have been amply publicised are unworthy not only of a Member of Parliament but of any self-respecting patriotic Indian citizen.

5. These are all acts which no Member of Parliament should indulge in keeping in view the dignity of the office of such membership. These acts seriously impair a Member's right to represent his constituents in Parliament and direct from the trust reposed in him as such Member. It is the Committee's view the Members of Parliament should observe the highest standard of rectitude in matters concerning drawal of allowances for, otherwise, they are liable to be accused of committing a fraud on public funds. There is no doubt that Shri Subramanian Swamy has deliberately violated the law by travelling on a passport which he knew was impounded and also when he drew TA/DA when he had no intention of attending the meetings of the House/Committee. He also did not appear before this Committee in spite of repeated directions in that behalf. His description of Parliament as "Our captive Parliament" and the innuendos he has made against the Members show his utter disrespect to the Parliamentary institutions of the country and amount to contempt of the House and its members. All these facts constitute a grave breach of the elementary standards of conduct expected of a Member of Parliament.

6. The Committee would, therefore, recomend that Shri Subramanian Swamy be expelled from the membership of the Rajya Sabha as his conduct is derogatory to the dignity of the House, its Members and inconsistent with the standards which the House is entitled to expect of its Members. In making this recommendation, the Committee would like to quote with approval the following observations of May (18th edition – p. 128):

> "The purpose of expulsion is not so much disciplinary as remedial, not so much to punish Members as torid the House of persons who are until for membership."

The Committee is conscious that this is the first time in the Rajya Sabha that a recommendation for expulsion of one of its Members is being made to the House. However, the Committee would be failing in its duty if it overlooked serious deviations, as in the present case, from the standards of conduct which the House has a right to expect of its members.

13

RAILWAY ACCIDENT INVESTIGATION REPORT ON DERAILMENT OF 371 DOWN CHURCHGATE-BORIVLI SUBURBAN TRAIN AT BANDRA STATION OF THE BOMBAY SUBURBAN SECTION OF WESTERN RAILWAY AT 15.32 HOURS ON 23rd OCTOBER, 1976 – REPORT

October 23, 1976 – February 3, 1977[1]

One Man Commission Shri P.M.N. Murthy, Additional Commissioner of Railway Safety, Western Circle, Bombay

Officers Present Shri M.L. Gupta; Shri L.F.X. Freitas; Shri R.H. Buch; Shri P.S. Chaudhuri; Shri P.C. Gupta

Appointment

The Commission was constituted under Rule 4 of the Statutory Investigation into Railway Accidents Rules, 1973 (notified by the Ministry of Tourism and Civil Aviation vide No. RS 13-T/(8)/71 dated 19th April, 1973).

Terms of Reference

To inquire into the Derailment of 371 Down Churchgate-Borivli Suburban train at Bandra Station of the Bombay Suburban Section of Western Railway at 15.32 hours on 23rd October, 1976.

---

1. Ministry of Tourism and Civil Aviation, Commission of Railway Safety, Government of India, New Delhi, 1981, i + 14 p.

Conclusions

42. *Cause*: (a) On consideration of the available evidence, I have reached the conclusion that the Derailment of No. 371 Down Churchgate-Borivli suburban train over the Down Local line at Bandra station on the Churchgate-Virar electrified suburban section of the Western Railway at about 15.32 hours on 23rd October, 1976, was the outcome of the palm pull rods on the brake hanger assembly of the leading right wheel on the trailing bogie of the 2nd coach [Motor Coach No. 510 B] getting detached at their foreend from the hanger. After detachment, the inner palm pull rod struck and bent the gauge and driving rods of the motor operated facing Points No. 136 on the Down Local line, resulting in the points gaping and causing the derailment of the coaches that followed (3rd to 9th). The processes which resulted in the palm pull rods becoming disengaged at their leading end, were initiated by the unseating of the brake hanger due of the top suspension pin working out on the run.

(b) *Responsibility*: With reference to para 41*(d)*, I am unable to assign responsibility for this accident on any individual railway staff.

43. *Relief Measures*: (a) Apropos Section II of the Report, the relief measures were prompt and satisfactory.

(b) According to the evidence adduced, Shri Y.Y. Syed, resident of Bahadur Ke Chawl, Behram Pada, Bandra who was standing on platform No. 2 and witnessed the accident rendered, considerable service in rescuing passengers from the derailed coaches, particularly the 3rd coach. The Railway Administration may appropriately convey their appreciation to him.

Recommendations

44. Since this occurrence, the Western Railway Administration has taken certain measures oriented towards securing a higher standard of maintenance of E.M. units such, as special checks of rakes by a separate gang at the time of going out from the Car Shed, surprise checks by Assistant Officers and Senior Supervisors on the quality of the work done at the stabling depots during the night, strict instructions not to re-use split pins and cotters, improvement of lighting in stabling yards, etc. This is indeed gratifying. However, considering that each EMU rake runs as many as 500 kms a day, such intensive utilisation of the stock cannot be viewed without concern until such

time as the existing infrastructure for their maintenance is strengthened with commensurate inputs. Towards this end:

(a) Adequate number of pit lines should be provided at a suitable terminal or intermediate station so that the undergear of all EMU rakes could be thoroughly examined once in 48 hours, i.e., after they have done about 1000 km. It is understood that this facility is proposed to be provided at Kandivli to the extent available funds permits. This accident highlights the need to push through this scheme with expedition and enlarge it as necessary, the requisite funds being allotted on priority;

(b) To enable a more purposeful examination of the rakes stabled at night, yard capacity should be augmented where necessary with additional lines. For want of the same, some EMU rakes are now per-force stabled on platform lines where adequate inspection cannot be carried out;

(c) Additional staff required for maintenance should be inducted into the infrastructure urgently, the inherent procedural delays in creation of posts, recruitment and training being obviated to the maximum;

(d) The existing methodology of maintenance inspection wherein gangs are allotted responsibility for each half a rake, i.e., 4.5 coaches (which, apparently is a relic of the days when EMU rakes were made up of 2 units with 8 coaches) should be rationalised and the work required to the done by each set of staff clearly spelt out. It appeared from the evidence recorded at the Inquiry that there was some ambiguity in the matter, particularly about pins and cotters on the brake gear, when a distinction was sought to be made between those visible from outside and others visible from down under. Also wheel tapping was being done only on a few rakes and not all;

(e) The 'Shed allowance' available on the Western Railway for the 45 rakes on line is many a time only 2 rakes, as against a minimum of 5 rakes (at least 10%) considered necessary. This is not a happy situation in as much as staff have to function under pressure to keep the rakes in service and more often than not, quality of workmanship may go by default. It is desired that steps are initiated to provide adequate shed allowance; and

(f) The instructions contained in Railway Board's letter No.

70/Elec/440/24 dated 17-2-1971 to carry out the POH of electrical equipment and bogies of EMUs annually (by adopting the unit exchange method as far as possible) instead of once in 18 months should be implemented without delay. The fact that arrears in POH are reported even basing on the 18 monthly schedule is rather disturbing and calls for an early probe into the attendant circumstances.

45. Pursuant to discussions following the statutory inquiry into this accident, the Railway Administration has suggested some modification in the fixtures to buttress the integrity of the brake rigging on EMUs:

(a) Replacement of split pins and cotters on the brake assembly by castle nut, lock washers, and split pins similar to those provided in the 1951 stock;
(b) Replacing the present safety brackets which are of MS flat section used for support width-wise, by brackets fabricated from MS angle iron section and improving also the method of fitment; and
(c) Providing safety chains for palm pull rods of motor bogies.

These proposals have been or are being referred to the Research Designs and Standard Organisation and are commended for urgent consideration.

46. According to extant specification, brake hanger pins are to be of class I case-hardened steel or class IV steel. Chemical and Metallurgical analysis of 7 pins taken out from the brake assembly on the rear bogie of the 2nd coach carried out by the Assistant Chemist and Metallurgist, Parel, Central Railway, revealed that none of them conformed to specifications. Some of the cotters seen by me were made of lugs tack-welded together and not from an integral piece as should be. May be, this was locally fabricated in the shops or obtained from Trade. In any case, necessary remedial measures are imminent to ensure the conformance of such vital safety items of specifications.

47. The mechanical POH of EMU rakes is at present done by the Mechanical Department in the Mahalakshmi Shops. The 'on line maintenance'—both Mechanical and Electrical—is however, done by the Electrical Department. In their letter No. E(NG) I-76 PMI/14

dated 17-7-1976, it was decided 'inter alia' by the Ministry of Railways that the entire responsibility for the maintenance of EMUs should be that of the Chief Electrical Engineer and that these instructions should be implemented by 30-9-1976. This has not been done on the Western Railway so far.

Arising out of close inspection of the detached pull rods in which bushes were found missing in the holes in use (as also a few others) and the view expressed that possibly they may not have been put in at the time of the last POH in July, 1976, I had occasion to inspect some EMU coaches which had recently been received in the car shed at Bombay Central after mechanical POH. On one coach No. 510 C— one of the anchor links was bent; coil springs on another had been painted only on the outside—the rusted inner portion was prominently visible. Case of a bell crank pin which had sheared off not being replaced during POH resulting in the brake cylinder falling off and a few other such shortcomings glossed over during POH were also complained of. Verily, this situation which apparently stems from the divided responsibility obtaining at present, is not conducive to efficient maintenance. It is desired that the POH of EMUs in its entirety be brought under the control of the Chief Electrical Engineer and the necessary organisational restructuring effected with the utmost dispatch in consonance with the Railway Ministry's policy directive referred to above.

Railway Board's Comments on Various Paras of the Report

Para 44(a)—Subject to availability of funds, action would be taken by the Railway Administration to expedite the creation of pit facilities at Kandivli stabling yard. A detailed work study is also being made by the Railway to determine *inter alia*, shortfall in facilities for implementation of 48 hourly pit inspection of EU coaches. Action, as necessary, would be taken by the railway administration in the light of the study made.

Para 44(b)—Keeping in view the future operating pattern, increased number of rake holding—the *vis-a-vis* availability of land, it is proposed by the Railway Administration to provide 8 stabling lines at Kandivli for a capacity of 13 rakes. This would avoid stabling of the rakes on the platform lines.

Para 44(c)—The maintenance staff required for a holding of 58 rakes has already been sanctioned by the railway administration. A work study is also under way to find out that additional staff would be required for a holding of 67 rakes in order to carry out systematic maintenance.

Para 44(d)—Instructions have been issued by the railway administration, allotting specific work to the staff. A directive has also been issued to enforce strictly the night checking including wheel tapping.

Para 44(e)—The Railway Administration will make efforts to keep shed allowance at the rate of 10 per cent of the rakes in traffic use.

Para 44(f)—Measures are being taken by the railway administration to rationalise POH activities. These measures primarily relate to better organisation, methods and system in Mahalaxmi shops, the aim being to reduce detention and to increase the output. Recently two major workshops schemes have been undertaken by the railway (i) at Kota for wagons and (ii) at Mahalaxmi for improved facilities of EMU coaches. Because of the expansion of the Kota workshop, some wagon workload has been transferred from Partapnagar shops to Kota. The capacity thus released at Partapnagar would be used for additional coaching out-turn, relieving in turn Mahalaxmi shops of some workload of OCVs and PCVs. The capacity thus finally released at Mahalaxmi is proposed to be used for additional EMU POH out-turn. As a result of these measures, not only the arrears of POH are being brought down but also there has been improved productivity in the Mahalaxmi shops. The arrears of POH on the basis of 18 months schedule have been brought down from 9.3 per cent as on 1-10-1976 to 3.6 per cent as on 1-5-1977. Mahalaxmi shops are also being expanded at a cost of Rs. 1.52 crores. Of this, Rs. 78 lakhs has already been spent and a sum of Rs. 30 lakhs has been made available in the current year. When the full scheme is completed, the shops would be able to handled yearly POH of bogies and electrical equipment and two-yearly POH of coach bodies for a holding of about 620 coaches.

Para 45(a)—The matter was examined by the RDSO who considered that the purpose will be served by the following modifications which are being implemented on both the Central and Western Railways:

(i) Replacement of ordinary cotters by bulb cotters.
(ii) Provision of a stopper plates on the EMU bogies.

Para 45(b)—The RDSO have issued a modified design of safety bracket using higher section of M.S. flats. Action is being taken by the Western Railway to provide these on all the coaches.

Para 45(c)—The matter is being further examined by the RDSO.

Para 46—Instructions have been issued by the railway administration to ensure that vital equipment conform to the extant specifications.

Para 47—It is appreciated that unified control is desirable and is possible even now. It is impracticable to bifurcate the workshops like Parel/Mahalaxmi or Matunga where POH of both conventional and EMU stock is being done at present. Back shop facilities for both these activities are common and if two different individuals are made separately responsible for POH of conventional and EMU stock within the premises of the same workshops, it would create substantial working difficulties. In consideration of the above, status quo has to continue. However, necessary organisational procedure orders have been issued to enable the Chief Electrical Engineer to monitor the POH of EMU stock in its entirety.

14

RAILWAY ACCIDENT INVESTIGATION REPORT ON DOUBLE COLLISION, FIRST OF OJA SPECIAL GOODS TRAIN WITH THE REAR OF WJD-12 UP GOODS TRAIN AND SUBSEQUENTLY OF NO. 78 UP VIJAYAWADA-MADRAS PARCEL PASSENGER WITH THE REAR OF OJA SPECIAL GOODS TRAIN BETWEEN THE UP DISTANT AND UP HOME SIGNALS OF SRIVENKATESWARAPALEM STATION OF SOUTH CENTRAL RAILWAY AT 21.15 AND 21.58 HOURS RESPECTIVELY ON 17th NOVEMBER 1976

November 20, 1976–February 5, 1977[1]

One Man Commission Shri K.N. Kamath, Additional Commissioner of Railway Safety, Southern Circle Bangalore.

Officers Present Shri S. Balasubramaniam; Shri P.K. Srinivasan; Shri M.A. Cherian; Shri K. Rajagopalan; Shri C.V. Ramanaiah; Shri S. Gopalakrishnan; Shri C. Prakasa Reddy
No representative of the Police was present during the Inquiry.

Appointment

The Commission was constituted under Rule 4 of the Statutory Investigation into Railway Accidents Rules, 1973, (notified by the Min-

---

1. Ministry of Tourism and Civil Aviation Commission of Railway Safety, Government of India, New Delhi, 1985, i + 17 p.

istry of Tourism and Civil Aviation vide Notification No. RS 13-7(8)/71 dated 19th April, 1973.

Terms of Reference

To investigate into the double collision, first of OJA special goods train with the rear of WJD-12 Up goods train and subsequently of No. 78 Up Vijayawada-Madras Parcel Passenger with the rear of OJA special goods train between the Up distant and Up home signals of Srivenkateswarapalem station of south central railway at 21.15 and 21.58 hours respectively on 17th November, 1976.

Conclusion

46. On full consideration of all facts, material and circumstantial evidence and the results of observations, I have come to the conclusion that the two collisions, first of OJA-Spl. Up Goods train with the rear of WJD-12 Up Goods train and thereafter, of No. 78 Up Parcel Passenger with the rear of OJA-Spl. Up Goods train that occurred between the Up Distant and Up Home Signals of Srivenkateswarapalem station at 21-15 hrs. and 21-58 hours respectively on 17-11-1976 were caused as a result of the Driver of OJA-Spl. having far exceeded the prescribed speed limit and driven the train in a rash and negligent manner and the Driver of No. 78 Up having failed to strictly observe the speed restriction and to keep a sharp look-out for any obstruction.

47. Responsibility

(i) *Collision of OJA-Spl. with the rear of WJD-12*

(a) Driver Shri C. Chittibabu of OJA-Spl. is responsible for driving his train in a rash and negligent manner. He contravened the important instructions stipulated on Form T-159/R and in the Subsidiary rules.

[Shri C. Chittibabu was appointed as a Shed Khalasi on 28-7-1954 and promoted as Second Fireman in June 1960 and as First Fireman in January 1968. He became a Diesel Assistant in September 1971 and as Driver 'C' grade in May 1975. He has had only one punishment so far, a censure in June 1956.

He was last medically examined on 8-11-1975 and was not recommended to wear spectacles.]

(b) Diesel Assistant Shri Kanna Reddy of the OJA-Spl. must also share some responsibility for failing to keep a good look-out and notice the Tail lamp of the train ahead sufficiently in advance and thus warn the Driver of the obstruction. He has contravened G.R. 122.

[Shri Kanna Reddy was first appointed as a Shed Khalasi in July 1955. He was promoted as Fireman 'C' in May 1961 and as Fireman 'B' in February 1970. After attending a course for Diesel Assistants at Kharagpur, he was posted as Diesel Assistant in June 1975.

He has had one punishment of withholding of increment for removing oil from Loco Shed in July 1957.]

(ii) *Collision of No. 78 Up with the rear of OJA-Spl*

Driver Shri R. Govindarajulu of No. 78 Up Passenger is held responsible for not regulating the speed of his train within such limit as would have enabled him to stop it short of any obstruction. He contravened the 'Important Instructions' (ii) and (vi) on Form T-159/R and those in para 3 (b) of Appendix V of the Subsidiary Rules. While judging the gravity of his offence, however, the mitigating factors discussed in para 44(ii) may be taken into consideration.

[Shri Govindarajulu was first appointed as a Shed Cooly on 5-12-1944. He was promoted as Fireman 'B' in May 1951, as Shunter 'B' in January 1955, as Driver 'C' in September 1956, as Driver 'B' in July 1971 and as Driver 'A' in September 1974. He has had ten punishments so far and his accident index according to the formula of the Railway Board works out to 396.]

48. *Relief Measures*: With reference to Chapter II of this Report, I am satisfied that the medical aid was prompt considering all circumstances.

The patients in the Civil Hospital at Nellore and Kavali and the Railway Hospital at Vijayawada were being well looked after, particularly so in the Railway Hospital.

Recommendations

49. This is not the first time that serious accidents have taken place during total interruption of communications. In 1969 two acci-

dents took place on the same day involving four passenger trains*. Though both these accidents occurred during day time, the visibility was very much restricted on account of stormy weather and the Driver was not even able to get his Fireman to walk ahead to guide him due to the strong wind coupled with blowing of sand. It will be seen in the present case that two adjoining sections—Tettu and Kavali and Kavali and Srivenkateswarapalem were being worked under this system, the total distance involved being about 24 km. If a Driver is to proceed at 8 km/h. on account of poor visibility during night or due to fog or mist or any other similar cause, it will take him three hours to cover the distance. In my view it would be too much to expect a Driver to keep a sharp look-out all the time for any obstruction during such a long period. It is, therefore, recommended that trains should be run on the authority of T-159/R only during day time and that too when visibility is clear, the speed being restricted to 8 km/h. The speed should be restricted further to 8 km/h. when the view is not clear on account of curve, fog, rain or any other cause. Running of trains during night under this Authority shall be prohibited save under exceptional circumstances as explained in para 50 below.

50. In para 3(b) of Appendix V of General and Subsidiary Rules of the South Central Railway it is stipulated that the speed should be restricted to 25 km/h over the straight and 8 km/h while approaching or passing any portion of the line where the view ahead is not clear due to curve, obstruction, rain, fog or any other causes whereas in para (ii) of the important instructions on Form T-159/R it is indicated that the speed must not exceed 5 M.p.h. during night or when visibility is not clear. There is no mention in Appendix V of the G. & S.R. regarding the reduced speed during night. If running on the 'Authority to proceed without Line Clear' has to be resorted to at night in exceptional circumstances, e.g., to take a passenger train held up at a small station with no facilities to a bigger station, the speed

---

* (1) Collision between No. 18 Up "Delhi-Madras Janta Express" train and No. 52 Up "Kazipet-Madras Express" train between Chirala and Vetapalemu stations of South Central Railway on 17th May, 1969.

(2) Collision between No. 54 Up "Hyderabad-Madras Express" train and No. 16 Up "New Delhi-Madras Grand Trunk express" train between Vetapalemu and Kodavakuduru stations of South Central Railway on 17th May, 1969.

should be reduced further. It is suggested that para 3(b) of Appendix V may be revised as under:

> "a Caution Order restricting the speed to 25 km/h during day and 15 km/h during night over the straight and to 8 km/h during both day and night when approaching or passing any portion of the line where the view ahead is not clear due to curve, obstruction, rain, fog or any other cause."

51. It is necessary that the 'Important Instructions' on Form T-159/R should be revised to keep in line with the conditions stipulated in Appendix V so that the staff may not get confused.

52. Sudden cyclonic storms are quite common in the coastal regions of South Central Railway (and also of Southern Railway) on account of which total interruption of communication occurs often in these regions. During discussions with the Railway Officers at the Inquiry one useful suggestion was made, viz., use of portable wireless sets for obtaining Line Clear during such total interruption of communications. It should be possible to identify these areas where such interruptions occur frequently and keep a few wireless sets at selected stations for being sent out to the affected stations as soon as the total interruption of communication occurs by the first train proceeding under the authority of T-159/R or by a push or motor trolley or other suitable means of transport. Paper Line Clear could then be obtained by these stations by contacting the adjoining stations over the wireless sets and exchanging Private Numbers. It is recommended that this suggestion may be considered by the Railway Board in the interest of Safety, and tried out in one or two selected areas where such interruptions are frequent.

53. According to para 8 of Appendix V referred to above the Guard has to keep a sharp look-out in the rear and be prepared to protect it if necessary. When trains are despatched at 15 minutes intervals it is most probable that they would be held up at the Home Signal for want of line at the station as happened in this case. In such a case, according to G.R. 125, the Guard has to protect the rear of the train if the train has been held up for over 15 minutes, by going back showing the hand Danger signal and placing one detonator at 600 metres and three detonators at 1200 metres from the rear of the train. To carry this out and return back to his Brakevan it would take the Guard nothing less than 30 minutes. Such protection would also

be necessary if the train is disabled and cannot proceed ahead due to any cause whatsoever as per G.R. 166. Considering that trains would be running at a restricted speed of 25 km/h during day time and an even lower speed during night, it is recommended that the distances for protection by detonators may be reduced suitably, say to 125 metres and 250 metres respectively, and a special para incorporated in Appendix V. This would make it easier for the Guards to comply with the instructions.

54. According to para 2 of Appendix V before any train is allowed to enter a Block section in advance when there is total interruption of communication, both the Drive and the Guard of the train have to be advised by the Station Master. In para 3(a) it is, however, indicated that an 'Authority to proceed without Line Clear' shall be given to the Driver of each train. Though Form T-159/R provides space for obtaining not only the signature of the Driver but also the signature of the Guard, and it is also stipulated that Guard of the train and the Station Master should certify under their signature about having translated and explained the particulars to the Drive and understood thoroughly by him in case he is illiterate, it was seen that the signature of Guards were not generally being obtained on the Form. The two Guards involved—of WJD-12 and OJA-Spl. both stated that they were not informed about the 'total interruption' between Kavali and Srivenkateswarapalem. It appears that the signature of Guards is not being obtained because of the distance and time involved in doing this. This is not a satisfactory state of affairs. It is essential that the Guard should also be posted with the information and the Railway Administration should ensure that the signature of the Guard is also obtained when trains are despatched on the authority of Form T-159/R.

55. It was seen that the Switchman of the South Cabin of Srivenkateswarapalem had informed the Switchman of the North Cabin, Bitragunta, by telephone about the accident at 21-55 hrs. The Switchman, North Cabin, however, conveyed this information to the Assistant Station Master only at 22-30 hrs. Even allowing for the fact that telephone communications were cut off at Bitragunta on the day and there was also a power failure, it should not have taken 35 minutes for the Switchman to inform the Assistant Station Master about the accident. The Railway Administration may look into the cause of the delay and take necessary remedial measures to prevent recurrence.

56. The Guard of BMD-23 has deposed (para 24) that fifteen minutes after his train was held up at Srivenkateswarapalem Up Home Signal he went to the rear of his train and protected it with detonators as per G.R. 125. The detonators were placed 600 metres and 1200 metres in rear of his train and he had shown his hand Danger signal towards the oncoming WJD-12. After the train had slowed down considerably he had picked up these detonators and gone back to his train hurriedly as, by then, he had noticed that his train had started moving ahead. The Driver of WJD-12 has confirmed that he had slowed down on seeing the Red hand signal shown by this Guard. But from the evidence of both it is very clear that the Guard had not gone so far behind his train. Most probably he had started from his brakevan only after seeing the headlight of WJD-12 at some distance and was, therefore, able to proceed only a much shorter distance and then showed the hand Danger distance and then showed the hand Danger signal to stop the train. Had he been one kilometre behind his Brakevan he could not have seen his train moving ahead. However, as he had managed to avert what might have been had managed to avert what might have been another accident, he may not be held responsible for having failed to protect the rear of his train. Nevertheless, even if his statement regarding placing of detonators is believed, he should have left the three detonators and removed only the intermediate the when returning to his Brakevan as per para (f) of G.R. 166.

57. There was no First-Aid Box at Srivenkateswarapalem station. It was understood that it had been removed for replenishment. In such contingencies it should be ensured that a spare box is supplied to the station before removing the existing box so that the same could be used in an emergency.

58. The Caution Order forms were being issued by the Cabin Switchmen. It is desirable that these are issued by the Station Masters as indicated in para 3 of Appendix V.

Railway Board's Comments on Various Paras of the Report

Paras 49, 50, 52 and 53: The rules for working of trains during total interruption of communication have already been revised in consultation with the Commission of Railway Safety.

Para 54: Instructions on the subject have been reiterated by the Railway Administration who have initiated a drive to educated all the staff in this respect.

Paras 55 and 56: Both the Switchman, Bitragunta and the Guard of BMD-23 Goods have already been punished by the Railway Administration.

Para 57: Instructions have been issued to all the Railways to obtain replenishment from the nearest health unit as soon as the items in the first aid box are used up and in case the first aid box has to be detained in the health unit or Hospital, a spare first aid box should be issued by the health unit or hospital.

Para 58: The concerned staff are being suitably educated by the Railway Administration to follow the extant instructions with regard to issue of 'Caution Orders'. This has been noted by CRS.

15

COMMITTEE ON PENAL RATES AND SERVICE CHARGES, 1976 – REPORT[1]

Chairman Shri C.P. Shah (replaced by Shri V.R. Desai)

Members Shri K.K. Pai; Shri Inderjit Singh; Shri N.R. Kulkarni; Shri S.H. Cassim; Dr. M.V. Patwardhan; Shri S.N.S. Raghavan

Observers Shri S.R. Avadhani; Shri V.M. Sunder Raj

Terms of Reference

(a) The Committee may consider framing guidelines on:

(i) the circumstances under which panel rates of interest could be levied by banks on their constituents and the justification for such levy;

(ii) the level at which such panel rates should be charged;

(iii) the normal period for which such panel rates could be charged;

(iv) the follow-up-action which banks should simultaneously initiate to restore normalcy to the accounts and to bring about discipline on the part of borrowers; and

(v) remedial measures to deal with persistent defaults and irregular accounts;

(b) The Committee may also, in particular, give guidelines for the application of panel rates in the case of sick borrowing units.

(c) The Committee may also review the varying practices followed by different banks in the matter of levying service charges over a wide range of their functions and suggest streamlining and

---

1. Bombay, Reserve Bank of India, 1976, (extracts from *Reserve Bank of India Bulletin*, June 1976, pp. 400-409)

rationalisation of the practices in this regard to help banks to evolve a common code of conduct.

(d) The Committee may also review the working of the informal understanding and the practices which have emerged among members in respect of the operation of the Inter-bank call money market and suggest further guidelines in this regard.

It was clarified to the Committee by Reserve Bank of India that, in dealing with terms vide paragraph (a)(iv) and (a)(v) above; the Committee was not required to deal with the large question of reconstruction and nursing finance in all its implications, but was expected to deal with them insofar as they have a direct bearing on the question of Penal rate. Likewise, it was also clarified that in dealing with term (c) above the Committee was to restrict its deliberations only to those service charges which are directly related to borrowal accounts.

The Reserve Bank prescribed a minimum lending rate at 10 per cent p.a. since June 1973, which was raised to 11 per cent p.a. in December 1973 and raised again to 12.5 per cent p.a. in July 1974. Effective from 15th March 1976, Reserve Bank have prescribed a ceiling on the lending rates of banks at 16.5 per cent p.a. in case of Indian Banks with demand and time liabilities of Rs. 50 crores or above and all foreign banks and at 17.5 per cent p.a. in case of Indian Banks with demand and time liabilities of Rs. 25 cores or above but less than Rs. 50 crores. The ceilings are not applicable to smaller Indian Banks with demand and time liabilities below Rs. 25 crores and to the specified exempted categories of advances made by all banks. It was against this background that the Committee was to recommend guidelines.

Contents

Terms of Reference; Existing Practices of Banks; Rationale for Penal Rates; Circumstances where Penal Rates are Justified; Pre-requisites for Charging Penal Rates; Penal Rates to Small Sector and Agriculture; Follow-up Action; Service Charges; Inter-Bank Call Money Rates and Practices; Processing Fees; Recommendations Regarding Processing Fees; Time Table; Recommendations on Other Issues.

Existing Practices of Banks

In response to a circular issued by the Indian Bank's Association, 33 banks sent detailed replies up to the 13th April 1976.

We give below an outline of the various practices followed by banks in applying in penal rates. The banks have advised that penal rates are applied after giving an opportunity to the borrower to regularise the account and only where defaults are frequent, persistent or deliberate.

(a) Circumstances where Penal rates are charged:

(i) Default in repayment of term loans, temporary loans and acceptance or payment of bills on due dates;
(ii) Drawings beyond the sanctioned limit or drawing power rendering of the account irregular;
(iii) Where credit facilities cannot be renewed in time because of the borrower not submitting financial data and other particulars;
(iv) Non-fulfilment of export obligations or misuse of export finance facilities;
(v) Diversion of funds for unauthorised purposes;
(vi) Non-submission of stock statements or non-compliance with other terms and conditions of the credit facilities;
(vii) Where inventory and receivables are in excess of the norms prescribed by Reserve Bank of India and these excess assets are not reduced by the borrower within the agreed period;
(viii) Where profitably, turnover, debt equity gearing, or other financial indicators are, according to the bank, not satisfactory and there is no effort made by the borrower to improve these despite opportunity and time given;
(ix) In lieu of commitment charge;
(x) Where borrowers have not taken out adequate insurance cover for stocks in which the banks have insurable interest or where the risk is not covered by the borrower; and
(xi) On inoperative accounts resulting from various causes.

(b) Level and Period of Penal Rates:

(i) Penal rates charged by the banks vary from 1 to 5 per cent above the normal rates. The overall interest rates including penal rates are in some cases, as high as 23 per cent. Some of the banks charge initially 19 per cent and escalate it by one per cent every week subject to a maximum of 23 per cent;

(ii) Majority of the banks seem to charge panel rate in the range of 2 to 3 per cent above the normal rates; and

(iii) Some banks initiate other measures if penal rates do not have the desired effect in a period of two years whereafter other measures may have to be taken.

(c) Application of Penal Rates:

(i) Penal rates are normally charged by most banks on irregular drawings or the amount in default in respect of term loans, where the irregularity persists for longer periods, penal rate is charged on the entire amount of the advance;

(ii) In case of bills, the practices of the banks fall in two broad categories: where penal rate is applied from the date of dishonour and where it is applied from the 6th or 7th day after the purchase of the relative bill;

(iii) Penal rates levied in respect of advances to priority sectors are generally lower than the rates charged from larger advances; and

(iv) Small borrowers with outstandings below Rs. 10,000 are exempted from penal levy by a few banks.

Rationale for Penal Rates

Practices of banks in the matter of penal rates are diverse and varied. Complaints have been heard on various forums that overall lending rates of banks (inclusive of penal rates) have at times gone up to 23 per cent it is, therefore, essential to streamline the system of penal rates and define the scope, circumstances and manner of their application.

There is no standard definition of penal interest in banking literature or operational manuals of banks and our enquiries reveal a wide variety and diversity of practices among banks and financial institutions in the concept and application of penal rates. In all cases, however, penal rate as is currently understood represents additional interest charged over and above normal interest rates, levied a penalty for defaults of the borrower in complying with the terms on which credit facilities were sanctioned to him. The term 'defaults' covers a wide range, such as default or delay in repayment of a term or demand loan or retirement of bills and non-compliance with or non-observance of other terms of the sanction.

Credit facilities are sanctioned by a bank on the customer accepting certain basic terms and conditions as apart of the credit arrangement. Unilateral violation of the terms of the credit facilities is considered as a breach of the understanding on the basis of which the bank has agreed to make the credit facilities available.

Any commercial contract which requires compliance with certain conditions by the parties thereto usually contains a provision for levy of penal charges on the default being made by any party in complying with the terms of the contract. In all business contracts it is common to make a provision for penal charge on these lines. Since grant of credit facilities is also a commercial contract between the bank and the customer, it would only be equitable if the agreement between them provides for levy of penal rate in situations which are tantamount to a breach of the basic terms and conditions of the agreement.

Where a borrower default in complying with the terms of the credit arrangement, several options are open to the bank. For instance, the bank could persuade the customer through personal discussions or correspondence to comply with the conditions of the advance and to setright the irregularities or it could take a more serious view of the customer's failure and recall the advance. It is not, however, necessary or practicable to resort to such an extreme step of recalling the advance and terminating the credit facilities. Instead, it would be better to charge a penal rate as an interim measure for disciplining the borrower and securing this compliance with the terms and conditions of the credit arrangement. Where the defaults are persistent or recurring, the credit facility assumes a higher credit risk. Interest rates normally charged by banks are based on credit ratings of their customers, higher rate being charged where the credit rating is lower and correspondingly the risk is higher. Advances with persistent defaults assume the nature of high credit risk proposals and the bank would be entitled to charge a higher rate so as to reflect the higher risk involved.

Although penal rates should not be treated as a measure for increasing the revenue of banks, the borrower's failure to honour the term loan instalment or bills on the due date inevitably throws out of gear the credit planning and resources budget of banks, particularly of small banks, and they would be entitled to compensate themselves for the additional cost and in convenience through levy of penal rate on the account of the defaulter.

It will thus be seem that penal rates cannot be objected to in principle and will have to be accepted as a justifiable part of the interest rates policy of banks, as long as they are applied with selectivity and discrimination.

Circumstances where Penal Rates are Justified

After enquiring into the practices and policies of banks, the Committee has come to the conclusion that the following are broadly the areas where the bank may be justified in charging penal rates on advances:

(a) *Default in Repayment of Loans*

(i) Where a specific repayment schedule has been stipulated for repayment of the term loan or a temporary facility, the customer is expected to negotiate in advance for extension of the repayment date, in case it is not possible for him to make the repayment on due dates, where the customer fails to negotiate in advance, the bank would be justified in charging a penal rate on the amount in default.

(ii) Even where the customer approaches the bank for rescheduling the repayment instatements, it is possible that the bank may not be fully satisfied about the validity of the reasons offered by the customer for not adhering to the repayment schedule in which case the bank would be justified in charging penal rate on the default amount for instance, where the customer's inability to honour the repayment instalment is due to diversion of funds for unauthorised purposes, mismanagement, speculative build-up of inventories or laxity in chasing up receivables, etc., the bank may not be satisfied about the validity of the borrower's explanation.

(b) *Irregularities in Cash Credit Accounts*

(i) Irregularities in cash credit accounts may arise as a result of drawings in excess of sanctioned limits or in excess of drawing power as calculated on the basis of the prescribed margins, where such an irregularity was arisen without prior arrangement with the bank, it represents a breach of the terms of the arrangement and the bank would be justified in levying panel rate.

(ii) Theoretically, the bank is free to stop operations in the account but before such an extreme step is taken, the bank would be justified in bringing home to the borrower the need for maintaining discipline by levying penal rate as a deterrent against continuance or repetition of such irregularities.

(iii) Initially, the bank may change penal rate on the amount of irregularity but if it persists for a longer period or if such irregularity recurs frequently it may be necessary to charge penal rate on the entire outstandings in the account. But in all cases it would be necessary for the bank to exercise its discretion carefully, particularly in view of the uncertainties faced by customers in anticipating their day to day cash flows.

(c) *Non-submission of Stock Statements and other Financial Data*

(i) A number of banks have voiced complaints of persistent defaults on the part of the customers in the submission of periodical stock statements within the stipulated date. As a result, drawing powers which are perforce calculated on the basis of the outdated stock statements are misleading. This renders it difficult for the bank to ensure that drawings are, in fact, being regulated within the drawing power computed on the basis of the current stock position of the customer. If a valid explanation is not forthcoming from the customer, and if such practices become frequent, the bank would be justified in charging penal rate on the entire advance inasmuch as the advance in such circumstances would be conducted without any indication of the actual drawing power in the account.

(ii) Likewise, several banks have expressed difficulties in receiving financial data and follow up information in time. Not only that the quarterly or half yearly data are delayed,

> but even yearly reviews or credit appraisals are inordinately delayed because of the lack of vital information. Advances are, therefore, required to be reviewed and continued on the basis of old data during which period the financial position of the customer might have considerably changed and possibly worsened. Inability of banks to effectively supervise the advance because of lack of data is a paramount cause for several industrial units becoming sick of getting into financially involved position without the knowledge of the bank, which requires timely information to notice the symptoms of incipient sickness. Timely submission of essential data is, therefore, a vital part of the follow-up system which alone would enable the bank to effectively supervise the conduct of the account and ensure that bank finance is being utilised for the purpose for which it is intended.

In view of this, therefore, the bank would be justified in taking stern action against the customer, including levy of penal rate if the required data are not forthcoming either because of wilful default on the part of the customer or due to his failure to build up an adequate management information system. This discipline would also give the borrower an incentive to plan his business, cash flow and management information system in such a way that the terms of the advance are complied with.

(d) *Default in Honouring Covenants*

As a measure of financial discipline, it is the practice of many banks to stipulate covenants relating to financial planning of the borrower so as to ensure that there is no diversion of bank credit for unauthorised purposes. The covenants require the customer to obtain prior consent of the bank before making other borrowing arrangements, taking up new projects or large scale expansion, making intercorporate investments and loans, effecting mergers and acquisitions, etc. Reference is invited in this connection to paragraph 86 of the Report of the Study Group to frame Guidelines for Follow-up of Bank Credit appointed by Reserve Bank of India, which has made detailed recommendations on this issue. Where the customer wilfully defaults in honouring important covenants stipulated by the bank, it would be in order for the bank to charge penal rate as a measure of discipline.

(e) *Panel Rate on Excess Borrowings Arising Out of Excess Current Assets*

The RBI Study Group Report referred to above has also made a suggestion that where the customer continues to carry excess current assets as compared to the norms stipulated for inventory and receivables the bank may charge penal rate on excess borrowings arising out of excess current assets. Reserve Bank of India have endorsed this suggestion in their letter DBOD No. CAS.BC.62/ C.446/75 of August 21, 1975 in which banks have been asked to consider, after giving a reasonable time to customers for reducing excess current assets, whether they should charge a higher rate of interest on the portion of borrowings considered as excessive. The Committee agrees with the suggestion made by Reserve Bank of India.

(f) *Demand/Usance Bills*

Where demand bills are not paid on presentation and where usance bills are not accepted/paid on due dates, banks would be justified in levying penal rate or overdue interest. If Reserve Bank's Policy of converting book debts into bill finance is to be encouraged, banks will have to exercise strict control on payment of bills without permitting and laxity in this regard. Besides, a discipline imposed by the bank would also assist industry trade in the management of there own receivables.

(g) *Export of Credit*

In respect of export credit, the directive issued by Reserve Bank of India from time to time stipulate that no bank shall charge interest on pre-shipment and post-shipment export credits by way of loans/ advances/cash credits/over drafts and by way of purchase, discount of bills or renewal of such credit at a rate exceeding the prescribed ceiling rates which are at present 8 per cent p.a. for post-shipment credit on deferred payment terms (available for the full period of credit allowed on each instalment) and 11.5 per cent/13.5 per cent p.m. on other post shipment credit pre-shipment credit up to stipulated periods.

The Reserve Bank directives further prescribe that where pre-shipment credits or post-shipment credits arc extended beyond the periods stipulated for ceiling rates, the banks may charge there normal rates of interest for the extended period. The Reserve Bank of India has further advised banks that in cases where packing credits are availed of but the exports do not materialise, the banks should charge a suitable rate of interest higher than their normal rate of interest from the date of the advance.

The Committee agrees with the present position in this regard. In drawing up the above list, the Committee has adopted the principle that penal rate should not be regarded as a revenue raising measure but rather as a measure to enforce discipline in the conduct of the account. The practice in some banks of charging penal rate in lieu of commitment charge is clearly not justified. Similarly, if a borrower does not comply with the insurance condition of the advance, the bank concerned with its insurable interest should be in a position to take out the cover at the cost of the borrower to repeated levy of penal rate which in any case cannot be a substitute for the insurance cover. As regards levy of penal interest on inoperative accounts, perhaps what is needed in action on the lines indicated in Section VIII of the Report.

Pre-requisites for Charging Penal Rates

While there could be several circumstances as illustrated above where the bank would be within its rights to levy penal rates, it is essential to emphasise that the policy of levying penal rates will have to be implemented with discrimination and selectivity. Unless the bank's decision to levy penal rate is preceded by consideration of all the attendant circumstances, the system of penal rate may become arbitrary.

For instance, where penal rate is intended to be charged for non-submission of financial data, it is necessary to make sure that the customer has been given adequate time to compile and submit the required information. Similarly, where penal rate is sought to be levied as a result of the default committed by the customer in honouring repayment scheduled in respect of term loans or temporary credit facilities, the bank will be well advised to examine the circumstances in each case in detail and exercise its discretion carefully. The default of the customer may be because of the strain on his liquidity arising out of cash accruals falling short of his earlier estimates on the basis of which repayment instalments were stipulated. In such circumstances, the bank should rather examine the reasons for the customer's inability to generate cash accruals as expected instead of straightway charging penal interest on the defaulted amount.

A similar approach should be followed in the case of irregularities Likewise, it would not be advisable to charge penal rate for accessional non-compliance with the terms of the advance. Further, distinction will have to be made between the conditions fundamental and incidental to the arrangement and it may not be necessary to charge panel rate where there is a breach of minor conditions.

To reiterate, the decision to charge penal rate should not be treated as a routine measure which may, in fact, lead to postponement of a more important decision for making an indepth study on the problems confronting the customer. In order to avoid indiscriminate levy of penal rate, we would suggest that decisions on penal rate should be taken at a fairly high level in each bank. The decision-making levels should be determined by each bank in the light of its own administrative structure.

Levels and Period of Penal Rates

On the basis of the data collected from banks, the Committee considers that it would meet with the requirements of the schemes on penal rates if penal interest is charged at rates varying from one per cent to 2.5 per cent p.a. over and above normal rates applicable to the advances. Subject to the condition that, under no circumstances, the rate should exceed two per cent p.a. above ceiling rates for advances prescribed by Reserve Bank of India for different classes of banks, i.e., 16.5 per cent or 17.5 per cent p.a. as the case may be.

The penal rate or overdue interest on all overdue bills should be levied at 18.5 per cent p.a.

All small loans up to a credit limit of Rs. 5,000 and all advances under Differential Interest Rates Schemes should be exempt from the levy of penal rate. Since the question of agricultural advances has been examined from a different point of view. Such exemption will not apply to agricultural advances. If the default continues for an unduly long period, the situation would call for a more serious remedy, inasmuch as the bank's interests during this period would have already been greatly jeopardized and a mere levy of penal rate would not have improved its position.

Panel Rates to Small Sector and Agriculture

In case of advances to small scale industries (SSI) and agriculturists, considering their limited capacity to bear additional costs and the need for adopting a sympathetic approach to remedy the difficulties resulting in irregularities or defaults in their accounts, a somewhat lenient view has to be taken in charging panel rates on such accounts. The Committee, therefore, suggests that the following approach should be adopted in dealing with advances to these sectors.

(a) *Small Scale Industries*

Greater selectivity and circumspection should be exercised as counselling and personal dialogue with the borrowing unit is necessary in order to resolve many of their management accounting and operational problems. The Committee, therefore, recommends that in case of small scale industries, the scale of penal rates should be slightly lower. We accordingly suggest that where credit limits of SSI units are less than Rs. 2 lakhs, penal rate should not exceed 1.5 per cent provided that the overall rate of interest, inclusive of penal rate, should not in any case, exceed the ceiling rates of interest prescribed by the Reserve Bank of India for various classes of banks, i.e., 16.5 per cent or 17.5 per cent p.a. as the case may be. In case of SSI advance to units having limits of Rs. 2 lakhs and over, the panel rate may be on the scales recommended by us in paragraph above.

(b) *Agricultural Advances*

(i) The Committee considered the question of penal rates on agricultural advances to small and marginal farmers and other direct agricultural loans. Taking into account the observations of the Study Team appointed by the Reserve Bank of India on overdues of Co-operative Credit Institutions and the general experience of banks in respect of overdues in agricultural finance, the Committee considers that it would be advisable to give a time of at least three months to such borrowers for making repayments of the loans or of instalments against advances granted to them.

(ii) If the bank is not satisfied with reasons for default even during the extended period, the bank may charge penal rate on the advance. However, penal rate should be charged only on the overdue instalments and not on the total outstandings, unless of course, the entire loan is recalled.

(iii) Where, however, the farmers borrower is not in a position to repay the loans on account of natural calamities, such as drought, flood and famine, etc., or on account of unforeseen contingencies such as death or physical incapacitation of the borrower or unusual circumstances beyond the control of the borrower, the bank should rather reschedule the repayment instalment than charge penal rate.

(iv) In the case of agricultural loans (excluding plantations, which should be governed by our recommendations in paragraph above), the penal rate should not be more than 2.5 per cent and the overall rate of interest, inclusive of penal rate, should, under no circumstances, exceed the prevailing ceiling rates prescribed by Reserve Bank of India in respect of interest rates for various classes of banks, i.e., 16.5 per cent or 17.5 per cent p.a. as the case may be.

Follow-up Action

Where panel rate is required to be charged on defaulted loan instalment or irregularities, it can serve as a deterrent measure only to a limited extent and it would be essential to enquire into the circumstances under which the default or irregularity continues. To a great extent the information available under the Information System introduced for large borrowers by Reserve Bank of India is pursuance of the recommendations of the RBI Study Group on Follow-up of Bank Credit would enable the bank to have a greater perception of the financial affairs of the customer. Although the Information System is applicable, to begin with, only to borrowers having credit units of Rs. 1 crore and above and is to be extended in due course to borrowers with limits of Rs. 50 lakhs and above it would be desirable to introduce this system gradually to borrowers having lower credit limits to improve the follow up of such advances.

It is possible that in quite a few cases, as in-depth study would be required to decide upon the remedial measures to be taken and the bank officials by themselves may not be able to undertake a detailed study of this nature. In such cases it would be advisable to seek the services of competent consultants. Where viability of the customer's operations is in question, appropriate remedial action including change in product mix, diversification, modernisation, etc., may be necessary.

A suitable programme for nursing the account may be called for in such cases. Where the bank comes to the conclusion as a result of the detailed study of the operations of the customer that uneconomic operations are due to mismanagement it may even be necessary for a thorough restructuring of the management of the unit. Once an in-depth study of this nature is completed and the bank comes to a definite conclusion, penal interest rate would not be relevant any longer as a measure for imposing discipline on the customer. In fact, where the bank decides to inject further funds for placing the unit on a viable footing it may be advisable not only not to change penal interest but even to extent concession in the interest rates originally stipulated for the advance.

This course of action would be possible only where the customer's co-operation is forthcoming for taking appropriate remedial measures. Where the financial affairs of the customer are deteriorating due to a recalcitrant attitude of the customer, a more serious action would be called for. In extreme cases, the bank would be well justified to call up the advance and terminated the arrangement.

The foregoing discussion really takes us to the subject of reconstruction or nursing assistance to sick units. In view of the limited terms of reference of this Committee, we consider that Reserve Bank of India should formulate guidelines for the banking system on this issue in constitution with banks and financial institutions.

Service Charges

As stated earlier, the Committee is not required to examine service charges levied by banks on the entire range of their services and is required to concern itself only with service charges related to borrowal accounts directly.

Service charges relating to borrowal accounts can be divided into two parts.

(a) *Out-of-pocket Expenses*

Reimbursement of actual out-of-pocket expenses incurred by banks consisting of such items as godown keeper's salary, travelling or conveyance expenses of bank's inspectors or field officers, legal charges, stamp duties and fees, etc., paid for documentation, charges paid to consultants for feasibility reports or consultancy reports, fees paid to appraisers in case of jewel loans, etc. In the opinion of the Committee, there should be no objection to banks recovering such actual charges from the borrowers. Moreover, from the data obtained from banks the Committee was found that such charges are reasonable and necessary. The levy of such charges may continue to be left to the discretion of each bank.

(b) *Incidental Processing or Service Charges*

Some of the banks levy special fees or service charges, either at a flat rate or on a percentage basis. Such charges differ from one bank to another, though there are quite a number of banks, which do not recover service charges of this nature. During the limited time available at the disposal of the Committee, it was not possible to obtain data from the banks concerned to see whether recovery of such service charges is justified. The Committee therefore, proposes to examine this matter further in consultation with the banks concerned and our further report will be submitted shortly.

In the meantime, the Committee recommends that no bank should increase its scale of such service charges, prevailing before the ceiling on interest rates were prescribed by the Reserve Bank of India, until our final report is submitted.

Inter-Bank Call Money Rates and Practices

Most banks have reported that fixation of voluntary ceiling on inter-bank call money rates including overnight call money and money on notice for all periods up to 14 days has been a welcome measure and has helped to keep the call money market orderly and the costs within reasonable limits Indian Banks' Association (IBA) has already appointed a committee to consider the question of similarly regulating rates on inter-bank deposits particularly from co-operative banks for periods beyond 14 days. The need for such regulation is genuine and urgent and this is a step in the right direction. The Committee is of the opinion that the Report of the IBA committee on such inter-bank deposits may be awaited before any further decision could be taken. The banks have fixed a voluntary ceiling of 12.5 per cent on inter-bank call money rate. The Committee hopes that the Reserve Bank would consider this as well as the ceiling rate put on bank advances while fixing the maximum and minimum rates on discretionary refinance provided to the commercial banks.

Recommendations Regarding Processing Fees

Accordingly the Committee makes the following recommendations after taking all the relevant factors and aspects into account.

(i) (a) no bank which was not already levying processing fees on borrowal accounts on a percentage per annum basis or as a percentage of interest income as on 15-3-76 should do so thereafter.

(b) many banks that were already levying such percentage processing fees had several special aspects that required to be tackled with consideration and understanding. These special aspects are explained by the chairman of the Committee in his separate letter to the Reserve Bank of India. Taking them into account the Committee recommends that all such banks may be given time up to 1st January 1978 to discontinue percentage processing fees in accordance with the following time-table and to bring them in line with our recommendations that follow hereafter in 11 (ii).

Time Table

A. The percentage processing fees should be brought down to one per cent per annum on the outstanding debit balances by 1st January, 1977.

B. They should be brought down to 1/2 of one per cent by 1st July, 1977.

C. They should cease altogether by 1st January, 1978.

(ii) Where a limit has been sanctioned and availed of by a customer, a flat rate of processing fee on a once-for-all basis could be levied at the discretion of the banks at a rate not exceeding 1/20th of one per cent with a maximum of Rs. 2,500.

(iii) This charge will not however apply to advances sanctioned to priority sectors, other than exports, where the total limits are less than Rs. 2 lakhs and to all export credit, and advances to weaker sections.

(iv) Since ceilings on interests rates are not applicable to smaller Indian banks with time and deposit liabilities below Rs. 25 crores, they should also be exempted from these recommendations regarding processing fees on borrowal accounts.

Recommendations on Other Issues

(a) *Commitment Charge*

It was felt by the Committee that in order to discourage large unutilised limits which tied up funds unnecessarily and prevented banks from making optimum use of their resources for needy borrowers there was a case for reintroduction the system of levying a commitment charge on unutilised units.

The Committee is aware that under the recommendations of the Tandon Committee the customers were required to indicate a fixed amount of loan component in the total limits sanctioned to them and that the rate of interest changeable on the fluctuating component was to be one per cent higher rate of interest for the fluctuating part of sanctioned limits, there should also be a provision for levy of commitment charge on the portion of the credit limits that remained unutilised even beyond the fluctuating component. The Committee recommends that Reserve Bank may consider this.

(b) *Folio Charges for Operations on Loan Accounts*

The Committee found that in many cases, in addition to processing fees, folio charges based on the operations in a borrowing account of turnover were also levied by banks, monthly, quarterly or half yearly. These charges are levied both on loan accounts as well as deposit accounts.

The Committee recommends, that banks may continue to levy folio charges as at present until RBI Working Group on Banking Costs, Operational Efficiency and Profitability of Banks has completed its costing studies and determined the basis on which such service charges should be levied for deposit accounts. Thereafter, the same basis may be applied for determining the folio charges on loan accounts also.

(c) *Processing Fees on Limits Sanctioned but not Availed*

In many cases, borrowers make applications for sanction of credit facilities to several banks, but avail them from only one bank where borrowers apply for credit facilities but do not avail of the sanctions, the bank is unable to recover its costs from any source. The Committee, therefore, came to the conclusion that banks may be allowed the discretion to charge a processing fee of Rs. 100 and a maximum Rs. 5,000 to a customer who does not avail of limit/s sanctioned broadly or substantially on the lines applied for.

The Committee was recommended processing fees in such cases on a higher scale than for limits sanctioned and availed of, because in such cases the entire effort in processing a loan application is wasted and the sanctioned credit facilities remain unutilised. It will also discourage similar applications to a multiply of banks.

(d) *Out-of-Pocket Expenses*

It may be recalled that the Committee had recommended in paragraph 35(a) of its report dated 22nd April 1976 that there should be no objection to banks recovering actual out-of-pocket expenses from borrowers, including travelling or conveyance expenses of bank's inspectors or field officers. The attention of the Committee was drawn to a circular letter dated 17th June, 1976 sent by the Department of Banking and Revenue, Government of India to Chairman and Managing Director of Public Sector Banks requesting them to stop using the conveyance or transport of the borrowers and to stop the recovery of conveyance charges from them. The Committee feels that out-of-pocket expenses incurred by banks for periodical inspection or visits to factories or plants are a necessary expense and there should be no objection to the recovery of actual out-of-pocket expenses incurred – this is usually provided for in the terms and agreement for the facility. If such expenses are not allowed to be recovered, banks may find that they are actually out-of-pocket when they carry out such inspections even when the party's account has been running in credit for a prolonged period, thereby earning no interest for the Bank. Thus, the question of using the conveyance or transport provided by the borrower or charging actual out-of-pocket expenses may need to be reconsidered and the Committee therefore may be allowed to be levied as at present.

CHAIRMAN INDEX OF COMMITTEES & COMMISSIONS IN INDIA 1947-76
Volumes 1 to 14